COMMUNICATING
WITH
MEDICAL
PATIENTS

Sage's *Series in Interpersonal Communication* is designed to capture the breadth and depth of knowledge emanating from scientific examinations of face-to-face interaction. As such, the volumes in this series address the cognitive and overt behavior manifested by communicators as they pursue various conversational outcomes. The application of research findings to specific types of interpersonal relationships (e.g., marital, managerial) is also an important dimension of this series.

COMMUNICATING WITH MEDICAL PATIENTS

edited by
Moira Stewart
Debra Roter

Sage Series

Interpersonal Communication 9

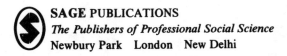

SAGE PUBLICATIONS
The Publishers of Professional Social Science
Newbury Park   London   New Delhi

For information address:

SAGE Publications, Inc.
2111 West Hillcrest Drive
Newbury Park, California 91320

SAGE Publications Ltd.
28 Banner Street
London EC1Y 8QE
England

SAGE Publications India Pvt. Ltd.
M-32 Market
Greater Kailash I
New Delhi 110 048 India

Printed in the United States of America

Library of Congress Cataloging-in-Publication Data

Main entry under title:

Communicating with medical patients / edited by Moira Stewart and
    Debra Roter.
            p.   cm. -- (Sage series in interpersonal communication : 9)
        Bibliography: p.
        Includes index.
        ISBN 0-8039-3216-2. -- ISBN 0-8039-3217-0 (pbk.)
        1. Physician and patient. 2. Interpersonal communications.
    3. Confidential communications--Physicians.   I. Stewart, Moira.
    II. Roter, Debra. III. Series: Sage series in interpersonal
    communication : v. 9.
    R727.3.C63   1989
    610.69'52--dc19   136775   88-36593
                                                                 CIP

FIRST PRINTING 1989

Contents

Series Editor's Introduction

After I finished reading *Communicating with Medical Patients*, I couldn't put it down. I especially wanted my family physician to read it, too. It is a book in which we have a mutual interest. It is a book about how we communicate and how that process affects the bottom line in medicine: quality health care.

We live in a time when the word "revolution" is overused, but the ideas in this book are focused on a truly different perspective on the doctor-patient relationship from that which most of us have experienced. Understanding human interaction has, in this perspective, been cast as an equal partner to technical knowledge for optimum effectiveness in health care.

Each chapter is detailed, but the book is broad in scope. An international list of distinguished authors represents both researchers and practicing physicians. They write about communication education and communication research, but, like so many areas of communications study, diciplinary lines are blurred. These authors represent the areas of family medicine, psychology, sociology, education, and psychiatry as well as communication. The variety of approaches is refreshing and instructive.

This book is driven by four key questions:

- What do we know about the way physicians and patients interact?
- Does our knowledge of physician-patient interaction suggest it plays an important role in outcomes desired by both physician and patient?
- If so, can we identify the most effective ways to achieve these outcomes?

- And, as we learn more about the nature and effects of physician-patient interaction, can the physicians and patients be taught ways to improve the effectiveness of the process?

The utility of the book should be obvious. Scholars will find it to be a valuable resource for scientific studies, instruments, and research strategies used in previous work as well as a preliminary research agenda. The emphasis on teaching throughout this book means it will also be used by educators who are charged with providing practical learning experiences for physicians or prospective physicians. In addition, the book is sure to find its way into classrooms populated by students of health care and communication—students who likely will be undertaking the next generation of research in this area.

—*MARK L. KNAPP*

Acknowledgments

This book would not have come to be without the energetic support and commitment of two key groups: the Centre for Studies in Family Medicine of the University of Western Ontario and the Task Force on the Medical Interview of the Society of General Internal Medicine. In the Centre, Drs. Ian McWhinney, Martin Bass, and Brian Hennen have encouraged Moira Stewart in her efforts over the past five years to develop international forums on doctor-patient communication. In the Task Force, Drs. Mack Lipkin, Jr., and Samuel Putnam have been particularly helpful to this project and to collaborative research ventures led by Debra Roter.

The first International Conference on Doctor-Patient Communication, where this volume was conceived, was funded by the James Picker Foundation, the National Health Research and Development Program of Canada, and the Ministry of Health of Ontario.

We are indebted to Margaret McCaffrey for her excellent work in editing the manuscripts to a consistently high standard.

Moira Stewart is a Career Scientist of the Ontario Ministry of Health, Health Research Personnel Development Program.

"There Were No Signs" from *Balls for a One Armed Juggler* by I. Layton is used by permission of the Canadian publishers, McClelland and Stewart, Toronto.

Foreword

Making the Subjective Objective

Eric J. Cassell

This interesting, evocative book is a notable contribution to a fundamental and continuing change in medicine. It should be read and thought about, not only for the specific ideas in its pages, but also for the future toward which it points: the return of patient and doctor to center stage.

Patients and their symptoms had been the focus of the doctor's attention for centuries until they were displaced by the rise of disease theory in the beginning of the nineteenth century. From then on the physical expression of the patient's affliction—alterations in the appearance of organs and tissue in the clinical examination and at autopsy, changes in physiology and biochemistry, the development of tests and measurements—claimed the profession's attention. Although science came late to medicine, disease theory prepared the way for its entrance and made possible the spectacular advances of the twentieth century. Medical science became the instrument of the physician's power.

During this century, and parallel to the molecularization of medical knowledge, the patient has gradually been reestablished in importance. Today the patient's perspective is influential, and growing in influence, wherever doctors take care of sick people. In a modern hospital the opposite appears to be the case: the technological imperative appears to obliterate patients' personal needs—their individual concerns are brushed aside by the anxiety to support the function of their organs. For that very reason, these wards no longer spearhead the advance of clinical medicine. It is not technology that has turned medicine upside down these days, but rather the power of the patient. The bioethics movement, the malpractice crisis, the rise of consumerism, and the public's enchantment with the chimera of existent wholism are only the most visible current signs of the patient's rise to centrality.

Virtually all medical schools have introduced courses in ethics, medical humanities, or the social sciences. Medical students generally endorse these programs as part of what is frequently termed their idealism, where sick people are placed above technology. It has been repeatedly shown that by their fourth year students have become skeptical and cynical about their ideals. As interns and residents they are rewarded primarily for their technical mastery, and appear to observers to become indifferent to their patients' needs, desires, concerns, and even suffering. Their own reports, however, tell a different story. In the face of their patients' sickness and misery, their previous humane concerns have become a burden. They are burdened as a result of the inadequacies of their training. Their identification of patients' non-disease needs is based almost purely on native skills; the tools provided during their education for responding to these needs are little better. In contrast, their understanding of disease and pathophysiology is excellent and nearly matched by the diagnostic and therapeutic skills they have been taught.

How could it be otherwise? The actions of clinicians, we are frequently told, are based on two kinds of knowledge: medical science and the art of medicine, or the abilities doctors require to apply their knowledge of science to sick people. These abilities are believed to be learned in practice and by precept, and this common belief both distinguishes and denigrates them in relation to science. Ultimately, the art of medicine is based on knowing about sick people; this knowledge is problematic, and that puts the art of medicine below the stairs.

Today, scientific knowledge is frequently considered to be the only *real* knowledge, while other kinds of knowledge are of lesser value. By science is meant natural science; the scientific deals exclusively with the objective (synonymous with measurable). Scientists believe that science deals with facts because only facts have meaning. Facts are things that can be verified, empirically demonstrated. Things that are not facts are doubtful and uncertain, matters of attitude and opinion. From the scientific perspective, questions about whether the man with a broken leg is in pain, or the woman who lost her child is suffering can *never* be answered because they are not open to empirical verification. Considering that medicine's warrant to exist is the relief of suffering, a profession grounded in the belief that it cannot have real knowledge of whether someone is suffering has lost its way.

What physicians know about patients and their suffering (as opposed to their diseases), however, is generally subjective, based on intuition and the interpretation of words, appearances, and behaviors. How can such information compete in medicine with the objective information of science?

Here is where this book stands out. These papers have returned to a saner definition of the scientific by subjecting communication with patients to systematic analysis, without pretending that verbal interaction can be reduced to numbers (the usual criterion of the scientific). They also show us how to remove the stigma of subjectivity from physicians' knowledge of their patients. Scientists and doctors are unique in their odd use of the words "objective" to mean only a thing which can be measured and "subjective" to mean ideas, judgments, percepts, meanings—like the information physicians derive about patients from their spoken language. Where did such nonsense come from? The knowledge contained in verbal interactions becomes objective (employing the word the way the rest of the world uses it) when the utterances are critically examined by the attentive listener. Doctors must work at the tools for discriminating analysis of their communication with patients in order to become a true partner with their knowledge of disease. This book provides guidance for that learning. In doing so, it helps pave the way for an understanding of medicine of which it will be truly said that doctors bring two forces to bear on their patients' problems: their knowledge of medical science and themselves.

Introduction

Moira Stewart
and
Debra Roter

Why are issues concerning the interpersonal relationships between patients and doctors viewed as distinct from other aspects of medical practice? How can they be integrated with the medical practice and education? To address these questions we have brought together the work of researchers, educators, and practitioners from two continents and many disciplines.

The convening of experts across geographic and disciplinary boundaries is no insignificant challenge. We have been struck by divisions within the field of inquiry into the doctor-patient relationship; isolation is obvious even to the uninitiated eye. For example, the powerful teaching techniques developed in Europe and Britain are virtually unknown to North American practitioners. There are similar gaps in our European counterparts' knowledge of North American developments in research and education. The geographic divisions are evident in journals read and work cited, and in the paucity of international forums.

Similar divisions result from professional identification and disciplinary training. Especially evident is the lack of communication between researchers on the one hand, and educators and practitioners on the other. Research findings that should inform the educational process are simply not included in the medical curriculum. Educators and practitioners often do not appreciate important research results partly due to language differences, different journals, and lack of communication between different disciplines.

With these issues in mind, the first International Conference on Doctor-Patient Communication was convened in London, Ontario, in the fall of 1986. An expert panel of educators, practitioners, and researchers from the United States, Canada, Britain, and Europe spent an intensive week exchanging thoughts and perspectives on communication in the doctor-patient relationship. Much of the work discussed during that seminal week is represented in this volume.

GOALS

With this volume, we are seeking a fundamental transformation of the traditional clinical method and the social relations it fosters between doctor and patient and between student and teacher. The vision, articulated by Ian McWhinney, that begins this volume is of a patient-centered clinical method. This transformation is not a trivial refinement in the practice of medicine; it requires a painful acknowledgement that something is amiss in the very fabric of medicine. McWhinney notes that the traditional method diagnoses disease, but does not aim to understand the meaning of the illness *for the patient*.

The patient-centered method aims not only to diagnose the patient's disease but also to understand the meaning of the illness for the patient. This method demands of physicians that they learn to respond to cues by which patients express their feelings, that they develop enough self-knowledge to respond appropriately to patients' feelings, that they have the ability to organize complex biopsychosocial information from the patient, and that they practice empathy and attentive listening. For example, McWhinney maintains that a knowledge of blindness—and a particular patient's experience of blindness—is as important to the physician treating the patient as is a knowledge of vision.

Discontent with the traditional clinical method is well-known, well-voiced, and long-standing. (See the Anthology of pre-1976 writings edited by Stoeckle, 1987). Both patients' and physicians' voices for reform have been heard, but not heeded. This has occurred, McWhinney maintains, because prior suggested reforms have not clearly specified implications for training and practice, or criteria for validating the effect of reforms.

The time for this specification is now. The patient-centered method requires a radical change in the very person of the physician, in the definition of the medical task, and in the basic epistemology of medicine. Medical education must encourage reflection, personal development, and the growth of self-knowledge. It must also teach communication skills that reveal the patient's world to the physician, and analytic skills that can encompass a complex web of relationships rather than single causal chains. Pathological diagnoses are not replaced; rather, the physician's ability to make accurate and meaningful diagnoses is enhanced. Finally, the patient-centered method must be validated by both process and outcome measures, and the criteria for validation of effect must be incontrovertible.

We agree with White (1988) and Odegaard (1986) that the doctor-patient relationship is the cornerstone of the task of medicine. This book was conceived to provide a mandate and charge to medicine: to transform the traditional clinical method by a more humane, patient-centered focus. This book is designed to synthesize a growing body of experience that provides a basis for the patient-centered method. McWhinney's impassioned plea for a new clinical method sets the tone; four sections of the book deal with issues related to the physician's own transformation, issues related to the medical interview, issues related to teaching and learning, and issues related to validation.

EXCELLENCE IN COMMUNICATION

The definitions of excellent communication in this book arise from underlying principles that communication should be patient-centered; patients should be involved in their own care, and patients should have a sense of control over their own treatment. The bias is toward a more active role for patients, leading to mutuality in the doctor-patient relationship. The writings reveal a conviction, based on two decades of research, that better communication will give patients an increased sense of control in the medical encounter over their problems and symptoms and over their own care. More important is the conviction that active patient involvement in care will lead to earlier recovery and higher quality of life.

We believe that physicians will also benefit from a change in the traditional biomedical model and in their relationship with patients. The analogue for the biomedical model in education is a teacher-learner relationship dominated by the teacher. We advocate a more learner-centered basis for training physicians so that they will become better and more effective healers.

Some readers may feel that in our enthusiasm for changes in medical practice and teaching we have been too uncritical. Criticism of patient-centered medicine is certainly not prominent in the book, although there is a commitment to rigorous evaluation. Controversy and confusion does exist regarding the model of relations advocated here, and we take this opportunity to clarify alternative models of doctor-patient relations and their implication for patient care.

TYPES OF DOCTOR-PATIENT RELATIONSHIP

Expectations for a relationship are complex; they are often unstated and sometimes changed depending on the patient's social world, physical condition, stage and type of illness, and a host of cultural and demographic factors. The direct expression of the doctor-patient relationship may change in keeping with changing needs and circumstances so that no single model is forever appropriate, nor is another forever inappropriate.

The most common forms of the doctor-patient relationship exist on a spectrum of high and low control. See Figure 1, taken from Hall and Roter (forthcoming).

If there is high physician control and low patient control, the physician will dominate, making decisions in what he or she perceives to be the patient's best interest. These decisions entail access to information and services. The patient's job is to cooperate with medical advice, that is, to do what he or she is told. This is the traditional form of the doctor-patient relationship and is still the most common. Strengths of the model are attributed to the comfort and support patients may draw from a doctor "parent" figure. Some argue that relief from the burden of worry is curative in itself and that the implied trust and confidence allow the curing art to do its powerful magic.

The reassuring and pat smile from the doctor is uncomplicated by detailed explanations, options, alternatives, and second opinions. Some patients benefit from this type of relationship at particular points in their illness, particularly those suffering from life-threatening and life-limiting conditions. Recognition and fulfillment of this need is important

PHYSICIAN CONTROL

PATIENT CONTROL	LOW	HIGH
LOW	DEFAULT	PATERNALISM
HIGH	CONSUMERIST	MUTUALITY

Figure 1.1   Types of Doctor-Patient Relationship

for both curing and caring. Prolonged commitment to this model, however, significantly limits the development of a mature relationship.

Since the balance of power is obviously imbalanced, this model assumes patient trust and physician altruism, with significant potential for patient exploitation. The President's Commission for the Study of Ethical Problems (1982) concluded that even when patient and physician have mutually agreed on this type of relationship, the result may be questioned. The commission argues that patients and doctors are often on so substantially unequal a footing that few patients really have an effective role in shaping the relationship. The possibility exists, then, that patients may adopt a passive patient role by default, not fully aware of alternatives or able to negotiate a more active stance.

A nationwide survey found that older, less educated patients who were more accepting of authority were more likely to accept this type of relationship (Haug and Lavin, 1983). This group probably would also be least aware of alternatives and most timid in negotiating a different kind of relationship.

Younger, better educated, and more skeptical patients would be much more likely to be assertive and demanding. In a reversed power relationship between doctor and patient, a patient's demands for information and technical services are accommodated by a cooperating physician. This type of relationship is consumerist in nature and redefines the medical encounter as a marketplace transaction. *Caveat emptor* rules the transaction, with power resting in the buyers who can make the decision to buy or not as they see fit (Haug and Lavin, 1983).

When the patient's requests are within the parameters of good medical judgement—and for most conditions these parameters are quite wide—little conflict need emerge. In acceding to demands that are contrary to standard practice, however, the physician is acting outside of his professional expertise and training, skirting the mainstream of medicine and risking criticism from medical colleagues. On the other hand, the physician may lose patients' goodwill and business.

The consumerist doctor-patient relationship has been criticized for its assumption of conflict and diminishment of trust, at least as reflected in any commercial relationship, and its risk of under-utilizing the physician's expertise. The consumerist pattern even suggests that patients who do not assume the assertive posture of the model are failing to act as responsible adults.

The mutuality model still stresses patient control, but is based on a more participatory alternative, the one most often advocated in this book. Each participant brings strengths and resources to the relationship on a relatively even footing. Because the power in the relationship is balanced, decisions are the result of what has been called a meeting between experts (Tuckett et al., 1985). The patient's job, in this model, is to become part of a joint venture.

Conventional wisdom reflected in most training programs holds that physicians bring to medical practice a world view based purely on the biomedical model, which emphasizes biochemistry and technology. In contrast, a patient's world comprises a complex web of personality, culture, living situations, and relationships that color and define the illness experience. Unchallenged, the biomedical view loses the context of the patient's life. As a result, not only may pertinent information be missed and incorrect medical diagnostic decisions be made, but also inappropriate treatment may be selected, seriously threatening the patient's quality of life. When the patient's illness framework is taken into account, the healing resources of both patient and physician are maximized.

What happens when the patient's and physician's expectations are at odds or when the need for change in the relationship cannot be negotiated? Poor "fit" and failure to change may be characterized by a lack of control and may be a relationship of default. In this case, a patient may drop out of care completely because of failed expectations, concluding that all doctors are incompetent, insensitive, or otherwise inadequate. Most often the physician will be unaware of the reasons for the loss of this patient; the patient will simply not come back.

We have described the prototypical forms of the patient-physician relationship, but reality is not so simple and straightforward. Rather, these prototypes are a point of departure and perspective for the discussions in this volume.

1

The Need for a Transformed
Clinical Method

Ian McWhinney

Method is central to any scholarly or professional discipline. Mastery of the discipline requires mastery of a method—techniques for gathering information and rules for classifying information and validating evidence.

A discipline's method evolves as knowledge changes and, in the case of applied disciplines, as objectives change. For over 100 years, medicine has used a traditional clinical method, which has been very successful in meeting certain objectives. However, mounting evidence shows that this method does not meet the needs of the late twentieth century.

THE ORIGINS OF THE
TRADITIONAL CLINICAL METHOD

The traditional method originated in France at the turn of the nineteenth century. Medicine had previously lacked a clinical method and a nosology that was universally accepted as useful. In the seventeenth century, Sydenham had demonstrated the predictive power of a nosology based on observations of the natural history of disease. However, the nosologies of his eighteenth-century successors did not have this power; they were "uncorrelated catalogues of clinical manifestations . . . lacking the prognostic or anatomic significance that would make the results practical or useful" (Feinstein, 1967).

In postrevolutionary France, physicians began to turn their attention to the physical examination of the patient. New instruments, such as the Laennec stethoscope, revealed a new range of clinical information. At the same time, clinicians began to examine the internal organs after death and to correlate physical signs with postmortem appearances. According to Foucault (1975), "The constitution of pathological anatomy at the period when the clinicians were defining their method is no mere coincidence: the balance of experience required that the gaze directed on the individual and the language of description should rest upon the stable, visible, legible basis of death." The result was a radically new classification of disease based on morbid anatomy, a far more powerful classification system than the nosologies of the eighteenth century.

English physicians, who had displayed little enthusiasm for the botanical classifications of the eighteenth century, became so convinced by the French clinico-pathologists that, according to Crookshank (1926), "to interpret in terms of specific diseases [became] almost the only duty of the diagnostician."

This transformation was the beginning of the modern era in medicine. It was not only an advance in medical knowledge; it was a change in the way sick people were perceived. Certain social changes were necessary for the new medicine to become possible: "a reorganization of the hospital field, a new definition of the status of the patient in society, and the establishment of a certain relationship between public assistance and medical experience, between help and knowledge . . . ." (Foucault, 1975). The reorganization of the hospitals and medical schools in the wake of the French Revolution prepared the ground for "a mutation in medical knowledge" (Foucault, 1975). The result was the clinical method we know today.

Tait (1979) described the emergence of the method in his study of the records at St. Bartholomew's Hospital, where the archives contain clinical case notes dating back to the early nineteenth century. In this early period, clinical records were an unstructured account of the patient's complaints and the physician's superficial observations. By the 1820s, when the Laennec stethoscope was being used, notes on physical signs in the chest began to appear in the records.

The first part of the record to become structured, however, was the postmortem report. This became evident about 1850. From 1850 to 1880, there emerged, slowly and unevenly, a more structured method for recording the history and physical examination. Then, quite abruptly, about 1880 the record of the examination began to assume the structure used today: history of presenting complaint, history of past illnesses, family history, systems review, and so on. The process that began in late eighteenth century France culminated a century later in a fully defined clinical method.

That same clinical method dominates medicine today. Advances in investigative technology have made the method far more precise, and advances in microbiology, physiology, and biochemistry have increased its power to make causal inferences. Its aim, however, is still to interpret symptoms and signs in terms of physical pathology. This is simultaneously its greatest strength and its severest limitation.

The strength of the method lies in three of its features. First, it tells clinicians precisely what they have to do to get the required results: take the patient's history, conduct the examination and investigation in the prescribed way, and you will either arrive at the pathological diagnosis or be able to exclude organic disease. Second, it simplifies, orders, and clarifies what would otherwise be a very complex process. Third, it provides precise criteria for validation. The pathologist tells the clinicians whether they are right or wrong. These features of the method are exemplified in the clinico-pathological conference.

LIMITATIONS OF THE TRADITIONAL METHOD

Crookshank (1926) remarked about the books on diagnostic method that appeared in the first quarter of this century that they "give excellent schemes for the physical examination of the patient, whilst strangely ignoring, almost completely, the psychical." The traditional method is strictly objective: it diagnoses diseases. It does not aim, in any systematic way, to understand the meaning of the illness for the patient or to place it in the context of his life story or culture. Subjective matters, such as feelings and relationships, are excluded from consideration; the physician is encouraged to be objective and detached. Individual physicians may act differently, but in doing so they depart from the method as represented in the literature. The objectivity of the traditional method accords well with its origins in the European Enlightenment.

Paradoxically, the successes of medical technology have exposed most vividly the limitations of the traditional method. Concentration on the technical aspects of care has diverted us from the patient's inner world, an aspect of illness the method does not routinely force on our attention. At the same time, the complexities and discomforts of modern therapeutics have made it even more important for us to understand the patient's experience. Our neglect of this may explain the remarkable growth in patients' published descriptions of illness, many of them critical of the care they have received. Baker (1984) found 147 of these publications, which she calls pathographies, published from 1960 to 1982. Of the 91 she considered worthy of study, 14 were written between 1960 and 1969, 63 between 1970 and 1979, and 14 between 1980 and 1982. Those written by physicians or their relatives are of special interest, for they often identify very vividly with the defects of the method.

A poignant example is one physician's account of his own experience with slowly progressive macular degeneration. "Through all of these years," he writes, "and despite many encounters with skilled and experienced professionals, no ophthalmologist has at any time suggested any devices that might be of assistance to me. No ophthalmologist has mentioned any of the many ways in which I could stem the deterioration in the quality of my life. Fortunately, I have discovered a number of means whereby I have helped myself, and the purpose of this essay is to call the attention of the ophthalmological world to some of these devices and, courteously but firmly, to complain of what appears to be the ophthalmologist's attitude: 'We are interested in vision but have little interest in blindness'" (Stetten, 1981). An endocrinologist who developed amyotrophic lateral sclerosis (ALS) writes:

> I travelled to a prestigious medical centre renowned for its experience with ALS. The diagnostic and technical skills of the people were superb, and more than matched the reputation of the institution. The neurologist was rigorous in his examination and deft in reaching an unequivocal diagnosis. My disappointment stemmed from his impersonal manner. He exhibited no interest in me as a person, and did not make even a perfunctory enquiry about my work. He gave me no guidelines about what I should do, either concretely—in terms of daily activity—or, what was more important, psychologically, to muster the emotional strength to cope with a progressive degenerative disease . . . . the only thing my doctor did offer me was a pamphlet setting out in grim detail the future that I already knew about too well. He asked to see me in three months, and I was too polite or too cowardly to ask him why—what benefit was there for me to make the journey again? I still recall that the only time he seemed to come alive during our interview was when

he drew the mortality curve among his collected patients for me. 'Very interesting', he said, 'there's a break in the slope after three years.' When a few months later, I read an article by him in which he emphasized the importance of a compassionate and supportive role for the physician caring for the patient with ALS, I wonder whether he had been withdrawn because I was a physician [Rabin, et al., 1982].

It would be invidious to blame the ophthalmologists or neurologists in these examples. They were only practicing the traditional clinical method as it is described and taught. According to this method, the personal experience of the patient with the illness is not relevant. Nor is it likely that the experience of these two patients was due to the fact that they were both physicians themselves. Many others, physicians and non-physicians alike, have described similar experiences. The fact that even physicians can have this experience when they become patients indicates how seriously defective our clinical method is.

The traditional method does not help the physician to understand the meaning of the illness for the patient, nor is it equipped to deal with the moral and spiritual problems patients experience. Our way of making clinical decisions has fostered the belief that these are technical matters, not moral choices.

Should a clinical method take account of spiritual and moral questions? Are these not outside the physician's domain? The profoundly disturbing effect of illness may lead people to a serious examination of their whole life, raising moral and spiritual questions such as: What are the important things in my life? How have I fulfilled my responsibilities to my spouse, my children, my parents? How will this illness change my ability to fulfill my responsibilities? Has lack of responsibility contributed to my present illness and to my family's sufferings? What is the purpose of my life and work? What has motivated my working life? Have I been faithful to my true vocation?

Healing in its deepest sense—the restoration of wholeness—requires a resolution of these questions. Healing is not the same as treating or curing. Healing happens to a whole person; that is why we can be cured without being healed, and healed without being cured. A person who remains in anguish of spirit even after physical recovery cannot be said to be healed. Even when cure is not possible, Viktor Frankl (1973) has observed that suffering can be borne more readily if its meaning is understood.

How, then, can a physician be a healer unless he or she tries to understand these aspects of a patient's illness? To ask this is not to place the physician in the place of the priest, who has a role that no other person can fill. Priests are ordained to be teachers in spiritual matters and carry the authority to administer the sacraments and provide absolution. When it comes to listening attentively to the sufferings of others, however, any person may be a healer. Physicians, like nurses, are close to suffering and are called to listen more frequently and urgently than others. Imagine what it would be like for patients who felt that, for the first time, they were able to pour out their hearts to a physician, and then to be told that these things should be discussed with a priest, since they are beyond the competence of a physician.

The literature on doctor-patient communication (Ley, 1983) also criticizes our clinical method. All too frequently we do not listen to our patients, perceive their needs, or understand their sufferings. Is it unfair to blame all this on our method rather than on ourselves? In blaming the method we are in fact blaming ourselves. Although clinical method is a tool, it has dimensions beyond those of a scalpel, a drug, or an endoscope. The personality of physicians, and their perception of themselves and their task, enter deeply into clinical method. Changing the tool, therefore, requires changing the person. If we are on the brink of transforming clinical method, we are also on the brink of changing the way physicians think and feel.

THE INFLUENCE OF PSYCHIATRY AND BEHAVIORAL SCIENCE

Since the purpose of psychiatry is to understand aspects of human behavior, we might have expected a transformed clinical method to have emerged from the integration of psychiatry and clinical medicine. So far, there is little evidence that either behavioral science or psychiatry have influenced the traditional method.

Psychiatry itself has been influenced by the traditional method, in that it has developed its own nosology of mental illness. This has doubtless been necessary, but it has focused attention on behavioral pathology rather than on the normal behavior of sick people, and on generalization rather than on an understanding of the individual patient. Psychiatry and behavioral science together have tended to follow the trend toward what William James (1958) called "medical materialism" or "nothing butness," explaining away man's moral and spiritual experiences as "nothing but" psychological mechanisms. Moral and spiritual problems faced by seriously ill patients and their physician have been considered irrelevant. Psychiatry and behavioral science, with some exceptions, have tried to follow clinical medicine in becoming as objective as possible.

There have been several exceptions. Psychiatry and clinical medicine have come together at some points in the last few decades to evolve different clinical methods. The effect of these confluences, however, has been either temporary or limited in range. None of them has yet transformed the clinical method as taught in the medical schools.

In the 1950s and 1960s, Donovan, a gynecologist who trained with Dr. George Engel at Rochester, wrote a series of articles on the doctor-patient relationship and some psychosomatic aspects of gynecology (Wilbush, 1981). He maintained that the question-answer method of interviewing, so characteristic of the traditional clinical method, biased the selection of information from the patient. Donovan himself used an open-ended, patient-centered method, which gave him a very different perspective on the patient's experience.

Using this method with patients believed to have menopausal symptoms, Donovan found no evidence of a clear-cut menopausal syndrome. In many of the women, the symptoms were only one aspect of personal problems which were often of many years' standing. He believed the inadequacy of the clinical method for investigating these patients had resulted in a superficial and inadequate diagnosis of their illness. Donovan's work does not appear to have influenced gynecology; his papers have been cited more often in the behavioral science than in the medical literature.

In the 1950s, Balint (1961, 1964), a psychoanalyst, began to work with groups of general practitioners to explore the doctor-patient relationship. The result was a series of insights that have had a lasting effect on family practice. One of his aphorisms was, "If you ask questions you will get answers: and nothing else" (Balint, 1964). Like Donovan, he realized the inadequacies of the traditional method for reaching any deep understanding of the patient's illness. The need was to listen, not to ask questions. Balint developed the concepts of attentive listening and responding to a patient's "offers" as ways of understanding his illness. One of Balint's most important contributions to clinical method was his distinction between traditional diagnosis, the search for pathology, and overall diagnosis, the attempt to understand the patient and the doctor-patient relationship.

Balint also saw physicians themselves as powerful diagnostic and therapeutic tools that must be understood and applied, hence the importance of physicians' self-knowledge. Balint's influence has been felt in family practice, but not yet in other clinical disciplines.

Another example is the influence of Engel's biopsychosocial model. Engel (1980), a psychiatrist and internist, uses systems theory as a model for integrating biological, psychological, and social data in the clinical process. System theory is rooted in engineering, cybernetics, Gestalt psychology, and operations research. The method of nineteenth-century science was to deal with problems by "cutting them down to size," separating them from their surroundings, and reducing them as far as possible to linear causal chains. System theory seeks to do the opposite: to enlarge the problems until all their significant relationships are included. A system is defined as "a dynamic order of parts and processes standing in mutual interaction" (Von Bertallanfy, 1968).

In nature, each system is both an organized whole and part of a larger whole. Natural systems are ordered hierarchically, with larger, more complex systems superordinate to smaller ones. A person is a hierarchy of systems ranging from the cell to the organ and organ system. A person is also the lowest unit of a hierarchy of social systems from family to community, subculture and culture. Each level of the hierarchy has its own rules and distinctive qualities.

The biopsychosocial model requires the physician to consider and integrate information from several levels of the hierarchy: the milieu interieur, the person, and the level of interpersonal relationships. Although these concepts have been widely accepted, I do not think they have yet been widely adopted as a clinical method. The reason for this may be that the model lacks the strengths of the traditional method: it does not give the clinician a precise prescription for action and it does not provide criteria for validation.

Engel is critical of the psychological and social judgments arrived at by the biomedical method, claiming that the biopsychosocial method is more scientific. The biomedically trained physician, writes Engel, judges interpersonal and social aspects of patients' lives by "tradition, custom, prescribed rules, compassion, intuition, 'common sense' and sometimes highly personal self-reference. Such processes . . . remain outside the realm of science and critical inquiry. Not so for the biopsychosocially oriented physician, who recognizes that to best serve the patient, higher-system-level occurrences must be approached with the same rigor and critical scrutiny that are applied to systems lower in the hierarchy" (1980).

It is important to add that the canons of rigor for reaching a clinical diagnosis are not the same as those for establishing the meaning of the experience for the patient. There is no empirical test for patients' perceptions of their illnesses, the quality of their relationships, or their feelings of responsibility. These can only be ascertained by a dialogue between doctor and patient in which the meaning of words and actions is continually being interpreted and reinterpreted. This method has its own rigor, different from that of empirical science.

More recently, Kleinman et al. (1978) have drawn attention to the frequency with which patients' explanations of their illnesses are discordant with the biomedical model. If the physician fails to explore the patients' understanding of their illnesses, and to negotiate some rapprochement between the two understandings, the outcome is likely to be unsatisfactory. Although illustrated most vividly when physician and patient come from different cultures, discordance can occur even within the same culture. Kleinman et al. maintain that the traditional clinical method has no objective to understand the meaning of the illness for the patient. They recommend a series of questions designed to attain this level of understanding, followed by an explanation of the doctor's interpretation of the illness, and, if necessary, a negotiation between the two views of clinical reality.

As with the biopsychosocial model, this anthropological approach has been widely accepted but, to my knowledge, has not yet had a major impact on our clinical method. Specific questions are suggested for inclusion in the clinical method, but patients often do not disclose their innermost thoughts and feelings in response to questions. Expression of feeling is more likely to follow when the clinician has responded to some subtle cue provided by the patient. This is not to underestimate the value of certain routine questions—only to emphasize that they are rarely sufficient in themselves.

A TRANSFORMED CLINICAL METHOD

The transformed clinical method will be patient-centered rather than doctor-centered. The essence of the patient-centered method is that the physician tries to enter the patient's world, to see the illness through his or her eyes. In the traditional doctor-centered method, physicians try to bring the patient's illness into their world and to interpret the illness in terms of pathology. The transformed method will, of course, include this process, but it will no longer have the dominance it now enjoys.

The physician using the patient-centered method invites and encourages the patient's openness, aiming in every case to understand the patient's expectations, feelings, and fears. These are not usually made explicit, but are expressed in subtle cues, which will be picked up only if the physician is listening attentively. Patients are encouraged to express themselves, even though it may mean that physicians delay the pursuit of their own objectives.

Expectations, feelings, and fears are specific to each patient. The meaning of an illness for a patient reflects his or her unique situation and experience of life. Understanding a person in this way requires physicians to rid their minds of preconceptions and prejudgments, including those preconceptions derived from theories and schemata of human behavior. Theories of human behavior come from the physician's world, not the patient's. As the enquiry proceeds, a theoretical frame of reference may help both physician and patient to understand aspects of the illness, but it is not a substitute for knowing the patient as an individual. Understanding patients in this way also requires in the physician certain personal qualities not usually emphasized in medical education: self-knowledge, moral awareness, a reflective habit of mind, and a capacity for empathy and attentive listening. The following case vignette illustrates why they are needed.

Case Vignette

A 19-year-old girl was playing baseball when she fell to the ground, after which she was unable to bear weight on her right leg. She had dislocated her patella.

She was referred to the orthopedic service of a large general hospital and, after investigation, an arthrotomy was performed with soft tissue stabilization of the patella. The early stages of her convalescence were monitored by clinic staff. The clinic doctor felt that her response to surgical treatment was unsatisfactory. She had not complied with instructions to practice quadriceps exercises in the immediate postoperative period, and her convalescence had been compromised by lack of cooperation with the physiotherapist. When challenged with this, the patient became hostile. Her hostility upset the doctor and their relationship deteriorated.

As her convalescence progressed, the patient continued to have pain, discomfort, and loss of function in her knee. In addition, she complained of profound fatigue and needed 18 hours of sleep each day. She experienced tremor, fainting spells, palpitations, episodes of tachycardia, upper abdominal discomfort, nausea, vomiting, episodic diarrhea, and excessive perspiration. The orthopedic clinic advised her that these symptoms were not due to postsurgical complications, and they suggested that she consult her family physician.

Following a physical examination and some laboratory investigations, the family physician concluded that the patient's symptoms were manifestations of anxiety. She was encouraged to return on several occasions. Over the course of the next few weeks, in response to the physician's active listening, she talked about her life. She had been raised in an evangelical atmosphere, where the strictness of her upbringing had influenced her relationships with peers and friends and her sexuality and its expression. She was the youngest child; constant competition with her very athletic brothers had caused her to excel in sports, which also compensated for her indifferent academic performance. She was able to recognize that she had compensated for poor academic achievement and poor social skills by investing all her time, hopes and aspirations in athletic activities and that she had become immensely competitive.

Over several weeks, the patient developed insight into her problems and gradually recovered from her injury. She was able to recognize that the one area of her life in which she had invested all her hopes and expectations of self-actualization had been destroyed. She recognized that her response to this had been to develop profound anxiety, with periods of depression and withdrawal.

The meaning of this patient's illness can be interpreted at more than one level. Its meaning in anatomical and functional terms is not difficult to define. To the patient, however, it had another meaning. Her athletic pursuits were her way of dealing with doubts about her personal attractiveness and of compensating for an indifferent academic performance. At one blow, the injury destroyed the basis of her self-respect and created a need to reassess her life. Understandably, this reassessment did not occur immediately. The injury was followed by a reaction to her loss. The personal meaning of the illness was therefore conveyed to the physician indirectly—through noncooperation, anger, food refusal, and physiological symptoms.

What did this illness require of the physician? First, he had to identify the patient's behavior and her symptoms as cues to her feelings. It required enough self-knowledge to respond to the patient's anger, not with anger, but with the question "Why is this patient angry and uncooperative?" He needed the analytical skill to exclude an organic basis for the patient's symptoms. He had to think in terms of a complex web of relationships rather than a single causal chain. The injury triggered a life crisis, which in turn delayed recovery from the injury. The physician himself became part of the web, both as a recipient of the patient's anger and, later, as a therapist. Finally, it required the skills of empathy and attentive listening to help the patient work through her problems.

Knee injuries do not usually cause life crises, but they always produce some disturbance in a person's life, as does every illness or injury. This is why understanding the personal meaning of an illness should be integral to our clinical method.

The need for empathy and attentive listening has been recognized in medical education. One response has been to introduce the teaching of communication skills. What has been their impact on clinical method, as practiced in the medical wards and the medical clinics? I believe the impact here has been minimal. An observer could test this by recording how often students and residents are asked questions like, "What are the patient's feelings about the illness?" "What does it mean to him?" "What are his fears?" "What are his expectations?"

The ineffectiveness of attempts to reform our clinical method is attributable, I believe, to two defects of the alternative models: the lack of a clear injunction and the lack of validation criteria. How can these needs be met? To provide a clear injunction, some simplification must be instituted. Just as the traditional clinical method simplifies the complexity of clinical data by reducing it to items like "presenting complaint" and "history of present condition," so the new method must simplify and reduce the data on the personal meaning of illness. Levenstein et al. (1986) have done this by asking physicians to focus on three items: the patient's expectations, feelings, and fears. Just as the traditional method tells the clinician what he has to do but not how to do it, so the transformed method does not tell the clinician *how* to elicit expectations, feelings, and fears. That requires learned skills, especially the skill of attentive listening.

Clinical method can be validated both by process and outcome measures. Validation of process in the traditional method is usually done by audit of the medical record. This gives the observer only a second-hand account of the interaction between doctor and patient. To validate a method that includes the exploration of a patient's inner experience, audit of the record is likely to be insufficient. In the videotape and audiotape, however, we have means of laying all the subtleties of an interaction open to critical observers. Levenstein et al. (1986) and Stewart (1984) have shown how explicit criteria can be used for measuring the "patient-centeredness" of an interaction.

The ultimate test of a method is its outcome. To test the accuracy of the clinical diagnosis, the clinician can go to the pathologist. The equivalent test for accuracy of the patient's inner experience is the patient himself. Patients can tell us whether the physician acknowledged their expectations and understood their feelings. Moreover, once we have valid operational criteria for measuring "patient-centeredness," we can examine the association between this and the patient's recovery from his illness. Already there is evidence of an association between "patient-centeredness" and a greater likelihood of recovery (Bass et al., 1986; Headache Study Group, 1986).

THE NATURE OF THE TRANSFORMATION

I regard this as a transformed clinical method rather than an addition to the traditional method for two reasons: first, it requires a radical change in the person of physicians and in their perception of their task; second, it requires a change in the epistemology of medicine.

Understanding the inner life of another person requires putting aside one's self. This involves "bracketing" our prejudices and theoretical formulations so that the patient's experience can be apprehended as it is lived through (Kestenbaum, 1982). It includes setting aside, temporarily, our explanatory frames of reference, be they pathological, psychological, or social. Only in this way can our perception be "without prejudice." Keen (1970) has described the method thus:

> Mature awareness is possible only when I have digested and compensated for the biases and prejudices that are the residue of my personal history. Awareness of what presents itself to me involves a double movement of attention silencing the familiar and welcoming the strange. Each time I approach a strange object, person or event, I have a tendency to let my present needs, past experience or expectations of the future determine what I will see. If I am to appreciate the uniqueness of my datum, I must be sufficiently aware of my preconceived ideas and characteristic emotional distortions to bracket them long enough to welcome strangeness and novelty into my perceptual world. This discipline of bracketing, compensating, or silencing requires sophisticated self-knowledge and courageous honesty.

Although medicine does not make its epistemology explicit, an examination of the medical school curriculum leaves one in little doubt that medical knowledge is defined as that which is verifiable empirically by the scientific method. In this, medicine has embraced the positivism that has dominated western thought since the Enlightenment. The transformation of clinical method requires medicine to acknowledge that the scientific method is only one of several routes to knowledge.

The distilled wisdom of the great philosophical and religious traditions recognizes three paths to knowledge: the sensory, the mental, and the transcendent. Each requires rigorous discipline if it is to lead to truth. The path to an understanding of meaning is the mental-phenomenological method (Kestenbaum, 1982; Wilber, 1983). This begins with the bracketing of our preconceptions, so that the mental phenomena may be directly apprehended. Our apprehensions are then "shared and confirmed (or rebuffed) via interpersonal communication and interpretation" (Wilber, 1983).

We need to reexamine what Foucault (1975) would call our "episteme," to redefine what medical knowledge is and how it can be obtained. Should not a knowledge of blindness—and a particular patient's experience of blindness—be as important to a physician as a knowledge of vision?

CONSEQUENCES FOR MEDICAL EDUCATION

In *Science and the Modern World*, Whitehead (1926) expresses with great clarity what is wrong with modern professional education:

> Professional education produces minds in a groove. Now to be mentally in a groove is to live in contemplating a given set of abstractions. The groove prevents straying across country, and the abstraction abstracts from something to which no further attention is paid. But there is no groove of abstraction which is adequate for the comprehension of human life. Thus, in the modern world, the celibacy of the medieval learned class has been replaced by the celibacy of the intellect which is divorced from the concrete contemplation of the complete facts. We are left with no expansion of wisdom and with greater need of it. Wisdom is the fruit of a balanced development.

I would go further and say that wisdom is declining in the modern world.

In discussing the remedy, Whitehead is critical of our preoccupation with intellectual analysis. He fears that, in our attempts to attain a balanced development, we will supplement professional training (the mastery of a set of abstractions) with a slighter study of a different set of abstractions, as could so easily happen if we add courses in behavioral science to the curriculum. Such courses usually deal with abstractions rather than concrete human experience. It could even happen if we add courses in the humanities, for, in the modern university, the humanities have not escaped from the pressure to analyze. In Whitehead's view, "The makeweight which balances the thoroughness of the specialist intellectual training should be of a radically different kind from purely intellectual analytical knowledge." The need is for "aesthetic education."

Medicine will not necessarily be made more human by adding courses to the curriculum. We need a transformed clinical method that will lead us naturally into the subjective aspects of medicine. We will also need to teach clinical medicine in a different way—a way that will foster, rather than stifle, the student's moral and aesthetic development.

Let me give some examples of how this might enrich medical education. We tend to forget that medicine has a very rich imaginative and descriptive literature. Through the ages, talented writers have reflected on the great themes of medicine: suffering, illness, healing, dying. As I mentioned earlier, some have given us graphic personal experiences of their own illnesses. Some have written perceptively on a physician's life and work. Even the literature of clinical description can include patients' subjective experiences. The writings of Oliver Sacks (1973, 1984) are a modern example of this genre. Sacks's case histories are not only good clinical histories, but also testaments to the human spirit in its triumph over suffering. Medicine has its own poetry—a poetry we can all experience if we learn to listen to our patients' stories.

I can visualize a course in the medical curriculum that would sensitize students to the feelings of their patients. Students could be asked to imagine the experience of losing a pregnancy, having inoperable cancer, losing one's vision, caring for a spouse with Alzheimer's disease, bereavement, being paraplegic, and so on. They could then meet in a small group with people who had gone through these experiences and read related clinical descriptions and imaginative literature.

If I am correct, there are far-reaching implications for medical education. If physicians are to change in the way I have suggested, their education will have to encourage reflection, personal development, and the growth of self-knowledge. The current environment of the medical school, with its information overload, frenzied activity and competitive ethos, in many ways discourages personal development of this kind. Medical scientists sometimes make reference to "the frontiers of knowledge." I think they have in mind a frontier that is "out there." The newest and most challenging frontier may be within us.

PART I

Transforming the Physician

The first series of papers in this volume deals with our most fundamental and ambitious goal: a radical change in the physician's very person. Such change refers to the intimate processes of growth through self-awareness and personal development that are necessary for full realization of healing potential. This is a dynamic process with changing challenges and demands throughout life. Weston and Lipkin begin with the evolution of the student to physician. The student learns to tolerate the difficulties and uncertainties inherent in caring for patients and sharing their burdens of grief and suffering. These authors have observed predictable phases in students' development and readiness to learn. Novice medical students appear to exhibit a higher degree of skill talking with patients than more advanced students, partly because the more advanced students are forced to concentrate on the biomedical approach to patient care.

The challenge of mastering the art of healing is not only intellectual, but also emotional and physical. The authors argue that, tragically, the social relations between teacher and student mirror those of the traditional doctor-patient relationship in that intellectual and biomedical concerns take precedence. Medical education provides little guidance and emotional support to students for the overwhelming burdens they are often ill-equipped to carry.

The second paper of this series is also concerned with the training process that has the potential to enhance physician self-awareness and personal growth. Jacques Frenette and Fernand Blondeau provide first-hand insight into the use of Balint groups as a vehicle to transform the physician. Their paper describes the effective use of Balint training for residents in primary care.

Balint training is a powerful technique for promoting physician self-awareness that is well-known and practiced in Europe, but not widespread in North America. The authors make suggestions for incorporating this useful technique into training programs.

A fuller exploration of physicians' self-awareness in the healing relationship is found in Mark Longhurst's chapter. Insight can be gained, he states, by reflecting what others think of one, understanding one's own learning style, experiencing the humanities and creative arts, and experiencing clinical practice. Longhurst shares the sometimes painful, but ultimately rewarding, process by which he has increased self-awareness through his relationships with patients, and concludes by raising the intriguing question of whether physicians need be "wounded healers" who have healed themselves. He suggests that acquisition of self-awareness is a healing process in itself.

2

Doctors Learning Communication Skills:
Developmental Issues

W. Wayne Weston
and
Mack Lipkin, Jr.

> To a newcomer, one of the most striking features about medical education is
> the scant attention given to the basic psychosocial aspects of the socialization
> process, specifically the urgent anxieties that confront medical students. Sci-
> entific detachment and objective rationality reign supreme at the medical
> centre, so that, for the most part, recruits are left pretty much on their own to
> deal with their own fears and inner conflicts [Coombs, 1978: 134].

Learning to communicate effectively with patients challenges students
and demands more than simply learning good interviewing techniques.
Students must be prepared to commit themselves to relationships with
patients where there are often no clearly defined limits or end points;
the students must learn to tolerate the difficulties, confusions, and
uncertainties inherent in closeness to and management of sick people,
and to use these relationships for their healing power. One of the central
tasks of physicians is to create a sense of security and comfort, both by
their interactions with their patients and by their very presence. "Being
with" sick people in this manner requires physicians to be able to don
the healer's mantle and to accept the awesome power bestowed on them
by the sick. Additionally, students have often not experienced the issues
inherent in the interview—grief, dying, aging, and human suffering of

AUTHOR'S NOTE: *The authors wish to acknowledge Gregory Carroll Ph.D. for his contributions to the conceptual approach in the chapter and Lisa Nachtigall for energetic assistance in
developing a scholarly base.*

all kinds. The students' skills of interacting with empathy, positive regard, and genuineness are still rudimentary. These skills, together with learning about healing, must be experienced, felt, and integrated into the student's professional identity. These tasks are not for the fainthearted or the immature; they make great demands on the skills and personal strengths of the young physician-in-training. This chapter concentrates on the development of these personal resources.

As Coombs stated above, medical school concentrates on teaching facts, leaving students to deal on their own, as best they can, with their personal, emotional responses to what they are learning about disease, disability, and death. Although often the most important therapy physicians have to offer is **themselves**, medical education typically affords students and young doctors little or no help in understanding this profound responsibility and special privilege, let alone in learning how to do it. Becoming a doctor requires more than learning a body of knowledge and a set of skills; it also requires a significant transformation in the person of the student.

If we accept the premise that learning in medical school is more than the accumulation of information and technical skills (it involves a fundamental change in the person of the student-physician), then educators must examine ways to understand this process. This developmental approach to understanding the learning process is predicated on two fundamental principles:

- Students' readiness, or ability, to learn certain concepts and skills depends on their stage of development.
- New learning builds on what was previously learned, therefore the sequence in which learning occurs may be a crucial variable in effective learning and development.

In this chapter we present a framework for understanding learning in medical school, considering changes both within the student and in the learning environment.

PERSONAL DEVELOPMENT

Learning and development are closely linked: both connote changes in individuals brought about by experience. Developmental change implies that what was learned was not simply added to a store of knowledge. When people develop, they change in **qualitative** ways, "in the sense of self, in the manner in which specific tasks are assumed, in the manner in which relationships with others are developed and managed, and in the manner in which major choices are made" (Knopke and Anderson, 1981: 105). Several authors have described psychosocial development in adults as a series of discrete stages, each characterized by specific major issues to be resolved (Belenky et al., 1986; Chickering et al., 1981; Daloz, 1986; Erikson, 1980; Levinson, 1978; Loevinger, 1982). These stages are important in learning because they reflect and influence students' major preoccupations: how they see their tasks and roles in learning and even how they structure their knowledge.

Personal development forms the context in which all learning occurs—what is learned and how it is learned is embedded within the student's developmental framework. Late adolescents are preoccupied with establishing ego and sexual identities, detachment from parents, and development of independence. Young adults must pursue vocational goals, develop a professional identity, and attain a capacity for intimacy. It is important for them to establish intimate relationships and to create their own family arrangements.

Many physicians in training postpone dealing with such issues until their twenties and thirties (Grose et al., 1983; McCue, 1985; Pfeiffer, 1983). Medical training is psychologically demanding and time consuming, restricting general learning and growing up. Young physicians may focus so much on their education that they have no solid identity apart from that of their professional role as physicians. They may have a staggering knowledge of disease but be naive about human suffering; they may know precise drug treatment but stand empty-handed and mute before the patient who desperately needs counsel and support to cope with a terminal illness; they may be masters of medicine's remarkable biotechnical resources but lack power to heal the human spirit.

Students' enforced reliance on parents and spouses for emotional and financial support often magnifies the strain of medical education, intensifying dependence and retarding development. Students can also be dependent on their professors, especially in schools with teacher-centered curricula. Such dependency may interfere with the formation of a strong sense of independence or identity. Erickson argued that identity formation is the major developmental task of adolescence and early adulthood. It is a time of life when young people can try out different roles, play at being adults, and experiment with themselves. Once choices have been made and integrated, they become part of the individual's history and a template for the future.

> In the health professions, for example, one person might be finishing medical school and studying in a residency; another might be finishing work on a baccalaureate degree and pursuing graduate study. The occupational choice provides structure and direction to a person's life activity, frequently to the extent that as more time and energy are devoted to finding this direction, other activities and pursuits become less valued and therefore less a part of daily life [Knopke and Anderson, 1981: 105].

Until they develop a clear, integrated sense of themselves, young adults are not ready to tackle the next developmental task: establishing true intimacy. Erikson (1963) described intimacy as "the capacity to commit himself to concrete affiliations and partnerships and to develop the ethical strength to abide by such commitments, even though they may call for significant sacrifices and compromises." Young physicians who are still struggling with these issues will also have difficulties in their professional lives, particularly in those disciplines where the professional use of self in a long-term relationship with patients is crucial to effective work. Also, this developmental arrest partly accounts for the failure of so many medical school marriages.

Such physicians in training, caught in the throes of delayed adolescent turmoil, are a challenge to their teachers.

> When things go wrong, residents resemble adolescents caught in role confusion; they are moody, anxious, unable to make decisions, hateful of self and work, and overly conscious of paths not taken [Grose et al., 1983: 489-490].

If the teachers, also, are struggling with their own developmental needs, serious problems may develop in the relationship between them unless they can recognize the sources of these difficulties. The teachers may be dealing with Erikson's stage of generativity versus stagnation (Erikson, 1980). Have they mastered the developmental tasks up to this point in their lives to produce a valuable body of work and promote others' growth and development? To what extent will their unfinished business from earlier stages lead to self-absorption and stagnation? "Adolescent" rebellion in students may provoke righteous indignation in their teachers, and they may both overreact to each other out of their mutual unresolved developmental needs.

COGNITIVE DEVELOPMENT

The ways in which individuals view education, how they make sense of what they study, and even how they find meaning in their worlds are strongly influenced by development.

Perry (1970, 1981) described a series of stages of cognitive growth in university students. As students grow and struggle to make sense of their life experience, they find their familiar patterns of meaning inadequate, and they reach out for broader and deeper understanding. Perry argued that each new position both includes and transcends the earlier ones.

The students' first position is **dualism**, the division of meaning into two realms: good versus bad, we versus they, right versus wrong. For every problem, there are absolute right answers known by the authorities whose role it is to teach them. Knowledge is seen as a thing "out there" to be memorized by hard work.

In the next stage, **multiplicity**, students attempt to make sense of a diversity of opinions. They may argue that the right answer is not known yet or that some poor authorities have created confusion or that the authority wants the students to find "the answer" in themselves. The next step is for students to recognize that there is legitimate uncertainty in some areas. They retain a fundamental dualistic structure by dividing the world into two domains: the right-wrong world of authority and the uncertain world of personal opinion. In areas where the right answer is unknown, one opinion is as good as another. "The capacity for meta-thought, for comparing the assumptions and processes of different ways of thinking, has not yet emerged. This is perhaps the most critical moment in the whole adventure for both student and teacher" (Perry, 1981: 85).

In the stage of **relativism**, students have discovered methods to evaluate different opinions. Some will be found worthless, and there will remain issues where diversity of opinion is inevitable. At this stage, education shifts from collecting what "they" want toward developing a way of thinking shared by both teacher and student. Students are no longer just holders of meaning but makers of meaning. This is the basis of independent thought. This stage is very anxiety-provoking—there are no absolutes to rely on, and the students may feel that everything is tentative and must be reevaluated.

The final stage is **commitment**. In the place of uncertainty and diversity of opinion, students realize that they must take the risk of making their own choices. "Knowing that 'such and such is true' is an act of personal commitment . . . from which all else follows. Commitments structure the relativistic world by providing focus in it and affirming the inseparable relation of the knower and the known" (Perry, 1970: 97). Perry argued that this stage often requires a dialectical logic. Complex issues are frequently portrayed as a polarity between opposing opinions. Commitment involves not taking a compromise position, but rather embracing the tension of opposites and transcending them.

Perry urged the teacher to be aware of the considerable difficulties and anxieties accompanying the transition from one stage to the next. Each stage of development constitutes a qualitatively different frame of reference for perceiving and responding to experience. Giving up old comfortable ideas, even voluntarily, is often accompanied by mixed feelings, even pain and fear.

Learners may defend themselves against ideas especially when new ideas require admitting personal limitations or failure. This defense may involve projection (blaming somebody else or circumstances) or rationalization (arguing the case for the old way). Smith (1982) pointed out that change is most likely to occur when learners are free to face the ambivalence within themselves and are not pressured by others to change. They need a climate in which they can safely express themselves freely and where they feel accepted, regardless of attitudes. The process of incorporation is often aided by identification with others.

DEVELOPMENTAL TASKS IN MEDICAL EDUCATION

Table 2.1 summarizes the many developmental tasks facing the student physician. Many medical schools are so preoccupied with making sure their students know all the facts that they ignore the profound consequences their teaching methods have on their students' personal and cognitive development. They emphasize avoiding error and having the right answers, coupling this with a curriculum crammed with information. There is little time for critical reflection. This may result in a

TABLE 2.1   Maturation of the Student-Physician

	FROM	TO
FOCUS OF LEARNING:	Facts	Principles
	Knowledge	Wisdom
	Practical value	Creativity & Deeper Values
APPROACH TO LEARNING:	Passive recipient	Active agent
	Errors are to be avoided, denied, punished	Errors are raw material for learning
	Dependence	Independence, interdependence
	Need for certainty	Tolerance of ambiguity
	Imitation	Originality
	Narrow interests	Broad interests
	Superficial concerns	Deep concerns
	Amalgamate	Integrate
COGNITIVE STYLE:	Dualistic search for the "right" answer	Evolving commitment to better answers
	Receiver of meaning	Maker of meaning
PERSONAL DEVELOPMENT:	Identity formation	Intimacy, early generativity
	Selfishness	Altruism
	Boundary maintenance: rigid or vague compartments	Boundary maintenance: comfortable distinction of roles
PROFESSIONALIZATION	Sense of self as student	Comfortable in role of doctor
	Needing to prove self	Comfortable with strengths & limits
	Few responsibilities	Many responsibilities
	Rescue fantasy	Good enough
	Rugged individual	Team member
CONCEPT OF MEDICINE:	A "trade"	A "craft"
	A *dogmatic* science	An *art that uses* science
	A hierarchy	A contract and a covenant
	MD as expert	MD also servant
	A job	A "Calling"

regression of students' cognitive development to Perry's stage of dualism. This focus on being right may also lead to intolerance for areas of study that do not have clear-cut answers.

The transitions from medical school to residency training and then to independent practice are often difficult, especially so for those entering primary care. The biomedical framework they have learned during their training rapidly proves inadequate for understanding many of the clinical problems they meet in practice. There is great diversity of opinions and few absolute answers. Students may react to this situation by discrediting their teachers or even the whole field.

Perry described two deflections from growth in students who are unable to tolerate the uncertainties and anxieties required for healthy growth. One approach is **retreat** into an extreme and rigid dualism. Students adopting this posture often present childlike complaints and demands and may manifest a moralistic righteousness and hatred of different points of view. The second form of regression and alienation is **escape**—the exploitation of multiplicity and relativism to avoid the responsibilities of commitment.

Brent (1981) described five developmental tasks for physicians to accomplish during their training. Although he focussed on residency training, we believe these issues are confronted first in medical school and may not be resolved until after many years in practice.[1] The first task Brent labeled **vulnerability/invulnerability:** "This developmental task requires that the resident be able to accept vulnerability in himself and others while still maintaining a self-image as a competent healer" (p. 418). Physicians must come to terms with their magical wishes to be omnipotent and with their unrealistic expectations that they will know everything important and will never make serious errors.

In the second task, **active versus passive**, the physician "needs to learn how to balance the desire to care versus the desire to cure" (p. 418). Physicians must come to accept the limitations of the power of medicine and learn effective approaches to providing comfort and support to patients, rather than ordering more tests or performing more procedures to avoid confronting the uncertainties and confines of medicine.

The next task, **helplessness/problem-solving**, refers to the need to find an effective approach to the health care system at large. Many physicians adopt a rugged, individual approach, complaining about the hospital administration or the government instead of finding a more effective way to bring about needed changes in the system.

The task of **boundary maintenance** is crucial. "The resident needs to discover how close he wants to get to other staff members, patients and work in general" (p. 420). Residents need to learn how to say no and when to ask for help so that they do not become over-extended. They need to learn how to use their relationships with patients for its healing power as well as for the personal rewards this offers, without becoming over-involved.

The fifth task, **professional identity**, involves "the delineation of a role for oneself . . . (and) . . . the development of an ability to judge one's own performance critically" (pp. 420, 421). Brent argued that this is the most important task of the residency. During this time, residents-in-training become physicians, beginning to see themselves as professional healers. It is crucial that individuals not allow their professional identity as physicians to become so hypertrophied that they lose all sense of themselves as human beings separate from this role.

Brent concluded that "residency is more than the acquisition of new skills and knowledge. It also involves the development of attitudes and the modification of self representations" (p. 421).

The experience of being in medical school, described from a student's point of view, helps to flesh out Brent's useful framework. Melvin Konner (1987), who had previously been a professor of anthropology, described how medical school transformed him:

> And of course, last but hardly least, I now tend to see people as patients . . . . I see the flaws not just because the veil has been torn from my eyes by everything from the anatomy lab to the gynecology surgery suite, but because I have come to think first of what is wrong. Where is the pain? What is the problem? How can I help you? My stance toward people . . . now has a large component of a desire to find out what is wrong—something is wrong with everyone—and to try and make it right. It is not the only thing that I think of, but it is always in the back of my mind [pp. 366, 367].

He argued that medical school is not only intellectually challenging but requires great emotional and physical stamina. Medical training not only teaches a body of knowledge but changes the person. Although he decried the long hours without sleep, the enormous burden of work, and the almost overwhelming sense of lurching from crisis to crisis, all with little or no emotional support from the faculty, Konner argued that this may be a necessary part of the socialization process. The transformation from student to physician must be a difficult and memorable experience, he argued, so that the student feels he has been through something special that other people have not. Only then will he feel like a real doctor. But there are terrible risks in this process: the loss of compassion and the development of professional arrogance, emotional constriction, marital break-up and frank emotional illness (Konner, 1987: 373, 374).

DEVELOPMENTAL SEQUENCE IN THE CURRICULUM

I'd be sitting talking with a patient, in would sweep twelve coats, grab the chart from my hand, never introduce themselves to me or the patient, discourse loudly over the bed in technical jargon as if they were dealing with a hunk of beef, then sweep out without a word. On to the next case . . . . I don't want to become that kind of doctor. And what's particularly strange to me is that the people in my class here don't seem that way at all . . . . So the question in my mind for the past two weeks has been, what's the hamburger machine that chops up nice kids and turns them into the doctors I got to know [Le Baron, 1981: 58]?

The learning environment changes in predictable ways from the premedical years through the clerkship to the postgraduate years of training. This sequence of change is often out of step with the student's developmental needs and may partially explain some of the difficulties the student experiences. For example, many medical schools are "dichotomized" into preclinical and clinical halves. As well, postgraduate training provides a distinct environment. (See Table 2.2 for some of the contrasts among preclinical, clinical, and postgraduate education.)

In the preclinical half, the teaching methods are primarily didactic, emphasizing basic sciences. Often there is such a volume overload of material to be learned and regurgitated on multiple-choice examinations that students give up trying actively to understand the material, resorting to learning it in a superficial manner just well enough to pass the exams. Then, usually abruptly, students are placed in a clerkship experience where learning is primarily experiential and where they are responsible, not only for most of their own learning, but also for patient care. They are expected to work long hours, often go without sleep, and frequently perform more than their share of scut work. Despite these difficult conditions, clinical clerks are expected to perform their tasks efficiently, skillfully, and without complaint. They are expected to take charge of their own learning, although during their two preclinical years they had very little time or opportunity to develop effective self-directed learning. They are also expected to relate their basic science training to the clinical problems of the patients they care for, even though most of their basic science training was provided by nonphysicians and they were given little guidance about the clinical relevance of what they were learning.

TABLE 2.2 **Sequential Changes in the Learning Environment for the Doctor-in-Training***

	Pre-Clinical Student	Clerkship	Postgraduate
1. Teaching/ Learning Methods:	Lectures Seminars	Apprentice	Apprentice/ supervisor
2. Emphasis:	"The basics"— facts and concepts	Application of: Knowledge, Skills Attitudes (often unplanned)	Problem solving Skills Attitudes (often unplanned)
3. Major Responsibilities	Learn (memorize)	Learning Patient care Scut work	Patient care Supervising
4. Evaluation:	MCQ's OSCE's Exams based on textbook learning	Performance review (subjective) Occasional direct observation Licensing exam (MCQ's, PMP's)	Performance review Specialty exam (MCQ's, PMP's, orals)
5. Competing Demands:	Volume overload	Scut work	Too many patients to treat and students to teach
6. Role:	University student	Student doctor	Novice physician
7. First-time Experiences:	Cadaver Initial contact with patients 1st Rectal exam 1st Vaginal exam 1st Venipuncture No longer top of the class 1st failure	Clinical responsibility 1st serious error 1st death 1st birth 1st cardiac arrest Choice of career path Experiential learning	Independent clinical responsibility Teaching medical students Self directed learning
8. Curriculum:	Precise	General	Vague
9. Characteristics of the successful student:	Memory Comprehension	Motivation Maturity Stamina Integration of learning Memory Comprehension	Organization Interpersonal skills Dedication Integration of learning Comprehension

*Partly based on Bartlett, R. H. and Judge, R. D. (1986) "Into the Fire: Basic to Clinical Science Transition," in Bartlett, R. H. et al (Eds.) *Medical Education: A Surgical Perspective*. Chelsea, MI: Lewis.

LEARNING COMMUNICATION SKILLS

Skill in communicating with patients is the single most important skill the student physician learns. Using effective interviewing skills, the physician is able to discover the patient's problems, discuss treatment plans, and develop a good working relationship. These skills are not learned in isolation. What students learn and how effectively they use what they learn depend on many things: what else they are learning at the same time and the relative values placed on the competing demands for their time; teachers' expectations of students at different phases in the curriculum; the inherent abilities of students depending on their own personal development.

Communication skills are a hierarchy, building on prior skills:

- *"Taking" a history of illness.* In most medical schools these skills are taught early, often in the first year. The student must learn basic questioning technique and must become comfortable asking about areas generally considered private, such as bowel and bladder function or sexual activity.
- *Interviewing* is more open-ended and less disease-centered than history taking; it is more a dialogue than a question/answer process. Students need to be well versed in their history-taking skills so that they are assured that they will not miss anything important. In the medical school culture, missing a disease is a cardinal error; not helping a patient talk about the personal anguish of illness and disability is rarely criticized. This is a much more difficult skill to acquire; it demands of students that they be able to listen empathetically and not feel guilty if they cannot cure the patient.
- *Giving information to patients* requires different skills than taking information from patients: being well organized, clear, avoiding jargon, and tailoring the information to what the patient is able to cope with. Unfortunately, many medical schools ignore this aspect of communication.
- *Accepting responsibility* for a patient is often assumed to occur automatically. It is often terrifying for students to shift from being mainly responsible for information gathering to first-line patient care. In primary care, it often takes time before students can understand the nature of comprehensive and continuing responsibility for patients beyond the obligation to deal with the patients' presenting problems in an episodic manner.
- *Developing a close relationship with patients* comes easily to some students but is very difficult for others. Almost all students have concerns about their competence in relating professionally. Some students are shy, others are more comfortable with things and ideas than they are with feelings, and others are not ready to develop intimate relationships because they have not yet resolved issues of identity.

- *Collaborating or negotiating with patients* about investigation and management demands that students develop skills in working together with people and that they develop comfort with not always being in charge.
- *Learning "survival strategies"* in difficult interviews is essential for students. They need to be prepared, in advance, to handle difficult situations before being thrust into trying predicaments. Students will often avoid opening up a perceived "can of worms" because they do not have any strategies to cope with what might happen.
- *Learning to relate effectively* with "difficult" people is a strong test of physicians' skills but, even more, a challenge to their maturity and character.
- *Becoming a healer* is the ultimate task, not achieved by all physicians. It requires mastery of biotechnical skills and development of special personal qualities. Such physicians have a strong commitment to "hang in" with their patients to the end, no matter what their problems. They are not afraid to get involved with people in a deep and personal way because they have a keen sense of who they are themselves; they have resolved the issues of identity and intimacy described by Erickson. They are at peace with themselves, and their presence brings to the patient a sense of comfort. It is curious that western medicine minimizes the positive impact of the patient's faith and hope in the doctor as a mere placebo response. Experienced clinicians recognize that patients' trust and belief in physicians and their hope for recovery often have a remarkable healing power.

It has been our experience, supported by some literature (Barbee and Feldman, 1970; Cohen, 1985; Helfer, 1970; Preven et al., 1986) that in teaching communication skills, students pass through predictable phases in their development and readiness to learn. Early in their first year of medical school, students are eager to have contact with patients and are interested in anything that patients will talk about. They listen attentively and rarely interrupt. They do not yet feel like doctors and are grateful that patients will let them practice asking questions. Also they do not know much about disease yet and have no responsibility for diagnosis or treatment, so they are not preoccupied with disease or with missing something. In assessing the interviewing skills of 177 first-year students, Preven et al. (1986) found them to have a higher degree of skill in technique (mean score 80.4%) compared to content (61.4%). They were very good at using language appropriate to the patient (95.5%), allowing patients to tell their own story (91.9%), and using open-ended questions (86.3%), but they had difficulty with obtaining a past medical history (22%), attending to patient's cues (46.1%), and determining current life situation (48.3%). Preven argued that their results reflect the good basic interviewing skills of novice student physicians.

As soon as medical students learn about diseases their interviewing methods change; they begin to focus on symptoms of disease and on the functional inquiry, ignoring what patients say about themselves and their struggle to cope with their illnesses. These second- and third-year students appear less caring. Instead of carrying on personal conversations with patients, they conduct interrogations. Cohen's (1985) experience as a sophomore medical student provides a dramatic illustration of this problem. He was an educational psychologist and director of research in education for the Department of Medicine; he entered medical school to learn, firsthand, about the stresses on medical students and about how they learned in medical school. He prided himself on his sensitivity to the psychological aspects of illnesses. Nevertheless, the pressure of time and the pressure to conform destroyed his good intentions.

> I was astounded by my behavior with that patient. Intensive training in interpersonal communications would not have altered how I behaved. Given the time constraint, I dispensed with small talk, barely retaining a semblance of amenity . . . . The focus of my thinking was on the patient's physical signs and symptoms and the physiological reasons for them [Cohen, 1985: 332].

Only after students have mastered the biotechnical approach do they become comfortable again to talk with patients about what the patient wants to talk about.

CONCLUSIONS

Learning communication skills in medicine involves more than focusing on interviewing techniques; it also requires attending to students' personal development. Educators need to be cognizant of their students' cognitive and developmental needs. Students need time to reflect on the personal meaning of their experiences with sick patients. The curriculum must provide a balance of challenge and support; phases in the curriculum need to progress in a logical sequence and should parallel the stages of student learning and development. As Mount (1986) put it:

I am speaking of your personhood, the need for each of you to see yourself, as well as every one of your patients, as a whole person. Even as it is only to the degree that you acknowledge and validate the personhood of your patient, rather than his disease, that you will succeed in touching his real needs and easing his suffering, even so it is only to the degree that you nurture all aspects of your own personhood that your long range effectiveness, both professional and personal, will be assured [pp. 291, 292].

NOTE

1. It is because, while some developmental aspects of medical training are related to the context of training, others relate to the personal development of the individual which may be independent of their training setting.

3

Balint Groups in Clinical Training

Jacques Frenette
and
Fernand Blondeau

Teaching doctor-patient communication focusses mostly on acquisition of skills, but self-awareness of the physician is also an important factor in communicating.

In many countries groups of primary care physicians meet regularly to discuss a patient, to reflect on their relationship with the patient, and to ponder their role in that relationship. The late Michael Balint started such groups in England in the 1940s. They emphasize enhancing the physician's self-awareness and they have become an important vehicle for teaching and learning about the doctor-patient relationship.

Michael Balint, a Hungarian psychiatrist, became interested in primary care when he accompanied his father, a family physician, on his house calls. In 1938, he organized his first group of discussions on medical cases with general practitioners in Budapest. The following year, he moved to England, settling first in Manchester and then in London. He became attached to the Tavistock Clinic in 1948. His wife, Mrs. Enid Balint, reported that the first groups, made up of social workers from the Child Guidance Clinic, were formed in 1948 (Balint, 1986). The next year he organized his first group of general practitioners. These two groups of professionals had experienced a lack of continuity between their university training and their real work.

The Balints wished to collaborate with family physicians in studying cases presented by each member of the group. These two-hour weekly meetings, where the main objective was to study the doctor-patient relationship rather than the clinical diagnosis, were the basis for Michael Balint's best known book, *The Doctor, His Patient and the Illness* first published in 1957. This work deals with

- the doctor as a drug;
- the patient's offer and the real reason for the visit;
- the traditional versus the overall diagnosis;
- the doctor's apostolic function or sense of what is right and wrong for patients to endure;
- the "collusion of anonymity," in which no one appears to be responsible for decisions taken on the patient's behalf;
- relations between generalist and specialist;
- the generalist's psychotherapy.

Their method adapted the Hungarian analytic training, where the trainee presents his first case to his training analyst.

First, free associations are far more effective than the condensation of a formal report in enabling the candidate to communicate the essence of what has gone on in the session with his patient. Second, the training analyst and his student, in addition to addressing themselves to questions of clinical technique in relation to particular problems of the student's patient, can, at the same time, recognize and study the interrelation of his patient's transference and the therapist's countertransference. Indeed the almost uncanny capacity which Balint had for understanding so well his candidate's patient was, at least partly, a reflection of the extent to which he could read his candidate's countertransference as a reflection of the problems of the patient the candidate was treating [Bacal, 1972].

Michael Balint (1957) believed that the general practitioner's "psychotherapy" was authentic, but different from that of the psychoanalyst: "The acquisition of psychotherapeutic skill does not consist only of learning something new: it inevitably also entails a limited, though considerable, change in the doctor's personality." He first encouraged the members of the group to spend more time with their patients to get a better understanding of their problems. Later he condemned the attitude of physicians who devoted two afternoons every week to psychotherapy with their "special patients" and the rest of their time to regular general practice. In 1966, he organized a research group on that problem. Two years after his death, the group published *Six Minutes per Patient* (Balint and Norell, 1976), in which they describe the "flash," or moment of mutual understanding, when the doctor and the patient identify the problem. One experienced family physician stated at an international Balint congress in Budapest, May 1986, that "in the family physician's everyday practice, these "flash" occurrences are rare. Our role consists more in showing interest, respect and understanding toward our patients."

Experienced leaders of Balint groups, such as Dr. Michel Sapir, psychoanalyst from Paris, reason that participants attend such groups to achieve optimum training. In the course of their medical training, they have learned to avoid being influenced by their intuitions, fantasies, and emotions, to revere medical knowledge and scientific proceedings, and, in case of failure, to seek the help of a specialist. After a few years of practicing primary care, they realize their limitations in the presence of numerous problems that require both thorough diagnosis and a different, more global approach (Sapir, 1982).

According to Michael Balint, group studies should give doctors a new outlook on their everyday experience and enable them to identify problems that may be unknown to the medical profession. These problems may be the cause of many fruitless efforts by the physician and useless suffering and irritation for the patient.

BALINT GROUPS AT LAVAL UNIVERSITY

Our experience with Balint groups in our residency training program in family medicine at Laval University was initiated by Dr. Jacques Bury, psychoanalyst, director of the Behavioral Sciences Program in our Faculty of Medicine from 1975 to 1978. Our students' early contact with family physicians at the undergraduate level is conducive to a keener interest in training for family medicine. Balint groups are the main behavioral science activity of our residency program.

The Objectives (Bernatchez et al. 1975)

Residents are taught to
- have a more global understanding of the patient;
- avoid a break between somatic and psychic medicine;
- learn to be attentive to the patient;
- avoid preconceived judgment on the cause or nature of the patient's illness;
- be more tolerant of their own and the patient's personal feelings;
- learn to accept the patient's omissions in describing symptoms or answering the doctor's questions;

- adapt more easily to the patient's real request;
- realize one's automatic reactions;
- find the nonsolutions or false solutions that the patient uses;
- help to find ways of discovering conflicts and perhaps help the patient to resolve them;
- find a way of "being with" the patient rather than applying psychotherapeutic techniques;
- improve their therapeutic and diagnostic methods.

Methods

Weekly 90-minute sessions are held from September to May for all family practice residents. One resident makes a spontaneous presentation of a patient seen in the family practice unit, the emergency room, the ward, or the outpatient specialty clinic. The resident may have seen the patient for the first time, for a few weeks, or even for more than a year. The central point of attention is the relation between the doctor and the patient. The resident relates the facts, together with his or her hesitations, fears, and personal feelings toward the patient. The participants listen, ask questions, and try to get a better understanding of what really happened. Have they been in a similar situation? What would they do in a similar situation in the future? Some participants are more active than others, spontaneously presenting other cases, asking questions, and formulating hypotheses. Other students rarely intervene. Some do not bring up a single case during a two-year period.

The group has two coleaders: a psychoanalyst or a psychiatrist trained in the psychoanalytic method and a family physician experienced in Balint groups. Leaders are chosen from another hospital so that they do not meet the residents during their rotations. The family doctor's participation is desirable as a role model and as a reference to the reality of the practice residents will be entering. Michael and Enid Balint commented: "we may say that the general practitioner's setting— though containing many elements of fantasy—is much nearer to reality than the psychoanalytical situation. In order that he should be able to cope with the problems emanating from his professional world, the general practitioner needs psychotherapeutic techniques which, we must admit, will be considerably different from ours. Although his techniques will use a good deal of our findings, they will not be either a superficial or watered down form of psychoanalytic technique" (Balint,

1966). The students must understand that Balint groups are not group psychotherapy or group psychiatric case supervision. The focus is on the Professional Ego (Balint, 1957). Sometimes, the participants make reference to personal feelings or significant events that affect their behavior in a professional activity, for example, the illness or death of a relative. They may also describe the symptoms of the patient and his or her psychological and social status to seek the help of the group in an attempt to reach a diagnosis and to establish a plan of action for a subsequent encounter. The leaders direct the group activity toward an understanding of the doctor-patient relationship, rather than toward either a resolution of the residents' personal problems or the identification of the psychological, social, or psychiatric disorders of the patients.

Evaluation

Every year in May, the last meeting is used for an informal evaluation of each group with their coleaders. Each resident had the opportunity to complete, beforehand, a formal evaluation, which is sent to the behavioral program director. Twice a year, the Balint group coleaders meet to share their experience.

The residents' answers to the questionnaire suggest that most of them are

- more conscious of emotional and conflictual aspects;
- impressed by the numerous cases where objective diagnosis of somatic illnesses is impossible;
- more capable of understanding the concept of global medicine, considering the psychological, social, and somatic aspects;
- more disposed to listen to patients and try to understand their version;
- more inclined to accept treatment of patients they would have refused formerly;
- more at ease with most of their patients;
- more able to recognize their spontaneous personal reactions;
- more able to use their personal emotions;
- more interested in primary care;
- convinced that the family doctor's role is more important than they thought before;
- more capable of dealing with aspects of patient's private lives;
- more conscious of colleagues facing the same or different difficulties.

DISCUSSION

It is difficult in a training program for residents in family medicine to evaluate the effect of one teaching activity on a resident's attitude and behavior; it is even more difficult to measure its influence by an "opinion questionnaire." Those students who choose a family practice residency are usually more interested in the doctor-patient relationship than those who have chosen a medical or surgical specialty. Family medicine residents benefit from other activities that influence the way they relate to patients: one-way mirror and video supervision, sessions on awareness and assertiveness, and rotations in psychosomatic medicine. From our ten-year experience, we believe that Balint groups play a major role, which "entails a limited, though considerable change in the doctor's personality" (Balint, 1964).

CONCLUSIONS

1. The Balint movement is an important international force for teaching and learning the physician's role in the doctor-patient relationship.

2. Balint groups of primary care (family) physicians have operated successfully over the past 40 years in most European countries.

3. Balint groups affect demonstrable change in the young physician and his or her role in the doctor-patient relationship when conducted as part of the residency training program.

4

Physician Self-Awareness:
The Neglected Insight

Mark F. Longhurst

THERE WERE NO SIGNS

By walking I found out
Where I was going.

By intensely hating, how to love.
By loving, whom and what to love.

By grieving, how to laugh from the belly.

Out of infirmity, I have built strength.
Out of untruth, truth.
From hypocrisy, I weaved directness.

Almost now I know who I am.
Almost I have the boldness to be that man.

Another step
And I shall be where I started from.

Irving Layton (1963)

Self-awareness is a prerequisite for a physician to become a healer, only then is the physician capable of effective communication with a patient. The doctor-patient relationship consists of a person suffering, the patient (from the Latin *patior* : "to suffer"), and a person behaving as a healer, the physician. People become patients when, in their own perception, they pass some point of tolerance for a symptom or a debility and seek out someone who professes to help (Pelligrino, 1979). How might a person become that healer?

> No sooner does one dissociate one's personal self from the clinical situation than one makes the patient likewise into an inanimate object [Stein, 1985].

The physician healer has had special status in most recorded civilizations. Society has always bestowed power on those attending the sick, power to be used with consummate skill, infinite care, and undivided attention. Not everyone could become a healer and not all chosen could withstand the engagement with people in the extremes of their human predicament. It is a profound experience to confront, as a physician, the fears and trepidations of someone else's illness, which might include their pain, dying, birth, disfigurement, and loneliness. These emotionally charged issues can be addressed with greater sensitivity by the physician who has a sense of self.

Systems theorists suggest that self implies an intentionally active agent, acting toward the world (thus shaping himself and his environment), and an organism acted upon by the environment (shaped by outer influences) in a continuous flow of reciprocal/dialectical moves, that take place in the field of action (Sandelin, 1981). The implication is that doctors are Janus-faced, both a whole and a part of a system, creatively responding to both the internal world of self and the outside world of ourselves and the patient (Koestler, 1979).

WHAT IS SELF-AWARENESS?

Self-awareness denotes the conscious understanding of the impact of our internal subjective world. This view of reality modifies our behavior (or the potential for that behavior) toward another person. In a therapeutic relationship, that behavior must be constructive, affirmative, and honest. The anthropologists would add that this sense of reality is influenced by what they call ethnocentrism: the interpretation of the world through a society's cultural norms. The individual, in our case the doctor, has a set of lenses that interpret the world for him. There are four main lenses (Grams, 1987).

Through the belief lens we see what is held to be true or factual. The attitude lens is a preset readiness to respond in a characteristic or predictable manner. The meaning lens measures the significance of a situation with reference to how one should respond. The value lens gauges whether something is good or desirable.

Each physician is part of a structure, for example, family, has roles and responsibilities, and is evolving on a developmental scale. In examining the physician's self-awareness, we must acknowledge the dynamics of this context.

During my early years in practice, I was not particularly successful in dealing with alcoholics. I believed that alcoholism was not a disease and that self-control was a valued characteristic attainable by all. My physician role, at best, was to treat disease in the hospital, at worst, to treat people in the home. My professional attitude was predictable. My professional development was still, in many ways, adolescent. My personal experience of alcohol reflected a family capacity to tolerate moderate social drinking at the right time and place but under control. Drinking did not make one sick, unless it was by choice (the hangover). However, in practice I was confronted with people being destroyed by alcoholism. I responded inappropriately to passive-aggressive personalities and the endless noncompliance of the alcoholic patient. I was arrogant, paternalistic, intolerant, and belligerent, but that was my perspective, my model of the reality of alcoholism.

AWARENESS OF EMOTIONAL RESPONSE

Self-awareness helps us find the source of our emotional response to a patient, which develops at a personal, not a professional, level. Once we have teased out that source, we must bracket, compensate, and silence the preconceived ideas and emotional distortions we bring to the relationship (Keen, 1970).

To illustrate, every time that Ralph came to the office I would become anxious, and I would dig right into the physical manifestations of his rheumatoid arthritis. When he left I always had a lingering sense of incompleteness. Why? Obviously I was dealing only with his disease and avoiding his illness. He was like my father, who has been handicapped for years. I brought all the baggage of my relationship with him to the relationship between Ralph and myself. I didn't need to psycho-analyze my self and my familial roles to realize that my anxiety was interfering with my capacity to relate to this person who was asking for my care. At a later point in time, Ralph and I were able to talk of this very dilemma, and a sense of well-being then evolved in our interactions. He told me that if I had asked him earlier where the anxiety came from, he could have told me that his anger at his disability (which mirrored that of my father's) was obviously immobilizing my capacity to respond to him.

To illustrate further, Bill was a noncompliant patient who created difficulty for his physician. Bill ate chocolate bars that increased his weight and blood sugar; he refused the brace on his left leg, the side of his stroke; he rarely took his anti-hypertensive medications; and he was abusive to the nurses at the lodge. The doctor became angry, told me she disliked the patient and wished she could "fire him" from the practice. I asked the doctor, "Why would a 60-year-old man act in such a noncompliant manner but yet still come to the office?"

The doctor had not given this patient any space to rest his anguish. She was, in fact, inhospitable. She would not "let him in." She somatized everything about him and offered only oblique subversive communication to any substantive issues. We began to examine what was happening to her as a physician and a person, to talk about old men, loneliness, disability, impotence, control, and limitation. As she acknowledged the fears that surround such issues, she began to manifest her real compassion and her attention focused on Bill as a person. He had sensed that she had that compassion in her; that's why he kept coming back. "Physician hospitality implies paying attention without intention" (Nouwen, 1979). It demands the creation of an "empty space" where the guest (the patient) can find his own soul and where his loneliness will be understood.

Howard Stein (1985) said of the physician self, "one can truly recognize a patient only if one is willing to recognize oneself in the patient." So, unless we permit ourselves to reclaim our part (by reaching inward without fearing loss of reality), the patient will not sense the connectedness in the relationship and will not risk the intimacy that is required in a healing relationship. The doctor will not see in the patient that which he cannot afford to see in his own defense.

R. D. Laing (1978) illustrated in his poem *Knots* that one can never truly know another's experience. We know directly only what we ourselves feel. Only with time, a safe learning environment, and experience can one become increasingly attuned to the suffering of another person. We learn to trust intuition that may seem irrational, illogical, and dreamlike and to confront that part of the patient that may be in us. We all harbor feelings; the appropriate use of those feelings makes the "wounded healer" (Nouwen, 1979) operational. Feelings of inadequacy, impotence, and any threat to their sense of wholeness and personal value may cause young, developing physicians to strive to fill the void with tests and objectivity.

ACQUIRING SELF-AWARENESS

How then does one acquire the self-awareness to see into one's perspective, to understand its emotional spectrum and its impact on behavior? Self-awareness may be acquired by:

1. *Reflection of Self in Others*
   A reflection of oneself as seen in the eyes of others can heighten awareness of self. The reaction of others is a measure of one's impact. This was highlighted recently in an encounter with a family practice resident. Some patients complained to staff that this doctor was arrogant, but the resident was unaware that she was perceived in this way. Eventually, during a mock simulated office oral, she received that feedback from the simulated patient (faculty acting as patient). She then realized, with pain, that this remote attitude affected her learning interactions as well. Her learning style had always been quiet and passive, always fearful of being exposed as lacking medical knowledge. While her peers were willing to plead ignorance in clinical situations ("I don't know how this should be treated, can you help me?") cornering all the interactions, our resident (in the eyes of the faculty) was seen as "knowing," her "posture" aloof and reserved. Similarly, with patients she was distant, impassive, and unreachable. She was unwilling or unable to ask for information that was potentially laden with uncertainty.

2. *Understanding Learning Style*
   An understanding of one's learning style and abilities can be critical to an accurate view of self. It wasn't until age 38 (utilizing a Learning Inven-

tory) that I understood that I learned through experience and often only after reflection. I was not concrete, observational, or experimental in my learning style. My inability to understand something immediately was not stupidity; I had needed time to reflect and evaluate. Once through that process, I retained the knowledge firmly.

3. *Experiencing the Humanities*

Experiencing, studying, and enjoying the creative world of arts and letters can aid self-awareness. The artist speaks of universal truths and values that are both common and unique to each person. The experience of studying painting, listening to a piece of music, or reading a poem may reveal secrets about ourselves. We take a risk in letting go of our social and learned reflexes and confronting unbounded, timeless emotions or thoughts that are unknown and may be uncontrollable. However, if we cannot experience emotion through art, we will not be able to do so with people, particularly as a physician with patients. A painting by Luke Fildes (1891) called *The Doctor* still stirs the hidden tears (and fears) of attending at the bedside of a dying child. As a teaching aid with residents, this painting is an effective vehicle for self-examination.

A further benefit accrues from study of the arts. David Thomasma (1982) commented that "with self-critical skills come personal development skills." Burnout is less likely if a professional realizes that there are personal dimensions of the mind and spirit unaddressed by his or her discipline. The humanities can provide an oasis of personal refreshment.

4. *Creative Expression*

Partaking in some creative, self-expressive acts is another means of acquiring self-awareness. As an amateur photographer, I studied briefly at the Banff School of Fine Arts with Paul Caponigro, a noted American photographer. We had to show our work to the group and be critiqued by our teacher. When my work was displayed, after seemingly endless minutes of examination, Paul turned to the group and said, "There are questions raised in every print, of something beyond the subject. Over the mountains, behind the building, inside the child, there is always a presence." To me he said, "Take time when working, be patient with what is in you, and what is out there, and focus on that 'thing beyond' the question you are asking, the mood you are experiencing." That particular feedback has been invaluable for my attentiveness to people with chronic disability, particularly pain.

5. *Humor*

Humor is a route to self-awareness. No one is more flawed than he who takes himself too seriously. The exercise of maintaining that serious, perfect self is in itself exhausting and may be destructive. Jim Unger, creator of the "Herman" cartoon, is a marvel at debunking the doctor. I cannot look at a plant in my office now without seeing the cartoon depicting the serious physician, a suffering patient seated before him, and beside him on the desk stands a potted plant, dead and denuded. The caption reads, "I always have trouble with living things." Science has confused us as healers by giving us such miraculous cures, but we are confronted daily with the fragile nature of these cures and the unscientific nature of man. There is more to disease and illness than is seen in a microscope or laboratory. Each patient requires an approach different from the last, and outcomes are always uncertain. A humorous perspective balances the power and the helplessness.

6. *Experience*

Experience is a critical avenue to self-awareness. Lane Gerber (1983), in his sensitive book *Married to Their Careers* talked with a young doctor about the death of his son. The doctor and his wife were immobilized with grief over their tragedy. Over time, they examined for themselves one of the unspoken preoccupations of modern man: the denial of death (Becker, 1975). The experience of their son's death was something that they had difficulty sharing; each was absolutely alone. As both doctor and parent, the father had denied the possibility of death and the experience of dying. With the passage of time and the opportunity for thought, the young doctor reflected, "We cannot live for someone and we cannot die for them . . . we have to do those things ourselves" (Gerber, 1983). This was an agonizing, painful, and tragic way to gain self-awareness. This denial of death is a cultural phenomenon, but as physicians we cannot be above the dying and death. Needleman (1985) suggested that the physician who has lived through the loneliness of another's death becomes the healer society wants.

As a means of learning self-awareness, we might revive an old educational model: the mentorship. In this unique relationship, the mentor fosters a protégé's development by believing in him or her and helping the younger person refine, support, and attain those images and goals that form a blueprint for life (Levinson, 1978). This may be the best medical model for self-awareness and growth as a communicating healer.

HOW DOES SELF-AWARENESS HELP?

If we conclude that one can work at attaining self-awareness, does it bring better awareness of the patient? When physicians are better attuned, have that sense of self, they can make the connections essential to healing. Self-awareness may build within us compassion and a sense of hospitality. The word "patient" carries with it a relationship, which must be recognized as part of the healing process (Pelligrino, 1983).

Kleinman (1982) talked of the "cultural self" and the need to acknowledge the part of us that is colored by our culture. Doctors, who are themselves a distinct subculture, with group values of control, precision, linear thinking, monochronic time (schedules), disease, and science, are often at odds with the patient's subculture. The physician who knows him or herself can ask the patient for information about the meaning of symptoms, signs, and behaviors. Richard Katz (1982) observed a profound communication between healer and patient in the Kung people of the Kalahari. The power of the healer was the catalyst in the therapeutic relationship. The healing effect of that power came from a conscious (or unconscious) willingness of a patient to believe that the healer, through science, intent, energy, and creativity would bring a reintegration of the troubled person. The development of self was the cornerstone in the healer's training. The Kung people trained their healers, in a mentor system, to comprehend the magnitude of that power and to employ it with skill and control. The most powerful healers had special qualities: an enhanced ability to induce an altered state of consciousness and an adeptness at controlling the expression of "healing energy." They worked with dying people; they projected a charismatic influence, and they had a separate identity within the community, being relieved of the routine of hunting and food gathering.

Does one need to be a "wounded healer" to be a true physician? Many people believe so: "He cannot heal until he has healed himself" (Pelligrino, 1983); "Learn that for a physician, healing of yourself takes place through the healing of others" (Tumulty, 1978); "The healer undertakes to heal himself, to become a whole person . . . as a first step he accepts and 'owns' his powers and potentials and, specifically, his own limitations" (DeVries, 1985).

The individual freedom to feel and think is also freedom to choose behavior that best meets the demands of reality. Feelings and fantasies are not dangerous, but deeds may be (Tahka, 1984). The doctor must acquire the broadest possible awareness of his own feelings, needs, and conflicts to bring the greatest good to the healing act.

PART II

Applying the
New Clinical Method

Implicit in this book is the conviction that the patient's world view is an integral part of any doctor-patient encounter. To make this conviction explicit, the opening chapter of this section reviews the pertinent literature on patient beliefs. Weston and Brown cite evidence that patients' beliefs influence their decision to see a physician and that knowledge of patients' beliefs may improve outcomes of care. The authors suggest that physicians ought to distinguish between the two parts of the patient's story: the facts dealing with disturbed body function and the meaning the patient ascribes to those facts. The authors provide a framework for reconciling patients' beliefs with physicians' ways of understanding the problem. There are three areas where this reconciliation is essential. The first is the definition of what the problems are. The second is deciding the goals of treatment, and the third is deciding the respective roles of the doctor and patient.

This reconciliation can be facilitated by the patient-centered method advocated in this volume. But, as McWhinney notes, just as the traditional method tells clinicians what they have to do but not how to do it, so the patient-centered method establishes as its goal the physicians' knowledge of the patients' world, but does not tell the physician precisely how to proceed.

The final three chapters in this section present three examples of clinical applications of patient-centered concepts. The three papers have in common the description of very specific skills that alter the traditional focus of the visit from a disease-centered perspective to a patient-centered one.

Focusing on the opening of the medical visit, Frankel and Beckman describe methods of negotiation used in identifying the patient's primary problems. They question the conventional assumption that the first problem voiced by the patient is indeed the single chief complaint, and they recommend that physicians give patients an opportunity to relate fully the concerns for which they seek care.

Based on the painstaking application of qualitative methods of analysis to over 70 medical visits, the investigators found that in 69% of the visits studied, physicians interrupted the patient's opening statement— after a mean time of only 18 seconds—and directed questions toward this specific problem. In only one of these visits did the patient return to and complete the opening statement regarding health concerns. The investigators found no evidence that the first problem elicited in this manner, the one generally receiving the lion's share of attention, had any more clinical significance than problems identified later in the visit.

The authors suggest that patients are best encouraged to complete their statement of the problems by physicians either remaining silent or employing acknowledgments such as "mmh hmh," "okay," or "I see." Repetitions or paraphrases of patients' statements interrupt patients' full disclosure of concerns because they often lead to a series of closed-ended questions that terminate the presenting complaint and begin a traditional history taking. Most interviewing texts claim that repetitions and paraphrases facilitate communication. Frankel and Beckman conclude by conceptualizing the components of information as content, context, and conduct, all of which help to evaluate the patient's primary concern.

The third paper in this section, by Antony Cox, describes a rigorous experiment to identify those interviewing skills that facilitate the disclosure of emotion and emotion-laden information by patients. While these studies were conducted with parents of children referred to a child psychiatric clinic, the findings are relevant to medical encounters. Cox raises fascinating questions about whether interviewing styles of physicians can be experimentally manipulated and, further, what effect this manipulation may have on patient disclosure of feelings.

An important finding of the study was the recognition that there may be limits on how much most physicians are willing or able to alter their interviewing style; for instance, some physicians had more difficulty in performing some techniques than others. An especially important finding was that greater persistence with active techniques to elicit feelings was necessary with patients who were not generally inclined to express emotions. Specific strategies included in the active style were: explicitly asking about feelings, reflecting feelings, expressions of sympathy, open questions, and questions about sensitive material. For patients who appear to show emotions freely, however, Cox found that the doctor need only be attentive.

Levenstein and colleagues present a framework for integrating the process of differential diagnosis with the understanding of the patient's unique experience of illness. Their model calls attention to the parallel search for both disease (through the traditional history, physical examination, and laboratory investigation) and the illness (through the patient-centered perspective of eliciting patients' ideas, expectations, and feelings). Specific verbal cues, such as prompts, facilitating behaviors, and cut-offs are defined with examples illustrated through a clinical case.

The authors observe that physicians commonly use the disease framework first, moving to the illness framework only if the former did not yield a clear pathological diagnosis. While there is no sequential order recommended, the authors note that under usual circumstances, it is more efficient to begin with the patient's perspective of the illness.

The papers in this section, being grounded in clinical experience, exemplify a growing body of knowledge of the repertoire of skills necessary for a patient-centered method of communication in the medical setting.

5

The Importance of Patients' Beliefs

W. Wayne Weston
and
Judith Belle Brown

Patients' beliefs influence their perceptions of health and illness. Beliefs dictate which symptoms will be considered appropriate to take to a doctor, how patients will understand the cause and treatment of their illness, what patients expect of physicians, what personal and moral meanings patients will ascribe to their illness and how they will answer the perennial questions "Why me? Why now? What did I do to deserve this?" Physicians who ignore these dimensions of sickness overlook a powerful source of information and a potent tool for healing.

In this chapter we will examine the importance of patients' beliefs, how we discover those beliefs, and how we use them to improve patient care.

Patients' beliefs include thoughts, ideas, convictions, opinions, and values about illness and health care. General beliefs about sickness are learned from cultural groups and social class, and have been well described by others (Eisenberg and Kleinman 1981; Helman, 1984). We intend to focus on the particular beliefs of individual patients, no matter what their origin. These idiosyncratic beliefs are often more difficult to predict.

Lipowski (1970) described illness as an experience that brings forth either an active response with a striving to master the illness or a defensive response, striving to protect the body, which is under attack. Illness may also be seen as punishment or weakness; patients may deny their illness because they are ashamed of being ill. For others, illness is experienced as a relief, an opportunity to seek respite from demands or responsibilities. This can develop into a chronic "sick role." In a related way, patients may use illness as a strategy to gain attention, money, status, revenge, or escape. Often, illness is an irreparable loss; it may be so overwhelming that the individual responds with severe depression or a sense of hopelessness. Conversely, it can also be an opportunity to gain valuable insight or understanding into one's life experience.

PATIENTS' BELIEFS INFLUENCE THE DECISION TO SEE A PHYSICIAN

White et al. (1961) reported that in a typical American community of 1000 people, 750 per month have an illness or accident, but only 250 see a doctor. In a study of women using health diaries, Freer (1980) reported that these patients brought to their doctors only 1 out of every 40 symptoms they experienced. Physicians, steeped in the study of human biology and largely ignorant of cultural and social determinants of health and illness, have limited awareness of illness behavior. They have a simplistic notion about why patients go to doctors: "good" patients recognize symptoms of serious disease and promptly report them to their physicians; they put up with the aggravations of nonserious or untreatable disease without complaining. This attitude holds that symptoms directly correlate with pathophysiology. When they do not, the physician believes the patients have underestimated or exaggerated their problems. This fails to recognize the difficult, often frightening process of coming to terms with the possibility that one is ill, perhaps seriously ill. Also, this way of thinking can result in considerable frustration for physicians and dissatisfaction for patients. Many patients deny their illness and delay seeking help; others seek advice first from the "lay referral system," which may include family, friends, pharmacists, and others. Patients learn from this lay system which symptoms are serious enough to take to a doctor.

Balint (1957) and his group of general practitioners argued that doctors often unwittingly convey to their patients what problems they are interested in and what problems they do not want to hear about. Patients may be "difficult" at first but are quickly "converted" to the doctor's value system and learn to be "good" patients—or else they leave the practice. When a patient finally decides to see a doctor it is because the symptoms have become unbearable, or the patient's worry and anxiety about the symptoms have become intolerable, or the patient feels a need to talk about other things and the symptoms are a ticket into the office (McWhinney, 1972).

THE MEDICAL MODEL DOES NOT EXPLAIN EVERYTHING ABOUT PATIENTS' PROBLEMS

When patients go to a primary care physician, approximately half the time their problems cannot be adequately explained by the conventional biomedical model (Morrell, 1972; Peabody, 1927; Research Committee, 1958). They do not have a disease (either organic or mental) that explains their presentation. How can the doctor make sense of this apparent incongruity? People who are upset by the cares and worries of living may experience a heightened awareness of normal bodily sensations. Because they feel distressed and unwell, they may easily misinterpret these sensations as symptoms of disease. In Western culture the medical model has a monopoly on explaining illness. It is difficult for a person growing up in a Western nation to imagine any other way to explain illness; it is almost inconceivable for many Western-trained physicians.

For most people the terms disease and illness are synonymous, but we wish to make a distinction between these two modes of ill health. Disease is an abstraction, the "thing" that is wrong with the body-machine when we are sick. The biomedical model explains sickness in terms of pathophysiology—abnormal structure and function of tissues and organs. Sickness is reduced to disease. The focus is the body, not the person; the social and cultural contexts are irrelevant to the physician's central task of diagnosis and cure.

Illness, on the other hand, is a patient's personal experience of sickness—the thoughts, feelings, and altered behavior of someone who feels sick. Many people can have the same disease, but the illness experiences of each person are unique.

Disease and illness do not always coexist. Patients with an undiagnosed, asymptomatic disease are not ill; people who are grieving or worried may feel ill but have no disease. Patients and doctors who recognize this distinction, and who realize how common it is to feel ill and have no disease, will be less likely to search needlessly and fruitlessly for pathology.

Even when disease is present, it may not adequately explain the patient's suffering. For example, the amount of pain a patient experiences relates not only to the amount of tissue damage but to the meaning of the injury. The same wounds suffered on a battlefield and on a city street have different significance: the soldier may go home but the civilian may not be able to keep his job. It should not be surprising that the soldier has much less pain (Beecher, 1956). To understand a patient's experience of illness a physician must attempt to enter into the patient's world, to understand the patient's beliefs about what is wrong, why it happened, and what should be done. When a patient presents for the third time in one week with a sore throat, it is helpful for his doctor to know that the patient thinks it is gonorrhea but is afraid to mention it. When a mother brings her child to the doctor repeatedly with minor upper respiratory infections and wants blood tests, it is useful to find out that her sister died of leukemia.

KNOWING PATIENTS' BELIEFS
MAY IMPROVE OUTCOME

In a study of patients presenting to their family doctors with headaches, The Headache Study Group (1986) found that the best outcomes after one year of follow-up were in patients who felt they had been given sufficient opportunity to tell the doctor all they wanted to say about their headaches on the initial visit. The diagnosis, type of investigation or treatment, or referral had no relationship to outcome. These results may parallel the work of Brody (1980) on the placebo effect. He states that patients are more likely to have a positive placebo response if three criteria are met.

1. The illness is explained to the patient in a coherent manner, consistent with his preexisting view of the world.

2. The patient has a group of individuals assuming socially sanctioned caring roles and emotional support.

3. The healing intervention leads to the patient's acquiring a sense of mastery and control over the illness.

A key feature of Brody's model is the patient being helped to make sense of his illness in terms that fit his own beliefs. Brody also argues for a much broader understanding of the placebo response than the conventional view that it is merely an illusion or some kind of trick; patients are more likely to recover if the conditions for a placebo response are present. Indeed, it might be more accurate to refer to it as a healing response.

Henbest (1985) demonstrated that when physicians elicit patients' ideas and feelings, patients are more likely to demonstrate a resolution of their concerns about their problems. Brody and Miller (1986) studied 50 patients with upper respiratory infection. Initially, almost half the patients were at least moderately concerned that their problem was serious and might lead to more serious problems later on; 25% believed their illness would be difficult to overcome. One week later, 32% of the study population was completely asymptomatic. These patients, compared with those who remained symptomatic for at least a week, were more satisfied with the amount of time their doctor had spent discussing their concerns.

PHYSICIANS AND THEIR PATIENTS' BELIEFS

The medical interview may be viewed as an arena of struggle between the natural attitude with its common sense lifeworld and the scientific attitude with its objectified world of abstract logic and rationality.... I am proposing an interpretation of the medical interview as a situation of conflict between two ways of constructing meaning [Mishler, 1984: 123, 127].

In analyzing medical interviews, Mishler identifies two contrasting voices: the voice of medicine and the voice of the lifeworld. The voice of medicine reflects a scientific, detached attitude. Typical questions that interest the doctor include: Where does it hurt? When did it start? How long does it last? What makes it better or worse? The voice of the lifeworld, on the other hand, asks about the meaning of illness events and how they may affect the achievement of personal goals. Typical questions used to explore the lifeworld include: What are you most concerned about? How does it disrupt your life? What do you think it is? How do you think I can help you?

Mishler argued that typical interactions between doctors and patients are doctor-centered: they are dominated by a technocratic perspective. The physician's task is to make a diagnosis; in the interview, the doctor selectively attends to the voice of medicine, often not even hearing the patients' own attempts to make sense of their suffering. What is needed, he maintained, is a different approach in which doctors give priority to "patients' lifeworld contexts of meaning as the basis for understanding, diagnosing, and treating their problems" [Mishler, 1984: 192].

Williams and Wood (1986) described a similar distinction between the different purposes of the doctor and the patient in the interview. "Whereas the doctor's objective is to explain the etiology of disease, the patient may be more concerned to make sense of the disruption caused by the disease" (p. 1435). They characterized the patient's account as a "narrative reconstruction" whose purpose is not so much to answer the medical question, "Why have I got arthritis?," but rather to answer the metaphysical question, "How have I come to be like this?" They emphasized the need for doctors to understand their patients' experience rather than hastily dismissing patients' idiosyncratic statements simply as evidence of their need to be better informed medically.

Cassell (1985) has a corresponding message:

> The story of an illness—the patient's history—has two protagonists: the body and the person. By careful questioning, it is possible to separate out the facts that speak of disturbed bodily functioning, the pathophysiology that gives you the diagnosis. To do this, the facts about the body's dysfunction must be separated from the meanings that the patient has attached to them. Skillful physicians have been doing this for ages. All too often, however, the personal meanings are then discarded. With them goes the doctor's opportunity to know who the patient is [p.108].

How can we transcend this apparent dichotomy between the patient's world view and the doctor's? The task is often likened to a process of negotiation. Like and Zyzanski (1986) defined negotiation as "the process whereby two or more parties attempt to settle what each shall give and take, or perform and receive, in a transaction between them." But this perspective is contractual rather than a true meeting of the minds. We prefer to describe this aspect of the encounter as a mutual task of finding common ground between the doctor and the patient in three key areas: defining the nature of the problem, establishing the goals of treatment, and identifying the roles to be assumed by the doctor and patient.

Defining the Problem

Without some agreement about the nature of what is wrong, it is difficult for doctor and patient to agree on a plan of management that is acceptable to both of them. The physician need not believe that the problem is the way the patient sees it, but the doctor's explanation and recommended treatment must at least be consistent with the patient's point of view and make sense from the patient's world. Examples of difficulties defining the problem are:

- The patient says he or she is disabled by a back problem and the doctor thinks he or she is malingering.
- The doctor thinks the patient's blood pressure is a serious problem but the patient insists that it is not — he or she is simply nervous in the doctor's office.
- The parent of a six-year-old child thinks there is something seriously wrong to explain the child's frequent colds—six a year. The doctor thinks this is within normal limits.

It does not take long in the front lines of primary care for physicians to realize that a strictly biomedical approach to illness is ineffective. Several studies demonstrate the inadequacy of the conventional medical model for explaining many of the problems patients bring to their doctors. Blacklock (1977) found that, of 109 patients who presented to their family physicians chest pain, in 50% the etiology was unproven after six months follow-up. In another study of 300 patients complaining of lethargy, fatigue, or tiredness, Jerrett (1981) could find no organic cause in 62.3% of patients evaluated in a general practice over a three-year period. Wasson et al.(1981), investigating 552 unselected male patients with abdominal pain who presented to an outpatient clinic, found no evidence for specific organic diagnosis in 79% of them.

Defining the Goals

When doctors and patients meet, they each have expectations and feelings about the encounter; if these are at odds or inappropriate, there will be difficulties. For example:

- The patient has a sore throat and expects to receive penicillin but instead is urged to gargle with salt water.
- The patient is concerned about innocent palpitations and is found to have high blood pressure. The doctor launches into treatment of the hypertension without explaining to the patient the benign nature of the cardiac symptoms.
- The patient demands muscle relaxants for chronic muscular pains, but the doctor wants to use "talking" therapy to resolve the "underlying" problems.

If physicians ignore their patients' expectations, they risk not understanding their patients, who in turn will be angry or hurt by this perceived lack of concern. Timing is important. If the physician asks for the patient's expectations too early in the interview, the patient may think the doctor is evading making a diagnosis and may therefore be reluctant to say much. On the other hand, if the physician waits until the end of the interview, time may be wasted on issues unimportant to the patient. The physician may even make suggestions that will have to be retracted.

Defining the Roles

One of the major differences between primary care and other medical disciplines is the duration of the doctor-patient relationship. The physician may see the same patient with different problems in different settings over a number of years, and may also see the patient through the eyes of other family members. This ongoing relationship colors everything that happens between them. If there are difficulties or differing expectations of their relationship, they will have problems in working together effectively. For example:

- The patient is looking for an authority who will tell him or her what is wrong and what to do. The physician, on the other hand, wants a more egalitarian relationship where doctor and patient share decision-making together.
- The patient longs for a deep and meaningful relationship with a parental figure who will make up for everything the patient's own parent never gave. The doctor wants to be a biomedical scientist who can apply the discoveries of modern medicine to patients' problems.
- The physician enjoys a "holistic" approach to medicine and wants to get to know patients as people. The patient seeks only technical assistance from the doctor.

We advocate that physicians be sensitive to patients' cues to what they want to talk about and how much they can and want to handle on their own. This depth of understanding takes time and is one of the reasons that continuity of care is so important.

6

Evaluating the Patient's Primary Problem(s)

Richard Frankel
and
Howard Beckman

INTRODUCTION

Despite the technological advances of the past 20 years, many consumers are dissatisfied with the health care they receive. This dissatisfaction manifests itself as noncompliance with treatment recommendations, malpractice litigation, the use of nontraditional health care providers, anger over waiting time, and frustration with the quality of interactions with physicians. Medical educators and practitioners have become aware that the physician-patient relationship in general, and the office consultation in particular, require improvement. This chapter reviews research on patient-centered interviewing and describes the tasks and skills necessary to identify and evaluate the patient's primary problems.

The American Board of Internal Medicine (1983) issued a statement describing the humanistic qualities required of the internist and guidelines for their evaluation in practice. Similarly, Lipkin, et al. (1984), representing the SGIM Task Force on the Medical Interview, published a model curriculum for teaching interviewing skills to internal medicine residents.

As interest in patient-centered interviewing and patient involvement in care has grown, so too has criticism of the classical biomedical model of disease. Barsky (1981) has observed, for instance, that patients seek the care of a physician for many reasons, only one of which is disease. Patients also seek physician consultation for life stress, psychiatric illness, social isolation, and, increasingly, education. Often the physician is perceived as the only person available to listen to and comfort distressed patients of all ages.

In 1977, George Engel proposed the biopsychosocial model of care, which identifies psychological and sociological factors that accompany and contribute to the expression of disease and to the patient's decision to seek medical care. The model gives equal weight to biomedical and psychosocial factors in the presentation of a problem and distinguishes between disease (a pathological condition of the organism) and illness (the individual's social or psychological response to disease).

Besides recognizing the interrelationship of biological, psychological, and sociological factors, the biopsychosocial model contrasts with the physician-centered interviewing style that dominates the delivery of most medical care in the United States today. Specifically, the model challenges the assumption that the patient is merely a conduit for the extraction of clinical information, regardless of the physician's interviewing style. Current research demonstrates that the quantity, quality, and impact of information obtained during the medical encounter is related to the interviewer's style, interest, and involvement (Beckman and Frankel, 1984; Greenfield, et al., 1985; Headache Study Group, 1986; Roter, et al., 1987; Suchman and Matthews, 1988).

The type of interviewing that best facilitates use of the biopsychosocial model has been variously termed mutual participation (Morgan, and Engel, 1969), co-participation (Quill, 1983), and patient-centered interviewing (Stewart, 1984). These approaches are unique in viewing patients and physicians as individuals who mutually participate and influence one another during the medical encounter. The physician brings technical knowledge and clinical experience to the relationship; the patient brings his or her life experiences, health beliefs, and goals for service. The success of the encounter depends largely on the skill of clinical negotiation and the development of mutual respect and trust (Benarde and Mayerson, 1978; Brody, 1980; Lazare, et al., 1975a; Siegler, 1982). This discussion focuses on skills and methods that use negotiation as a primary strategy for opening the medical encounter.

We define the opening of the interview—one of its most important components—as the initial greeting, solicitation, and evaluation of the patient's primary concern(s). Whether a new or return visit, this portion of the interview should focus on those problems and concerns that both provider and patient agree are important. The accurate recognition of the primary concern(s) or problems(s) is central to providing care that will be relevant, satisfying, and medically sound.

The tasks of the opening segment of the interview are to:

1. define the specific concern(s) or problem(s) for which the patient seeks professional guidance;

2. understand the concerns in the context of the patient's life circumstances;

3. develop rapport with the patient, paving the way for a successful therapeutic outcome;

4. satisfy both participants by creating a therapeutic alliance;

5. utilize time efficiently.

DETERMINING THE PRIMARY PROBLEM(S)

One of the most complex tasks in evaluating the patient's primary problem(s) is accurate determination of the reason or reasons that the patient seeks medical care. Traditional medical education teaches that there is a single chief complaint. This assumption appears to cause tremendous difficulty in medical interviewing. In reviewing hundreds of transcripts, simulated patient interviews, and videotapes, we have observed several problems with the chief complaint model. The most common problem is that the provider assumes the first concern voiced by the patient is the chief complaint.

In a recently published study of opening moments in physician-patient encounters, Beckman and Frankel (1984) observed that patient responses to the physician's opening solicitation were completed in only 23% of 74 visits studied. In 6 return visits, no solicitation for concerns was made, and the provider began the encounter by focusing on identified problems from earlier visits. In 51 (69%) of the visits, the physician interrupted the patient's opening statement—after a mean time of only 18 seconds—and directed questions toward a specific concern. Importantly, in only one of these 51 visits was the patient afforded the opportunity to return to, and complete, his or her opening statement, i.e., the concerns for which they sought care.

Since 34 of the 51 visits were interrupted after the patient's initial concern, we hypothesized that the interrupting physicians assumed that the patient's first complaint was the chief one and began, at that point, to obtain the history of the present illness. To test this hypothesis, a group of internists, blinded to the nature of our study, were asked to rate the clinical importance of an abstracted list of all the concerns expressed in the 74 visits. They rated concerns that occurred first, second, and third in the patient statements as equally important clinically. We concluded that serial order is not related to the clinical importance of patient concerns, rejecting the hypothesis that the patient's first stated concern is more important than subsequent concerns.

These data also explain why Burack and Carpenter (1983) found that patients typically wait to share psychosocial concerns until late in the visit and that patients and doctors agree on the chief complaint in only 76% of somatic problems and 6% of psychosocial problems. In summary, physicians, both in training and in practice, often make implicit assumptions about the patient's chief complaint, most often without soliciting the patient's full range of concerns or priorities for treatment.

These findings are also consistent with the recommendations of Lipkin et al. (1984), who suggested that listening helps to elicit the full range and priority of patient concerns, and Nardone, et al. (1980), who suggested symptom lists rather than a chief complaint, to avoid premature and limited hypothesis testing. Several other investigators report findings showing that patients often have more than one concern to discuss (Good and Good, 1982; Greenfield, et al., 1985; Starfield et al., 1981; Wasserman, et al., 1984). The mean number of concerns in these studies ranges from 1.2 to 3.9 in both new and return office visits.

Platt and McMath (1979) have observed that one cause of "clinical hypocompetence" in interviewing is the failure to consider more than a single problem, and suggest asking "Anything else?" or "What else?" after each item in the patient's opening statement. We find that completion can be facilitated by either remaining silent or employing acknowledgment tokens such as "mmh hmh," "okay," or "I see" until the patient indicates the end of the statement of concerns. The following example shows that, given sufficient time and opportunity, the patient will mark the conclusion of his or her opening statement of concerns.

Physician: What problems are you having?

Patient: My back has been hurting me, I've had headaches for three weeks, and recently I have been having a hurting in my chest which causes me to have to sit down after I've walked only half a block.

(1.0 second pause)

Physician: Go on.

Patient: That's all I wanted to talk about today.

Barriers to completion of patients' statements of concerns have also been identified. Beckman and Frankel (1984), for example, found that recompleters, defined as repetition of the content or sense of the patient's previous statement, interrupted the patient's full enumeration of concerns. For example, if a physician responds, "You have chest pain?" to a patient's initial statement, "I have chest pain," this will usually lead to a series of closed-ended questions that terminate the solicitation of the presenting complaint and begin the history of present illness segment. In our study, recompleters accounted for 35% of the interruptions of patients' opening statements. Other causes of interruption were closed-ended questions (46%), elaborators (10%), and statements (10%). Although recompleters are regarded as generic facilitators in most interviewing texts, our findings suggest that their benefit depends on their location in the encounter.

Concern over the time required to permit patients to fully express their concerns is frequently cited as a barrier to more open-ended facilitation. In fact, we found (Beckman and Frankel, 1984) that no completed opening statement took more than 150 seconds. Although physicians may believe that patients will discuss their problems indefinitely if given the opportunity, there is evidence to the contrary, as the following example of an actual completed opening statement shows:

Physician: How have you been doing?

Patient: Oh, well, I've been doing okay, except for Saturday, well, Sunday night. You know I've been kinda nervous off and on but I had a little incident in my house Saturday and it kinda shook me up a bit.

→Physician: Okay.

Patient: And my ulcer has been burning me off and on like when I eat something if it don't agree with me then I'll find out about it.

→Physician: Mmh hmh.

Patient: But lately I've been getting this funny, like I'll lay down on my back and my heart will go "brrr," you know like that. Like it's skipping a beat or something and then it will just start on back off beating like when I get upset it will just start beating boom, boom, boom and it will just go back to its normal beat.

→Physician: Okay.

Patient: Is that normal?

Physician: That's a lot of things. Anything else bothering you?

Patient: No.

This exchange took less than 60 seconds. It required three acknowledgment statements (indicated by arrows in the transcript) and a question by the physician to confirm that the patient was finished. In that short period of time the patient provided a cohesive and uninterrupted statement of concerns and, in so doing, stated her agenda for the day's visit. Interrupting the patient before she had completed her statement would have given the physician an incomplete picture of the patient's needs, preventing him from effectively using the time allotted for the visit. With a complete statement of concerns the physician could understand the range of patient concerns, develop a short- and long-run plan, and negotiate which problems were of primary importance so that time could be appropriately allotted to deal first with those issues that required the most attention.

In addition to more effectively organizing the visit, there is evidence that eliciting the full range of concerns early in the visit reduces the occurrence of late concerns that Barsky (1981) has termed "hidden" agendas. Although some patients may hesitate in sharing concerns they perceive as psychosocially sensitive early in the visit, Beckman, et al. (1985) found that patients who completed their statement of concern in the opening moments of the encounter were significantly less likely to raise concerns toward the end of the visit.

At the conclusion of a successful opening, the physician should have determined the spectrum of available concerns that the patient chose to offer and defined the concerns so that an agenda may be established. Rapport is facilitated by politeness, mutuality, and positive regard for the patient's input and point of view. Achieving rapport early in a relationship is useful in treatment planning and negotiation, and may actually influence the outcome of care. At the conclusion of a successful opening, the physician is ideally situated to begin the evaluation of the concern or concerns that both participants believe are most important.

EVALUATION OF PRIMARY CONCERN(S)

Nardone et al. (1980) have conceptualized the information necessary to evaluate the patient's primary concern(s). They view this portion of the interview as having three overlapping components: content, context, and conduct.

Content

In 1969, Morgan and Engel described seven logical dimensions for evaluating symptoms: chronology, bodily location, quality, quantity, setting, aggravating and alleviating, factors and associated symptoms. Reiser and Schroder (1980) in their text, *Patient Interviewing: The Human Dimension*, described the order in which dimensions of the symptom should be evaluated. While useful for structuring written histories and case presentations, rigid adherence to logical structure may be a barrier to data collection. Nardone et al. (1980) and Beckman and Frankel (1984) noted that the logic of clinical decision making is often stressed in texts on interviewing without regard for context or logic of social interaction within which information is gathered. Many interviews are flawed by inattention to patients' signals of concern about a particular aspect of their problem. When interviewers use sequences of closed-ended questions organized exclusively around the seven dimensions of a symptom, they often prevent the patient from elaborating, questioning the meaning of an aspect of a problem, or providing their own attribution for the problem.

Teachers of interviewing must recognize the organization of the seven dimensions of a symptom as relevant to post interview activities such as presentations and written history taking, but that in the elicitation of the history, the interview should flow from the patient's descriptions of these dimensions. As an example, a physician begins the evaluation segment of the interview by asking, "When did your chest pain begin?" The patient responds, "Three days ago." The physician then asks, "Can you show me where the chest pain bothers you most?" By overdirecting the questioning, an important component of chronology has been ignored. In the following example, encouraging the patient to elaborate on the question of chronology produces a clinically important piece of information.

Physician: When did this chest pain begin?

Patient: About three days ago.

Physician: Go on.

Patient: That was when I was working in the backyard. I lifted five 100-pound bags of concrete and developed this pulling in my chest.

We consider all patient responses as potentially complex rather than simple. In soliciting information about aggravating factors, for example, we suggest that the interviewer resolicit (indicated by arrows in the transcript) after the patient offers one or more aggravators. For example:

Physician: What have you found that makes your headaches worse?

Patient: Lack of sleep.

→Physician: Anything else?

Patient: Now that you mention it, I believe that stress seems to be related also because by the end of the work day I usually have a headache.

→Physician: Anything else?

Patient: No.

Physician: Is there anything that relieves your headaches?

Elaboration of the initial description produces clinically relevant information about the context of the symptom.

Lazare et al. (1975a) suggested two additional components: the patient's goal for seeking care and the patient's request to the provider. Lazare defined the goal for care as the outcome the patient would like to achieve as a result of treatment, and the request as the method or means by which the patient would like the provider to be of help. Lazare hypothesized that eliciting and fulfilling the patient's goal(s) and request(s) will produce increased satisfaction, compliance, and ultimately clinical improvement. Starfield et al. (1979) found that patients reported improvement in problems in 49.4% of visits where there was agreement between physician and patient, and only 26.7% improvement in cases where the physician alone identified the problem as important.

Good and Good (1982) evaluated 460 office visits to four different practices and found 13 major request categories. Although requests varied depending on the practice site, 61% to 96% of patients wanted an explanation for their symptoms and results of laboratory tests, and had requests for symptomatic treatment, medical advice, and/or a diagnosis. In a subgroup from a holistic health center, the most commonly expressed patient goal was to share their experience of a problem with, and to receive a sense of being cared for from, a responsive physician. In fact, soliciting the patient's request often simplifies the physician's job because the patient's desire for help is more limited than the physician assumes.

Context

All problems, whether scientific or superstitious, exist within a system of beliefs, attitudes, and theories. The second component for evaluating a problem is identifying the emotional, social, and cultural milieu in which a problem occurs. Kleinman, et al. (1978) suggested that eliciting patient attitudes and beliefs about disease and treatment substantially increases therapeutic success. Snow (1974) counseled that understanding a patient's beliefs about a problem can help to generate more realistic plans for treatment, educate the patient, and prospectively identify potential therapeutic problems. Snow's description of the beliefs of southern rural blacks about hypertension has been instrumental in explaining why treatment often fails in urban areas where southern rural blacks have migrated (Snow, 1983). Kleinman et al. (1978) asserted that the consequences of neglecting the patient's view of the illness are noncompliance, dissatisfaction, litigation, criticism of the medical profession, and increased use of alternate health care providers. Their approach is especially important in determining the meaning of an illness to the patient and soliciting expectations for care. They suggested several useful questions to determine the impact of a problem on the patient's social and emotional context:

1. What do you think caused your problem?

2. Why do you think it started when it did?

3. How severe is your sickness?

4. What are the most important results you hope to achieve?

5. What do you fear most about your sickness?

We have found the solicitation of patients' attributions so important and useful in our own practice that we now teach it as the eighth major dimension of a symptom. We have also found that eliciting patient attributions increases participation in the process of care, demonstrates respect for the patient by including his or her perceptions of the problem, and helps to create a therapeutic alliance, one of the major goals of the consultation.

For example, a 46-year-old male presented in our clinic high blood pressure. A traditional evaluation was performed; he was diagnosed as having essential hypertension and was given hydrochlorothiazide and clonidine. He returned to the clinic monthly but his blood pressure continued to be elevated on each occasion. After three visits we asked the patient why his blood pressure was still elevated. He stated that he wasn't taking his medicine because it had nothing to do with the cause of his blood pressure. When asked what caused his high blood pressure, he said that a person had put a hex on him and that he was currently seeking its removal through a faith healer. We discussed the risks of sustained, uncontrolled hypertension and negotiated an interim treatment plan. The plan consisted of taking the medication until the healer had completed his healing program. When the healer concluded that the hex was removed, we would discontinue therapy for one month. If the high blood pressure was resolved, no further medical treatment would be considered. However, if his blood pressure continued to be elevated, he would agree to reinstitute his medical therapy. The patient was pleased with the plan and expressed relief at being able to share his explanation for his problem without being ridiculed. At the conclusion of the healer's intervention, we discontinued his medication. His blood pressure rose and, as agreed, he reinstated his medication. His blood pressure has been controlled for the past 18 months.

Seeing the problem in the patient's context often results in a major shift in the provider's conceptualization of the problem. In the evaluation of headache, for example, failure to address the complete context of the patient's concern often creates a barrier to successful communication. A patient who attributes headaches to a brain tumor, threatened stroke, or a subarachnoid hemorrhage, is unlikely to be satisfied by simple reassurance. Instead, some patients' fears are heightened by the fact that the physician did *not* explicitly refer to, or exclude, their particular theory or attribution.

Determining attribution, health beliefs, and expectations is best accomplished after the content of the problem has been established; otherwise many patients will conclude that the physician is unable to diagnose the problem. Equally important is the wording of the attribution question. Bass and Cohen (1982) found, for example, that when patients were asked "What *worries* you about this problem?," the majority of patients responded with, "I'm not worried." When the same patients were asked, "What *concerns* you about the problem?," more than a third (33.8%, N=125) voiced previously unrecognized concerns.

The major challenge of added responsibility for exploring belief structures is, of course, time. Common sense and experience suggest, however, that time-intensive activities such as eliciting a complete data base, elaborating patient descriptions, and exploring attributions are far more efficient as predictors of effective long-term treatment and overall quality of care than a narrow, symptom-specific approach.

Conduct

Perhaps the most frequently investigated portion of the interview to date has been its conduct or dynamics. Investigators have studied behaviors that increase satisfaction, foster participation, and encourage honest open-ended interaction between physician and patient. In virtually all cases, patient satisfaction and physician "interest" have been positively related.

Carter et al. (1982) and Inui and Carter (1985), for instance, reviewed studies of behaviors associated with positive and negative outcomes. To summarize a few of the most widely recognized associations, Wasserman et al. (1984) found a highly significant association between empathy and patient satisfaction. They also found that encouraging statements were associated with increased patient satisfaction, and that use of these statements increased the perception of providers as a source of information and advice.

In terms of empathy, Francis et al. (1969) found that provider warmth was associated with increased patient satisfaction. Similarly, Stewart (1984) found an association between patient satisfaction and the opportunity to share opinions during the interview. In addition, Benarde et al. (1978) found a positive association between patient-provider respect, eye contact, question answering, and the physician's emotional sensitivity. Carter et al. (1982) also found a positive relationship between opinion sharing and patient knowledge about illness, and compliance with medical recommendations. They further found that patient satisfaction was correlated with the opportunity to give an orientation to the problem(s). Finally, Carter et al. (1982) found an association between the patient's understanding of the problem(s) and release of tension.

Although the literature supports these physician behaviors, a comprehensive model of the interview process has not yet been tested. As a result, systematic application of the research findings has been slow in coming. For example, in 1977, Roter, found a positive association between patient satisfaction and the opportunity to ask questions. Almost a decade later, West (1983) and Frankel (1987), in reviewing transcripts and tapes of primary care visits, observed that patient opportunities to ask questions were infrequent at best.

The skills of being patient-centered and interested in building rapport fundamentally challenge the notion of emotional neutrality in routine practice. Interviewers new to behaviors that demonstrate encouragement, empathy, transfer of control to the patient, and support may initially feel uncomfortable using the biopsychosocial model. Teachers of interviewing need to encourage and support learners as they explore new feelings and approaches to interviewing. There must also be positive reinforcement of behaviors that promote *interactional* rather than *individual* competence. Mutuality, respect, and compassion are dynamic concepts achievable only in the context of social interaction and social exchange.

SUMMARY

In this chapter, we have addressed a relatively small, and specific, aspect of the medical encounter. Research is beginning to accumulate on other aspects of the encounter, such as compliance and the delivery of diagnostic information to patients, that depend on interactional skills and social context for their success. We have made great strides in developing theoretical frameworks for health care that are currently being adopted and taught in medical schools and postgraduate programs in primary care and family medicine. We are just beginning to understand the implications of the biopsychosocial model and its impact on the delivery of coordinated, comprehensive health care. The initial results are very encouraging, suggesting that enhanced communication between physicians and patients, and expanded understanding of the role of psychosocial factors in disease and illness will lead to better, more comprehensive, and mutually satisfying care in the future.

7

Eliciting Patients' Feelings

Antony Cox

INTRODUCTION

Symptoms of anxiety and depression are common among those attending primary health care facilities (Goldberg and Huxley, 1980). Even
where these feelings are not manifestations of a formally abnormal
mental state, they may be important to the patient's care. For example,
they may be relevant to compliance, or for prognosis (Leff et al., 1985).
In child psychiatry, parents' feelings toward the index child and their
partner are crucial to the assessment. Exposure to hostility and marital
discord are important factors in the genesis and persistence of child
psychiatric disorders (Quinton and Rutter, 1985).

Given this importance, what interviewing techniques facilitate expression of emotion? We examined this question as one aspect in a
series of studies of interviewing techniques in initial interviews with
parents of children referred to a child psychiatric clinic. The findings
can be considered relevant to medical interviews in other settings.

METHOD

The initial assessment interview with parents of children referred to
this child psychiatric clinic has clearly defined aims to gather a range
of information about the referred children, their development and their
family, including feelings and attitudes. The project was conducted in
four phases.

1. Methods of measuring facts and feelings elicited during the interview were developed. Satisfactory inter-rater reliability was obtained for the measures used (Rutter and Cox, 1981).

2. A naturalistic study of initial interviews with parents by trainee psychiatrists was undertaken to determine the range of approaches ordinarily followed in routine clinical practice (Cox et al., 1981a; Hopkinson et al., 1981). Analysis of association between interviewing style and response was used to generate hypotheses about the effect of style, which were tested in the third and fourth phases.

3. Four interview styles were systematically varied in the first experimental study of 24 mothers.

4. Two interview styles were systematically varied in the second experimental study of 16 mothers (Cox et al., 1988).

FIRST EXPERIMENTAL STUDY

Interview styles were systematically varied (Rutter et al., 1981) according to four styles. The styles ranged from high to low usage of active verbal techniques that the naturalistic study had suggested would be effective for obtaining good quality factual data or actively expressed feelings. The techniques for obtaining factual information were

- raising topics listed as relevant to the assessment;
- detailed probing;
- requests for detailed descriptions of behavior or events.

The active techniques for feelings were

- expressions of sympathy;
- inquiries about feelings;
- reflections or interpretations of inferred feelings.

The four styles used were based on levels of these techniques: low/low, low/high, high/low, and high/high. The styles with an active factual approach required interviewers to raise relevant topics not mentioned by the informant. They also actively probed and clarified family problems, such as parental mental health or marital difficulty, and sought detailed examples of relevant events and behavior. In the passive factual approach, the interviewer followed the informants' leads on topic, encouraging them to explore whatever they raised by repeating what they had said or by open encouragement to say more.

In the styles with an active approach to feelings, expressions of emotion were responded to verbally by sympathy and reflections or interpretations of feeling. In addition, mothers were asked about how they felt. In the styles with a passive approach to feelings, the interviewers avoided the use of these techniques as far as possible, simply exhibiting a generally sympathetic and accepting posture. Each mother of a newly referred child was interviewed twice, approximately two weeks apart. A different style was employed on each occasion by a different interviewer. Two experienced interviewers were trained in the different styles, using role-play and feedback. In this first experimental study, six mothers received the active factual/passive feeling style first and the passive factual/passive feeling style second, and six had the same styles in reverse order. Six mothers had the passive factual/active feeling first and the active factual/active feeling style second, and six had the two styles in reverse order. Each interviewer did an equal number of first and second interviews and an equal number of interviews with each style. For each pair of styles, a three factor repeated measures analysis of variance was performed to test for differences between styles, interviewers, and effects.

Results of the First Experimental Study

Results from eliciting factual information were quite clear (Cox et al., 1981c). The results related to feeling techniques (Cox et al., 1981b) were complex. In the total number of active expressions of feeling, there were no differences between styles. Mothers in interviews employing active factual/active feeling and passive factual/active feeling techniques expressed no more feeling than the other two groups. Factual materials that could be expected to be associated with strong feeling, such as criminal records, marital discord, and parental mental health matters were termed self-disclosures; there were no differences in the numbers of self-disclosures according to interviewing style.

Discussion of First Experimental Study

Analysis suggested several reasons for lack of difference in results between styles. First, in this experimental study the interviews have been paired so that mothers had a different approach to facts in the two interviews but the same approach to feelings. Individual differences between parents may have been enough to obscure differences between groups. Second, certain techniques, which cut across the prescribed styles, emerged as effective in facilitating expression of feeling or self-disclosure. For example, the active factual/passive feeling style employed, at relatively high levels, techniques that tended to immediately facilitate the expression of emotion: open questions and requests for self-disclosure.

The less active techniques facilitated expression of feeling and self-disclosure by virtue of the lower interviewer intervention rate employed so that in those styles techniques that were not specifically effective in facilitating expression of emotion were nevertheless more often followed by expression of feeling. Reflections of feeling, inquiries about feeling, and sympathetic statements were equally effective with all styles. Open questions held an intermediate position, being somewhat more often followed by expressions of feeling in the two less verbally active styles. Analysis showed that both interviewers had modified their natural techniques in the desired direction where factual techniques were concerned and were also comparable with each other. As indicated, the results for factual techniques were relatively clear-cut. In feeling techniques, both varied in the desired manner but one interviewer generally used more active feeling techniques than the other. If only interviews meeting criteria based on median counts were included, levels of expressed feeling were significantly higher in this first experimental study when active techniques were used. However, informants readily expressing feelings may have stimulated interviewers to use more of the prescribed techniques. This experimental study therefore left unexplained questions about feeling techniques and their effects.

THE FOURTH PHASE:
SECOND EXPERIMENTAL STUDY

The issues were examined further by a second experimental study with 16 mothers, comparing only two styles: active factual/passive

TABLE 7.1   **Mean Number Requests for Feeling, Interpretations, and Expressions of Sympathy, 60 minutes (S.D.)**

	Interview Style				
	A	*B*	*Analysis of*		
			Variance F ratio:		
			between Interviewers		
			F	*df*	*P*
Interviewer 1	30.9 (13.0)	53.0 (19.5)	47.09	1.12	<.0001
Interviewer 2	11.5 (8.8)	29.3 (10.2)			

N.B. Style B by interviewer 1 was paired with style A by interviewer 2.

A = Active factual/passive feeling
B = Active factual/active feeling

feeling and active factual/active feeling. This time the mothers had the same approach for facts but a different one for feelings. Otherwise the design was the same, as were the interviewers who had had the benefit of more detailed feedback from the results of the first experimental study.

Both styles were verbally active and there was no difference in the range or quality of factual data obtained in the two conditions.

In the active feeling style, expressions of sympathy, reflections of feeling, and questions about feelings were used more often, and, as in the first study, these techniques were much more often immediately followed by expression of emotion. However, despite the feedback, differences between interviewers in the use of these techniques remained, so that although both had changed the level of use, a low level for one was a high level for the other (Table 7.1).

TABLE 7.2   Interview Style

Mean no. feelings expressed	A	B	Analysis of Variance F ratio: between Styles		
			F	df	P
First 30 minutes (S.D.)	53.6 (16.6)	58.2 (19.2)	1.40	1.12	n.s.
Whole interview Prorated to 60 minutes (S.D.)	98.8 (24.2)	119.5 (26.2))	16.11	1.12	<.002

A = Active factual/passive feeling

B = Active factual/active feeling

More feelings were expressed with the active factual/active feeling style, but the difference was not apparent in the first 30 minutes (Table 7.2). Certain types of feeling are of particular diagnostic importance, such as negative feelings about spouse, child, or self. Different styles did not elicit different amounts of these types of feeling.

Strong correlations were found between pairs of interviews with the same mother in the amount of feelings expressed and also between the use of the prescribed feeling techniques and the amount of expressed emotion. Since these results suggested an informant effect, the impact of the style on the latter part of the interview, depending on the mother's level of emotional expressiveness in the first 15 minutes, was analyzed. Mothers were subcategorized on a median split into high and low expressers of emotion. The active factual/active feeling technique tended to sustain a high rate of emotional expression in high expressers or to increase it in a proportion of low expressers. The active factual/passive feeling style kept low expressers' rates low and reduced rates in over 50% of the high expressers A change from passive to active feeling style always led to sustained or increased rate of expression; a change from active to passive feeling style usually decreased the rate. These results suggest that the influence of informants reduced the intended differences in applied style.

Pairs of interviews were compared to see which style detected types of feelings that the other failed to detect. The active feeling style performed significantly better in this comparison. There were also interesting context effects: mothers more often expressed negative feelings about themselves after the interviewer reflected feelings with a sympathetic tone, while criticism of spouse was most often expressed after requests for information about sensitive data. Positive feelings were more often expressed after other feelings rather than at the beginning of an utterance, emphasizing the importance of encouraging sufficiently long utterances. Finally, the feeling techniques, whether prescribed or not, tended to facilitate the expression of feeling while structuring statements, clarifications, multiple choice, and closed questions tended to inhibit the expression of emotion.

SUMMARY

Some information about feelings will emerge from initial interviews with parents, no matter what the interviewer does. This is probably true of all initial medical consultations, despite quite marked differences between informants in the extent to which they express feelings. The setting, the expectations, and an attentive, interested interviewer will likely produce a considerable amount of relevant data on both facts and feelings; these factors were not varied in the studies described. They are relevant to technique and, indeed, may have overriding importance for what is reported or expressed. Nevertheless, it appears that many different techniques are relevant to facilitating emotional expression, and obtaining sensitive data. These include asking about feelings, reflecting feelings, expressing sympathy, open questioning, questioning about sensitive material, and encouraging longer utterances, which are more likely to occur if interviewers talk less. Since such passive methods appear quite effective, there may be a case for using active methods more sparingly since maximum revelation of feelings on first contact is probably not optimum. However, interviewers need to be aware of differences between informants—more persistence with feelings techniques may be needed with less expressive interviewees. There are limits to how much most people can alter their interviewing techniques, but since there are several ways of achieving similar ends, there may be methods to suit most interviewers and most clients.

CONCLUSIONS

These studies are examples of the most difficult research strategy in doctor-patient communication literature: the experiment. When interviewers were asked to change their question-asking or responding techniques for feelings, the difference in the number of feelings expressed by informants was not large. However, explicitly asking for feelings or responding more actively to their expression, elicited more emotions from interviewers after 15 minutes of an interview, if they were less emotionally expressive individuals.

When the physician wants feelings to be aired, the preferred technique depends on the patient. With those who tend to show emotion freely, the doctor needs only to be attentive, but with those who are more inhibited, the physician needs to question directly about feelings and to be more actively responsive when they are expressed.

8

Patient-Centered
Clinical Interviewing

Joseph H. Levenstein
Judith Belle Brown
W. Wayne Weston
Moira Stewart
Eric C. McCracken
Ian McWhinney

The task of the physician is twofold: to understand patients and to understand their diseases. In the process of medical history taking, we have a well tried clinical method for understanding diseases; we have no equivalent method for understanding patients. For three reasons, this lack is especially serious for primary care and family medicine.

First, as Carmichael (1980) has pointed out, a large proportion of the problems presented to primary care physicians is not diagnosed in the usual sense of the term. In these patients, a pathological diagnosis is not a realistic goal; the physician must have some other way of understanding the illness. The key to this understanding is an understanding of the patient.

The second reason relates to differing criteria of success in primary care and other fields of medicine. For primary care physicians, the focus is on preventing disease, not diagnosing it. More to the point, their role is to care for patients in the face of the effects on functioning of their diseases or life-problems. This role can only be fulfilled if physicians understand patients and their world.

The third reason relates to management, described by Stephens (1982) as "the quintessence of family medicine." Management in pri-

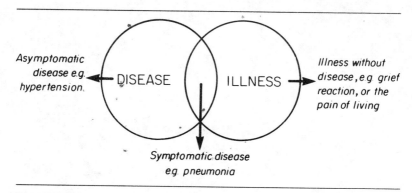

Asymptomatic disease e.g. hypertension.

Illness without disease, e.g. grief reaction, or the pain of living

Symptomatic disease e.g. pneumonia

FIGURE 8.1   **Two Modes of Ill Health: Disease and Illness**

mary care is tailored to individual needs. Although technological aspects of management may be standardized, there are numerous individual variations, even in patients with the same diagnosis. Thus, even when there is a clear-cut pathological diagnosis, the physician still needs to know the patient as an individual, with a unique experience of life, if the management is to be fully effective. A patient-centered **method** must include the process of differential diagnosis: it must aim to understand the patient through patient-centered interviewing and to diagnose the illness, if possible, in terms of physical pathology.

The twofold purpose of the process is best expressed in terms of the distinction between disease and illness. Disease is an abstraction, the thing that is wrong with the body-machine; illness is the unique experience of a person who feels ill. See Figure 8.1.

Several other authors have described a similar distinction between disease and illness (Cassell, 1985; Kleinman et al., 1978; Marinker, 1981; Mishler, 1984;) and we think this indicates that the differentiation has face validity. Our contribution to the growing appreciation of this conceptual distinction is to make explicit how physicians can apply these concepts, in practical terms, in their day-to-day practice. See Figure 8.2.

A patient consulting a physician has a certain agenda in mind. We have chosen to define this in terms of ideas, expectations, and feelings. The doctor also has an agenda: the correct diagnosis of the patient's complaints. For individual patients the physician may have a more specific agenda based on previous knowledge of the patient and the family.

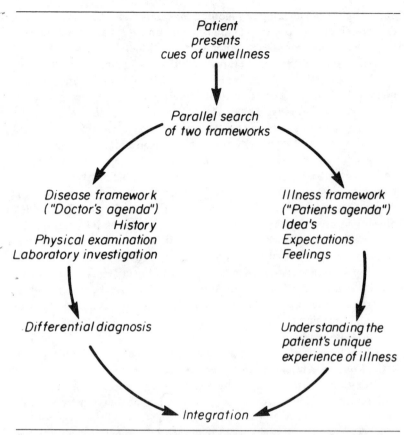

FIGURE 8.2   The Patient-Centered Clinical Interview

In the patient-centered method, the physicians aim is to ascertain the patient's agenda and to reconcile this with their own. In the disease-centered, or doctor-centered method, physicians pursue their own agenda and make little attempt to understand the patient's. The patient-centered method includes the disease-centered whenever appropriate.

The term "patient-centered medicine" was introduced by Balint et al. (1970) who contrasted it with "illness-centered medicine." An understanding of the patient's complaints, based on patient-centered thinking, was called "overall diagnosis," and an understanding based on disease-centered thinking was called "traditional diagnosis." The clinical method was elaborated by Stevens (1974) and Tait (1979). Byrne and Long (1984) developed a method for categorizing a consultation as doctor-centered or patient-centered, their concept of a doctor-centered consultation being close to other writers' "illness" or "disease"-centered methods. Wright and MacAdam (1979) also described doctor-centered and patient-centered clinical methods. A patient-centered clinical method has much in common with the psychotherapeutic concept of client-centered therapy (Rogers, 1951).

Byrne and Long, in their analysis of 1,850 general practice consultations, suggested that many physicians develop a relatively static style of consulting that tends to be doctor-centered: "The problem is that the doctor-centered style is extremely seductive." Clinical teaching in medical schools tends to emphasize a doctor-centered approach (or disease-centered, as we prefer to call it). According to this model, physicians ascertain the patient's complaints and seek information that will enable them to interpret the patient's illness within their own frame of reference. This involves diagnosing the patient's disease and prescribing an appropriate management. One of the criteria of success is a precise diagnosis, such as myocardial infarction, stroke, carcinoma of the colon, child abuse, attempted suicide, or alcoholism. In pursuit of this goal, physicians use a method designed to obtain objective information from the patient.

While there is substantial agreement on the need for family physicians to be patient-centered, there is no definition of what this means in operational terms. It could be argued that physicians' styles are so different, and clinical situations so varied, that no single method could cover all possible doctor-patient interactions. We do not accept this view. The method of differential diagnosis is designed to apply to any clinical situation. We see no reason why medicine should not develop an equally rigorous patient-centered method that can also be applied to any situation. Indeed, we believe it is essential for primary care to develop such a method.

In this chapter we describe patient-centered interviewing developed by Levenstein (1984) in his own practice and further developed and tested during visits to the University of Western Ontario in 1981 and 1982. Together with diagnosis, such interviewing exemplifies the patient-centered clinical method. We believe this method answers the question, "What is the minimum that can be expected of any primary care physician at any patient visit?"

PATIENT-CENTERED INTERVIEWING:
THE PATIENT'S AGENDA

The essence of the patient-centered method is that the physician tries to enter the patient's world, to see the illness through the patient's eyes by behavior that invites and facilitates the patient's openness. The physician seeks to allow patients to express all the reasons for their attendance, so that the physician can understand each patient's ideas, expectations, and feelings about the illness.

Each patient brings to the doctor's office ideas about the nature and the cause of the problem. Furthermore, each patient comes with expectations of the visit, not necessarily made explicit. Also, each patient has feelings about the problem or problems. Sometimes these feelings may be the major factor in the illness, as when the patient fears cancer.

Obviously each patient's accounts of symptoms and their underlying meanings reflect their own unique world. Categorization may help the physician, but the classification of clinical phenomena, be it physical, psychological, or social, comes from the doctor's world, not the patient's. It is not a substitute for understanding each patient as an individual. Entry into the patient's world is a difficult art, requiring empathy, nonjudgmental acceptance, and genuineness. It also requires skill in certain techniques, which we are convinced can be learned and taught. Moreover, physicians cannot be patient-centered unless they know themselves and are prepared to change their own attitudes and behavior.

The key to the patient-centered method, as its name implies, is to encourage as much as possible to flow from the patient. The crucial skill is to be receptive to cues offered by the patient. By attentive listening, the doctor is able to respond to these cues, thereby helping the patient to express his ideas, expectations, and feelings.

Failure to take up a patient's cues causes doctors to cut off patients and thereby miss an opportunity to gain fuller insight into their illnesses. It can also be frustrating for the patient, since the doctors are giving precedence to their own priorities.

These concepts have been compiled into a set of specific definitions for assessing that part of patient-centered care referring to the patient's agenda.

DEFINITIONS OF TERMS

Ideas

Most patients have their own thoughts about what is wrong with them, what might be causing it, and what might be its implications. Often patients are reluctant to express ideas for fear they might sound foolish or because, traditionally, the patient's role is more passive and it might sound presumptive or insulting to offer a diagnosis to the doctor. Physicians often need to encourage patients to express these thoughts.

Expectations

Each patient visiting a physician has some expectations of the visit. These expectations are the individual's stated reasons for the visit, and often relate to a symptom or a concern, for which is anticipated an acknowledgment or a response from the physician. The presentation of the patient's expectations may take many forms, including a straight-forward statement of the problem, a question, or a request for service. While a statement of expectations normally initiates an office visit, it may occur at any stage of the interaction. For example, a patient may say, at the end of the visit, "By the way, doctor, I've also got a pain in my knee."

Not all expectations are made explicit. For example, if a patient with hypertension comes for a follow-up visit there is an implicit expectation that the blood pressure will be taken.

Feelings and Fears

Feelings reflect the emotional content of the patient's illness. They may be the predominant aspect of the illness, as in a grief reaction, or be a contributory factor, as in the anxiety of a breadwinner with a myocardial infarct. Patients may not necessarily articulate feelings explicitly; they are frequently under the surface, or even unconscious, often emerging during the process of the interaction. Feelings may reflect the patient's life experience, personality, or defence mechanisms. They may arise directly from the stated expectations, as when a patient who has requested a checkup discloses during the course of the interview that she is anxious about the effects of dyspareunia on her marital relationship.

One feeling, fear, is an almost universal feeling in the doctor-patient interaction. To a greater or lesser extent, the patients are confronting the unknown, and it is rare that they would not have some fears and fantasies about their illness, management, or its effect on their lives. As with other feelings, fears may have their source in the "here and now," or in past events, or may reflect the patient's personality and life experience.

Prompts

Prompts are signals from patients that their ideas, expectations, or feelings have not yet been acknowledged or sufficiently explored. Prompts may be verbal or behavioral or may arise from the content of the consultation. For our purposes, we define prompts as either statements that are out of context, or restatements of a problem that has already been mentioned, as with the patient coming for an annual physical examination who mentions his sore knee and, later, since it has not been dealt with, says at the end of the visit, "And what about my knee, doctor?"

PHYSICIAN BEHAVIORS

Facilitating behavior is any verbal comment by the physician that encourages the patients' expressions of their ideas, expectations, or feelings. **Facilitating behaviors** may include open-ended questions, open-ended statements, reflections, and confrontations. In analyzing physician behavior we document whether the doctor acknowledges or cuts off the patient's expression of ideas, expectations, feelings, or prompts. **An acknowledgment** is defined as a verbal indication that the physician has heard the patient.

We define all statements not acknowledged by the physician as **cut-offs**: the physician blocks the patient's further expression of ideas, expectations, or feelings by changing the subject, using closed-ended or rhetorical questions, or not acknowledging a prompt. For example, patients may present an expectation such as "I'm having trouble sleeping" and doctors, working from their own agenda, might reply, "How has your appetite been?" Even if a patient's expression is acknowledged, it can be subsequently cut off. For example, patients may present an expectation such as, "What do you think of these warts?" and doctors, preoccupied with their agenda, reply "Warts, mm, well, let's set up this chest X-ray."

A **return** occurs when a physician has cut off a patient but subsequently returns to the patient's ideas, expectations, feelings, or prompts. A **return** is considered as an acknowledgment of the patient's problem and is not counted as a cut-off. For example, the physician who previously cut off the patient's mention of warts may say, "Let's have a look at those warts now. In what way do they concern you?"

AN ILLUSTRATIVE CASE

The following example, based on recent experience, illustrates the definitions.

A 68-year-old male patient, who has recently had surgery for a benign stricture of the sigmoid colon, presents for a routine follow-up office visit. The patient, a retired Roman Catholic priest, has recently moved into a retirement home for aging clergy. These facts are known to the doctor.

The Disease-Centered Interview

Doctor: Hello, Father Smith, how are you today?

Patient: Fine—except for my headaches . . . (expectation)

Doctor: . . . and your operation, how's that going? (cut-off)

Patient: Fine.

Doctor: Bowels working?

Patient: Yes.

Doctor: Appetite?

Patient: A bit poorly.

Doctor: Have you lost any weight? (exploring the disease framework)

Patient: No.

Doctor: Well, obviously your loss of appetite hasn't affected anything, so it can't be too bad . . . . Any nausea or vomiting? (cut-off)

Patient: None.

Doctor: Any pain at the operation site?

Patient: Not really.

Doctor: Are you eating the bran we recommended?

Patient: No.

Doctor: You must please stick to our recommendations. We don't want any recurrences.

Patient: (Sighing) Yes. (prompt)

Doctor: Good, well the operation seems to have been a success and there don't seem to be any complications. Have you any other complaints?

Patient: I have this headache. (prompt)

Doctor: Is your vision affected? (exploring the disease framework)

Patient: No.

Doctor: Any weakness or paralysis of your limbs?

Patient: No.

Doctor: Where are your headaches?

Patient: At the back of my head.

Doctor: Do they throb?

Patient: Yes.

Doctor: How long do they last?

Patient: About four hours.

Doctor: What takes them away?

Patient: I just lie down.

Doctor: How often do they come?

Patient: About twice a week.

Doctor: How long have you been having them?

Patient: Ever since I've been at the home. (prompt)

Doctor: Good, well you needn't worry—it can't have anything to do with your operation. They are tension headaches. Perhaps we can give you some paracetamol for them. The home you have just moved into seems to have beautiful gardens. (cut-off)

Patient: Yes.

Doctor: It really is good of the church to care for its elderly and it must be comforting to have company.

Patient: Yes.

Doctor: Well good. Come and see me in a month's time and we'll see how things are going. Take care.

The Patient-Centered Interview

Doctor: Hello, Father Smith, how are you today?

Patient: Fine, except for my headaches. (expectation)

Doctor: What about your headaches? (facilitating behavior)

Patient: Well, I've been getting them about twice a week at the back of my head and they bother me so I can't do anything, and I have to lie down.

Doctor: You can't do anything . . . what's that like for you? (facilitating behavior)

Patient: Its frustrating, they're interfering with the writing I want to get done and nobody seems to understand . . . (feeling)

Doctor: Understand? (facilitating behavior)

Patient: All the other priests are so old and decrepit in that place. All they can talk about is their aches and pains. I'm ashamed to say they make me sick. (feeling)

Doctor: Why are you ashamed? (facilitating behavior)

Patient: Well, I shouldn't really talk that way about them, they mean no harm . . . I feel, so quilty about it. (feeling)

Doctor: What do you mean guilty? (facilitating behavior)

Patient: I feel that my anger is unjustified, I'm so frustrated that no one understands that I wish to write. (feeling)

Doctor: It must be frustrating . . . (facilitating behavior)

Patient: Yes, it is and my headaches—my headaches make it worse. (prompt)

Doctor: When did they first start?

Patient: Ever since I've been at the home.

Doctor: Why do you think that is? (facilitating behavior)

Patient: I . . . don't know, I haven't really thought about it . . . do you think it's tension?. . . . I mean, the people at the home . . . is it possible? (Idea)

Doctor: What do you think?

Patient: Well, the whole situation at the home does trouble me. (feeling)

Doctor: Would you like to talk about it more? (facilitating behavior)

Patient: No, not now, perhaps later.

Doctor: Well, feel free to discuss it anytime you like.

Patient: Mmm, mm, I will.

Doctor: Well, how are things going after your operation?

Patient: It seems okay.

Doctor: What do you mean, it seems okay? (facilitating behavior)

Patient: Well I don't seem to be eating well and I can't stand that bran. In fact I have no appetite for food. (expectation)

Doctor: What do you think that could be due to? (facilitating behavior)

Patient: I wonder if it's due to the tension I'm feeling? (idea)

Doctor: Mmm, mmm.

Patient: I will really think about what we've said and come back to see you again.

Doctor: Fine, anything else today? (facilitating behavior)

Patient: Fine, everything is fine, except I get a funny feeling on my scar. (expectation)

Doctor: A funny feeling? (facilitating behavior)

Patient: Yes, it seems a bit numb . . . I am afraid it may be serious. (feeling)

Doctor: It's probably a little nerve that supplies the skin that was cut during the operation. Nothing to be concerned about.

Patient: I'm glad it's only that. I was quite worried. (feeling)

Doctor: Anything else you'd like to discuss? (facilitating behavior)

Patient: No, everything else is fine.

Doctor: Good. Would you like something for your headaches?

Patient: Thank you, but I don't think it's necessary.

Doctor: I'd like to see your wound in a month's time, but we can get together earlier if you'd like to.

Patient: Fine, I'll be in touch, Doctor.

In the disease-centered method, the physician's utmost priority is to check out any possible postoperative problems. Anything unrelated to it is of secondary importance. He thus single-mindedly pursues his objectives. When he finally does discuss the headaches he does so in a closed-ended way, not allowing the patient any opportunity to express his own ideas or feelings. He misses subtle cues throughout. In discussing the patient's social context, the doctor preempts any expression of feeling by the patient by using value judgments to describe his circumstances—none but the most assertive patients would contradict him.

From the physician's viewpoint, disease-management is fine: there are no postoperative complications and he has treated the patient's tension headaches with Paracetamol. However, the patient's world has not entered into it at all.

The physician using the patient-centered method allows the patient to guide the interview. He recognizes that the patient's expectation of the visit is that his headaches will be dealt with and, by using open, nondirective, facilitative verbal (and nonverbal) behavior, has elicited several ideas and feelings related to the patient's life. He picks up subtle cues and encourages the patient to expand. He also concentrates on the one aspect ostensibly related to the postoperative course, i.e., loss of appetite. However, it appeared to have an entirely different connotation when explored in the patient's context.

In short, while the doctor was aware of his own agenda, he understood that to learn about the patient and his illness, he had to do it through the patient's world.

RECONCILING THE TWO AGENDAS

At some stage the physician must apply the disease framework to arrive at a diagnosis. There is no necessary sequential order, with the patient's agenda being explored first, the doctor's agenda second. The patient may provide cues at any stage of the process. Under usual circumstances however, physicians must begin with the patient's agenda, since the understanding gained may determine how the physicians follow their own agenda. If, for example, they discover that the patient's reason for attendance is to obtain a certificate of sick leave for an illness that is already subsiding, they may not need to apply the disease framework at all.

We believe it to be quite common, even in family medicine programs, for physicians to use the disease framework first in all cases, moving to the patient's agenda only if the former does not yield a clear pathological diagnosis. We are convinced, however, that the patient-centered method, integrating the doctor's and the patient's agendas, should be universally applied in primary care.

In some cases, there will inevitably be a conflict between the patient's expectations and the physician's assessment of those needs. If the patient's main concern is itchy feet, and the physician finds a blood pressure of 230/140, the doctor will obviously try to convince the patient that the hypertension is a more pressing concern than the presenting problem. A conflict of this nature will normally result in negotiation followed by an agreement. The patient's expectations must be addressed, but only after more urgent problems have been dealt with.

Of course, physicians may not be willing or able to meet the patient's expectations. For example, they may be unwilling to prescribe penicillin for a cold. Even in this case, however, physicians will be able to deal with the situation more effectively if they know that this is what the patient expects.

In observing many doctor-patient interactions, we conclude that a failure to apply the patient-centered method correctly leads to a dysfunctional interview and an unsatisfactory outcome.

CONCLUSIONS

1. The patient-centered clinical method is an important concept for students and practitioners. The key concept is the distinction between the disease

framework (What is the diagnosis?) and the illness frame-work (What is the patient's experience of illness: ideas, expectations, and feelings?).

2. Physicians need to integrate both frameworks and develop specific skills for eliciting the patient's own ideas, expectations, and feelings using facilitating behaviors and refraining from cutting off the patient.

PART III

Teaching and Evaluation

Particular communication skills can be taught by specific pedagogical techniques such as systematic practice with patients, review of interviews on videotape or audiotape, and discussion with tutors.

Maguire and colleagues address the important question of whether interviewing skills acquired during medical training are maintained after the training period has ended, and if these skills are used only with particular types of patients.

A series of well-designed and controlled studies are quite stunning. The improvements in skills attributable to training were evident four to six years later when these same physicians were established in their own practices. In fact, the impressive ratio of total performance scores of trained to untrained doctors was only slightly less than it had been immediately after training, demonstrating an inconsequential decay of skills over the many years. As well, the impact of interview training with psychiatric patients extended to interviews with physically ill patients.

These findings are the happy corollary of the usually discouraging observation that doctors become fixed in their style of interviewing; the benefits of performance feedback are likely to persist throughout the doctor's professional life.

Schofield and Arntson deal with another part of the training process, the relationship between the community-based preceptor (the clinical teacher) and the trainee during the "apprenticeship" period with an established physician (equivalent to North American residency training).

The focus of the training program is the "training of trainers" through a three-day intensive program. As in the work of Maguire and associates, the teaching strategies include direct observation of physicians' interviewing behavior and structured feedback. Schofield and Arntson describe the six tasks for the physician to achieve during a visit with a patient.

1. Define the reasons for the patient's attendance.

2. Consider other continuing problems and risk factors.

3. Choose with the patient an appropriate action for each problem.

4. Achieve a shared understanding of the problem with the patient.

5. Involve the patient in the management and encourage the patient to accept appropriate responsibility.

6. Use time and resources appropriately and establish or maintain a relationship with the patient that helps achieve the other tasks.

Evaluation of performance is standardized and based on a taped record of an authentic visit with a patient in the doctor's own office or of a visit with a simulated patient.

Fascinating distinctions among the goals and priorities of trainers and trainees are also discussed by the authors, who conclude their paper with a discussion of the difficulties of addressing the conflicting needs of the teacher (trainer) and the learner (trainee).

Kurtz addresses the issue of integrating communications training into the medical school curriculum. Most medical schools offer training in communication as a single, self-contained course, offered entirely in the preclinical or early clinical years, concluded by one evaluation in which communication skills are isolated from other clinical concerns. She suggests a structured program, integrated with other parts of the medical school program. The curriculum is based on a helical process of teaching in which the student revolves through communication sessions over the four-year curriculum, practicing old skills while adding new and more complex material each round.

While instruments for evaluating communication skills are presented, to some extent, in all of the chapters in this section, the most sophisticated approach to scale assessment of reliability and validity is provided by Kraan and associates, who constructed a 68-item checklist useful for evaluating interview skills of medical students and practicing physicians. The analytic procedures used in this chapter are a model for further work; these subscales must now be validated in other parts of the world.

Each of the papers in this section on teaching and evaluation presents a different and important aspect of skills training, and together provide insight into the most innovative programs available and most sophisticated attempts at evaluation.

9

Consultation Skills
of Young Doctors—Benefits
of Undergraduate Feedback Training
in Interviewing

Peter Maguire
Susan Fairbairn
Charles Fletcher

INTRODUCTION

The traditional apprenticeship method of training medical students to take histories often does not provide students with enough interviewing skill to enable them to obtain a full and accurate account of patients' problems (Maguire and Rutter, 1976a). Furthermore, training has seldom extended to teaching students how to handle the second part of a consultation: explanation of findings and discussion of plans for investigation and treatment.

Most students, however, can acquire these skills through training, which includes four components: literature dealing with the information to be obtained and the skills to be used; systematic practice with patients; feedback of performance by audio or videotape replay; and discussion with a tutor (Maguire et al., 1978; Wakeford, 1983).

Much performance feedback has been done in departments of psychiatry, and only immediate benefits have been assessed. Are interviewing skills so acquired maintained after qualification and used with all types of patients (Carroll and Monroe, 1979)? And is performance with simulated patients comparable to performance with real patients? Special circumstances in the Manchester medical school allowed these

TABLE 9.1   Training Program for Each Quartet

Week	3 Feedback Students	1 Control Student
1	Interview to assess skills before training followed by feedback session	Interview to assess skills before training
2	First practice interview followed by feedback	No interview
3	Second practice interview followed by feedback	No interview
4	Interview to assess skill after training	Interview to assess skill after training

important questions to be studied. Experiments in performance feedback had been carried out four to six years previously on a random sample of students during a fourth year psychiatric clerkship. For a quartet of students, three were given feedback and the fourth was taught conventionally, serving as a control. Interviewing skills were assessed by videotape recording before and after their training, so all students were equally accustomed to this method.

Performance Feedback Training

Before feedback training began, each of the three "feedback" students within a quartet was asked to interview the same patient (Table 9.1). They were given the task of trying to establish the patient's main problems within 15 minutes. They were also informed that their interviews would be videotaped to allow rating of their interviewing skills and that they should write up a history afterwards based on the information they had elicited during the 15-minute interview.

As the main purpose of the experiment was to compare the three feedback programs, the order in which students interviewed the patients was so balanced that the first, second, and third positions were equally represented among the three feedback groups.

The students assigned to the control group saw the same patients under identical conditions, but a day later. It was considered that separating the control students from the feedback groups would reduce the chance of their feeling antagonistic because they were not to receive any feedback until after the experiment was over.

The patients who took part in these and subsequent interviews were inpatients or day patients suffering from an affective disorder, neurosis, or alcoholism. They were selected by medical staff who were independent of the study.

Training

When these interviews were completed, the three students in the feedback groups met with a tutor. They were given two printed handouts. The first handout described the areas of information that they should follow. These areas included details of the patients' problems, their impact on the patients' daily life, the patients' view of these problems, his or her predisposition to develop similar problems in the past, and questions designed to elicit any other difficulties. The second handout focused on the techniques that they should use. It was divided into three sections: beginning the interview, pursuing the main task, and ending the interview (Maguire and Rutter, 1976b).

After discussing these handouts with the tutor, the students arranged to see him or her for individual feedback between two and four days later.

Each student in the television group watched a television replay of this first interview with the tutor. The tutor discussed the student's performance in relation to the standards set in the handout.

METHODS

Samples

All 186 doctors from the "feedback" and control groups who were still practicing four to six years later as house officers, registrars, or trainees in general practice in the Manchester area were contacted. We asked them to attend the department of psychiatry to interview three patients. The interviews would be videotaped. A total of 148 (84%) provisionally agreed to participate. A random sample of 40 was obtained for the study, and of these a stratified sample of 36 doctors was obtained. The 18 doctors who had had performance feedback ("trained") and the 18 who had been control subjects ("controls") were closely matched for age and sex, their interviewing skills before training, and the time after training.

Patients suffering from a psychiatric (anxiety or depression), life threatening (angina or breast cancer), or chronic disabling illness (arthritis, asthma, emphysema) were recruited from the wards and outpatient clinics of Withington Hospital. Simulators were recruited through local advertisements, interviewed, and selected for further training. All simulators chose which category of illness they felt most able to portray, and each was shown a relevant but anonymous case summary. They were given a week to think it through. They were then interviewed in a television studio, and these interviews were replayed and discussed. Further practice and discussion were arranged when needed until the portrayals were authentic.

INTERVIEWS

Each doctor was asked to obtain a history of the presenting problems from three patients in 15 minutes or less per patient. Participants were then told the results of physical examination and relevant investigations, and the diagnosis. They were also given a treatment plan and a prognosis and asked to assimilate this information for five minutes. They then returned to the patients for ten minutes to explain and discuss findings, diagnosis, and proposed treatment. They were told to mention the prognosis in appropriate terms. These discussions were recorded on videotape for later rating.

Each doctor saw two simulated patients and one real patient, and covered each category of illness (psychiatric, life threatening, and chronic disabling). To avoid possible order effects, the three categories of illness were equally divided among first, second, and third interviews.

ASSESSMENT

All 108 videotapes were assessed by a trained psychologist (SF), who did not know which doctors had been given performance feedback. She used an interview rating scale to assess how well doctors began and ended their interviews, used the main interviewing skills, and performed overall (Maguire et al., 1978).

Beginning the interview was assessed by checking for the presence of 24 items of behavior contained in three subsections: greeting and seating, self-introduction, and orienting the patient. Ending the interview was assessed by checking for the presence of 10 items in three subsections: summarizing, checking accuracy, and concluding. The 11 main interviewing skills were each assessed on a five-point scale.

Overall ratings were also assessed on five-point scales to indicate the degree of self-assurance, warmth, empathy, and competence shown throughout each interview. A score of less than 50% of the possible maximum indicates clinical inadequacy in these skills; 70% is an acceptable score. Experienced teachers of interviewing in the department of psychiatry score 80% to 90% of the maximum.

Assessments were based on how well information was given to the patient, how this information was tailored to the patient's own view of what is wrong and what treatment to expect, and checking of the patient's acceptance and understanding of the information (Pendleton et al., 1984; Tuckett et al., 1985).

A three-point rating scale was used to score how well the doctor had handled and explained the topic. Two further three-point scales assessed exploration of the patient's views and negotiation on an agreed conclusion in the light of these views. The first topic that the doctor mentioned was noted, and interviews were also rated on the extent to which the doctor used methods to improve recollection and compliance (Ley, 1983).

RELIABILITY OF ASSESSMENT

From the 108 recorded interviews, 15 were drawn at random so that category of illness, trained and control groups, and stage of the study (early, middle, and late) were equally represented. These videotapes were independently assessed by two of us (SF and PM), and the kappa coefficient was used to determine variation between assessors (Cohen, 1960). Significant agreement ($p < 0.01$) was obtained on all items in the main skills section and on the overall ratings. Complete agreement was obtained on the items in the sections on beginning and ending the interview. Generally, agreement was 90%.

STATISTICAL ANALYSIS

The effects of training and the category of illness on the scores for beginning and ending the interview were determined by analysis of variance, using the assessments of main skills and overall performance.

RESULTS

Comparability of groups. Before training, the trained and control groups obtained similarly low scores (means 15.6 and 15.8 respectively out of a possible maximum of 44) on the main interviewing skills. At the end of the feedback training, the trained group achieved significantly better mean scores (23.6 [SD 5.5]) than did the control group (17.8 [4.9]). The score ratio of the trained group to the control group rose from 0.99 before training to 1.32 after training.

Main interviewing skills. Both trained and control doctors had improved their main interviewing skills (by 25% and 35% respectively) after training (see Figure 9.1), but the trained group maintained their advantage in the subsequent four to six years. The ratio of total scores of trained to untrained doctors was now only slightly less (1.28) than it had been immediately after training. The effect of training was most evident in clarifying patients' statements, using open questions, and responding to verbal clues about patients' problems (see Table 9.2). The control group did as well as the trained group on only one skill: avoiding the use of jargon. They failed to achieve reasonable scores (50% or more) on clarification, use of open questions, and covering psychosocial problems.

Beginning and ending interviews. Neither group scored well on beginning interviews (trained group mean 9.7—40% of maximum, control group 7.4—31%). Few doctors summarized what they had learned from their patients, checked its accuracy, or made concluding

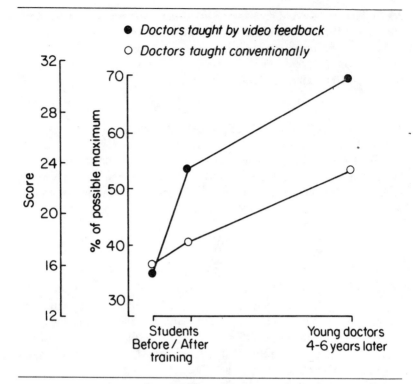

FIGURE 9.1   Comparison of Mean Scores for Main Interviewing Skills Obtained by Medical Students Before and After Training and While Working as Doctors Four to Six Years Later

statements. Consequently, they scored only 9% (trained 0.93, control 0.93) on ending interviews.

Overall ratings of performances. The trained group was considered to be more competent and empathic than the control doctors (Table 9.3). They were also perceived as somewhat warmer and more self-assured.

Category of illness. Trained doctors made greater use of the main interviewing skills when interviewing both physically and mentally ill patients. (Table 9.4). The benefits of training with psychiatric patients had therefore extended to other types of patients. These scores, however, obscured an important finding: both trained and control groups covered psychosocial problems more fully with psychiatric patients (Table 9.5) than those with a physical illness.

TABLE 9.2   Comparison of Overall Scores of Trained and Control Doctors Four to Six Years After Training

Skills	Trained Doctors Mean (SD) Score	% Of maximum score	Control Doctors Mean (SD) Score	% Of maximum score	Ratio of Trained to control scores	F value (df 1,34)	Significance
Clarification of patients' statements	2.78 (0.72)	70	1.63 (0.86)	41	1.71	50.60	p<0.001
Using open questions	2.30 (0.86)	58	1.67 (0.64)	42	1.38	12.73	p<0.001
Noticing verbal clues to patient's problems	2.83 (0.84)	71	2.11 (0.66)	53	1.34	12.73	p<0.001
Inquiring about patients' psycho-social problems	2.32 (0.75)	58	1.81 (0.58)	45	1.28	13.90	p<.001
Preventing needless repetition	2.85 (0.49)	71	2.24 (0.64)	56	1.27	20.50	p<.001
Keeping patients to the point	2.96 (0.55)	74	2.35 (0.62)	59	1.26	29.62	p<.001
Verbal and visual encouragement	2.96 (0.47)	74	2.37 (0.62)	59	1.25	18.8	p<.001
Getting precise information	2.61 (0.63)	65	2.10 (0.70)	53	1.24	14.3	p<.001
Using brief questions	2.59 (0.58)	65	2.14 (0.51)	54	1.21	8.8	p<.006
Reducing use of jargon	2.80 (0.49)	70	2.33 (0.58)	58	1.20	13.9	p<.001
Avoiding use of jargon	2.61 (0.60)	65	2.40 (0.53)	60	1.09	3.40	p=0.74
TOTAL SCORE	29.61	67	23.15	53	1.28		p<.001

First topic mentioned. Over half the participants (64, 54%) began with an explanation of the test results. Some began by explaining the purpose of the interview (14, 12%), diagnosis (15, 12%), or recapitulation of the patient's key problems (12, 10%). Occasionally the patient's plans (9, 7.5%) and the proposed treatment (3, 2.5%) were considered first. Only one interview began with an attempt to categorize the information to be given, for example, "I would like to start by telling you what I think is wrong."

TABLE 9.3   **Comparison of Overall Scores of Trained and Control Doctors Four to Six Years After Training**

	Trained Doctors		Control Doctors				
	Mean (SD)	% Of maxi-mum	Mean (SD)	% Of maxi-mum	Ratio of trained to control scores	F value (df 1,34)	Signifi-cance
SKILLS							
Self assurance	2.9 (0.58)	72	2.5 (0.54)	63	1:16	6.9	p<0.013
Warmth	2.6 (0.65)	65	2.2 (0.64)	55	1:18	8.2	p<0.007
Empathy	2.8 (0.66)	70	2.0 (0.61)	50	1:40	27.2	p<0.001
Competence	2.8 (0.50)	70	1.9 (0.47)	48	1:50	68.9	p<0.001

Handling of topics. There was no difference between trained and untrained doctors in their mean scores for handling the six main topics (Table 9.6). Most scores were low; treatment was the only topic with a mean score over 50%.

Information giving. To see how well doctors just gave and explained information, marks for obtaining patients' views and for negotiation were excluded from the analysis. Scores on all topics except prognosis then increased, but except for those for diagnosis (60%) and treatment (62%), all remained well below 50%.

Distribution of discussion scores. The mean scores shown in Table 9.6 conceal the fact that there were some very good discussions, particularly relating to treatment, and, to a lesser extent, diagnosis. For most of the other topics, performance was poor or the topics were omitted altogether.

Obtaining patients' views and negotiating. There were no good attempts to obtain patients' views or to negotiate concerning all the topics. However, when these aspects are considered for each topic separately, patients' views were satisfactorily obtained about treatment

TABLE 9.4   **Comparison of Main Interview Skills Four to Six Years
After Training According to Category of Patients' Illness**

Category of Illness	Trained Doctors		Control Doctors		Ratio of Trained to Control Scores
	Mean (SD) Score	% Of Maximum Score	Mean (SD) Score	% Of Maximum Score	
Life threatening	29.55 (2.85)	67	23.00 (4.27)	52	1.28
Chronic disabling	29.49 (2.81)	67	22.77 (3.43)	52	1.30
Psychiatric	29.77 (5.42)	68	23.68 (3.10)	54	1.26

For effect of category of illness on main skills $F=0.25$, $p=0.78$.
For trained v. untrained $F=45.60$, $p=0.001$

in 24% of discussions, and good negotiation took place only slightly less often. In the other topics these aspects of the discussions were usually omitted and were seldom handled well.

In most discussions the doctors were proficient in avoiding medical jargon, using short words, answering questions, and giving specific advice, especially early on in the exposition. They were not as good at repeating or reinforcing advice and encouraging patients to ask questions. Only a few participants made any attempt to check whether a patient had understood what had been said or to categorize the information given.

Type of patient. All the doctors thought they had been talking to real patients. When told that some were simulators, they could not differentiate between real patients and simulators. There was no difference between the mean scores on interviews with real and simulated patients.

DISCUSSION

It might be argued that although medical students given performance feedback acquire and retain certain interviewing skills, they have no impact on diagnosis and management. General practitioners, specialists, and ward nurses who use these skills, however, are much more

TABLE 9.5   Comparison of Mean Scores Four to Six Years After Training According to Inquiry About Psychosocial Problems

Type of Illness	Trained Doctors		Control Doctors		
	Mean (SD) Score	% Of Maximum Score	Mean (SD) Score	% Of Maximum Score	Ratio of Trained to Control Scores
Life threatening	2.17 (0.79)	54	1.56 (0.70)	39	1.39
Chronic disabling	2.17 (0.52)	54	1.78 (0.55)	45	1.22
Psychiatric	2.61 (0.85)	65	2.11 (0.32)	53	1.24

For nature of patient's problem $F=6.45$, $p=0.003$, df 1, 34.
For trained v. control doctors $F=13.94$, $p=0.001$, df 1,34.

likely to detect psychiatric morbidity than are those trained conventionally (Goldberg et al., 1980; Faulkener and Maguire, 1986; Maguire et al., 1981). Although there is no direct evidence that accuracy of physical diagnosis is improved by using these skills, they do considerably increase the amount of accurate and relevant information obtained about patients' presenting problems, their etiology, and their impact on patients and their families (Naji et al., 1986). Their application to patients with organic disease must therefore lead to more effective management. Moreover, surgical patients have been found to rate students who have acquired these skills as more empathic and understanding than those who lack them (Thompson and Anderson, 1982).

Byrne and Long (1976) found no relation between age and interviewing skills among general practitioners and concluded that doctors become fixed in their style of interviewing soon after qualifying. The benefits of performance feedback should therefore persist throughout a doctor's professional life. While there has been one report that the effect of performance feedback did not persist, this concerned preclinical rather than clinical students (Engler et al., 1980).

The only skills for which the trained doctors scored less than 60% of the maximum were the use of open questions and coverage of psychosocial problems. The control group's mean scores were less than 50%—too low for adequate history taking on these skills. The reluctance of these young doctors to ask patients with physical illness if it had led to anxiety and depression or adversely affected their job, personal rela-

TABLE 9.6   Mean Scores Four to Six Years After Training For Handling Main Topics

Topic	Possible Total	Mean Total Scores			Mean scores excluding patients' views and negotiation	
		Trained Doctors	Control Doctors	All Doctors (% of possible)	Possible	All Doctors (%)
Previous tests	10	1.9	2.4	2.2 (22)	6	2.01 (34)
Diagnosis	8	2.9	3.1	3.0 (38)	4	2.39 (60)
Aetiology	8	2.1	2.1	2.1 (26)	4	2.58 (40)
Future tests	10	2.9	2.5	2.7 (27)	6	2.38 (40)
Treatment	10	5.8	5.1	5.5 (55)	6	3.72 (62)
Prognosis	8	1.6	1.5	1.6 (20)	4	1.21 (30)
Patients' views (all topics)	12	2.1	2.1	2.1 (18)		
Negotiation (all topics)	12	1.7	1.5	1.6 (13)		

tionship, or sex life mirrors that of interns and residents in the United States (Duffy et al., 1980). There are probably several causes (Rosser and Maguire, 1982). If patients are asked how they feel about their illness, they may express strong emotions like sorrow or resentment, which the doctor may find difficult to handle. Patients might also be prompted to ask about the nature and prognosis of their illness or complications of treatment. Few doctors have been trained to handle such reasonable but difficult questions. Some doctors are interested only in their patients' physical illnesses and do not want to become embroiled in emotional and social matters. This reluctance to explore how patients perceive their illness and have been affected by it has also been found among consultants and surgeons, who often overlook psychiatric morbidity in their patients (Bridges and Goldberg, 1984; Maguire et al., 1981; Nabarro, 1984; Psychiatric illness in medical patients, 1979; Rosser and Maguire, 1982).

The tendency of young doctors to use closed or leading questions may have been due to their reliance on completing routine checklists of symptoms, which they had been instructed to cover as medical students.

It may also reflect a false assumption that closed questions save time. Control doctors performed best on avoiding jargon and keeping patients to the point, both of which require toughness. These are of obvious relevance to doctors working under pressure and may have improved by necessity.

The poor performance of both trained and control groups in beginning and ending interviews is disappointing. Few doctors explained the purpose of the interview or the time available. They had questioned the value of this mode of beginning as students and still rejected it. Their failure to check that the information they had obtained from patients was accurate and reflected key problems may have been due to their hurrying to complete their interviews within the allotted time.

The young doctors demonstrated fairly poor performance on giving information and advice. Unfortunately, the doctors were weakest in the techniques that have been found to increase patients' satisfaction and improve their compliance (Becker and Rosenstock, 1984; Brody, 1980; Haynes et al., 1979). It was, however, gratifying that in 25% of the discussions the doctors did negotiate about treatment. Fewer than half of them used the techniques Ley believes improve compliance. Their reluctance to discover the patients' views of their predicaments and to mention prognosis paralleled their tendency to avoid asking patients about social and psychological aspects.

The fact that the benefit of interview training with psychiatric patients extended to interviews with physically ill patients is encouraging, justifying the continuation of this training. It might be even more effective with both undergraduates and postgraduates if it were also given in other clinical departments, focused more on the weaker areas of performance, included practice with physically ill patients, and promoted discussion of the reasons for the reluctance to cover psychosocial problems, how to handle strong emotions and difficult questions, and, especially, how to give information and advice (Bridges and Goldberg, 1984; Goldberg et al., 1980; Shaw and Garth, 1975).

RECOMMENDATIONS

1. Undergraduate training in communication should include these four components:

    a. literature providing information to be covered in the course and the skills to be used;

    b. systematic practice with patients;

    c. feedback of performance by audio or videotape replay;

    d. discussion with a tutor.

2. Assessment of communication should include the following:

    a. rating the beginning and end of the interviews;

    b. 11 specific skills (Table 9.2);

    c. four global skills (Table 9.3);

    d. rating the giving of information and advice.

3. Because undergraduate training of this sort is shown to offer benefits four to six years later, it is highly recommended.

10

A Model for Teaching Doctor-Patient
Communication During Residency

Theo Schofield
and
Paul Arntson

In the United Kingdom, general practice is the only primary medical care discipline. Each doctor has a registered list of patients whom he or she will tend to see for three or four visits a year, each visit lasting between five and ten minutes.

EDUCATIONAL SETTINGS

Doctors entering general practice in the United Kingdom have completed their medical school education and at least three years of hospital practice. Two of these years may be part of a rotation structured to provide appropriate experience for general practice. Vocational training (hereafter called residency training) includes one year during which young doctors are actually working in general practice. During this time, one of the partners in a community-based practice acts as trainer or clinical teacher. There is usually only one trainee (resident) in each practice, but each week a group of residents will come together, for a half or whole day of small group teaching.

Each region and district is responsible for setting the curriculum for this year, and each clinical teacher is responsible for its implementation.

During this third year of training, residents develop a relationship with the teacher and can take part in informal discussions of cases. All sources on GP training emphasize that it is in this relationship that the values, attitudes, adaptation to change, and self-assessment necessary to be a competent GP are really learned.

In this setting, we have conducted two studies, which are reported here. The first was an evaluation of our attempt to introduce systematic teaching of doctor-patient communication through courses for the clinical teachers. The second was a study of the relationship between the resident and the clinical teacher, viewing this relationship as a powerful educational tool in itself.

AN APPROACH TO TEACHING

In their critique of educational research and teaching of interviewing, Carroll and Monroe (1979) described three crucial components of effective teaching: provision for direct observation and feedback on students' interviewing behavior, structured feedback, and explicit statements of interview skills to be learned. Our approach includes these first two elements, but differs significantly from other programs in the third; we emphasize the tasks to be completed in a visit, rather than a prescriptive list of the skills or strategies to be mastered.

We have described a cycle of care in which patients come to the doctor with not only a problem that has causes and effects, but also with their own understanding of health, including their ideas about the nature of their problem, concerns about its significance, and expectations about the visit or the help that may be offered.

After the visit there will be short-term outcomes, which can be measured as patient satisfaction, changes in knowledge, and a reduction in concern; intermediate effects, particularly changes in patients' behavior and compliance; and long-term effects, or changes in the patients' health.

This model recognizes, however, that patients' understanding of health will remain the most powerful influence on their behavior. One crucial task during the visit, therefore, is to explore and develop that understanding.

From this model, we have derived a list of tasks that can be achieved either in a single visit or in a sequence of encounters (Table 10.1). Although these tasks have a logical sequence, we do not intend to prescribe an actual sequence in practice. The last two tasks—use of time

TABLE 10.1   Tasks to Be Completed in a Doctor/Patient Interview

1. To define the reasons for the patient's attendance, including: the nature and history of the problem; their etiology; the patient's ideas, concerns, and expectations; and the effects of the problems.

2. To consider other, continuing problems and risk factors.

3. To choose with the patient an appropriate action for each problem.

4. To achieve a shared understanding of the problems with the patients.

5. To involve the patient in the management and encourage the patient to accept appropriate responsibility.

6. To use time and resources appropriately.

7. To establish or maintain a relationship with the patient which helps to achieve the other tasks.

and resources and maintenance of the relationship—run throughout any visit.

When we teach this model to community doctors, we also use a diagnostic process to assess the doctors' effectiveness in completing the tasks. Their strengths are identified and reinforced, and only in areas where they are less effective are alternative or supplementary strategies and skills considered. This approach differs from traditional teaching, particularly in medicine, by identifying and giving adequate attention to the doctors strengths rather than focusing immediately on their weaknesses. This is such ingrained behavior in doctors observing each other's consultations that we had to formulate rules for teaching and feedback.

1. *The doctor begins the discussion.*
   The injunction that the doctors go first in discussing the visit emphasizes their ownership of their own work and means that they are setting their own agenda for the teaching. If they identify the less effective aspects of the visit themselves, the role of teacher changes from external critic to helper.

2. *Strengths are reviewed first.*
Identifying the strengths of the consultation first increases the acceptability of the feedback, reinforces desirable behavior, and enables these strengths to be used in other settings.

3. *No weaknesses are discussed without recommendations.*
Coupling criticisms with consideration of alternative skills or strategies ("How could this have been done better?") ensures constructive rather than destructive feedback.

We record the visit in the doctor's own consulting room, but we also use these methods with simulated patients on our courses.

We use two teaching tools: a map (Table 10.2) on which we can record our observations of the consultation as it proceeds, and a rating scale (Table 10.3) on which both learner and teacher can record their judgment of how appropriately and effectively each task is performed. This is also used as a basis for the subsequent discussion. Neither tool, however, was designed as a research tool.

The sequence of events in analyzing a visit is as follows.

1. The learner and teacher observe and usually map the recorded visit.

2. The learner and teacher briefly clarify any matters of fact.

3. The visit is evaluated on the rating scale.

4. The learner discusses those tasks that he or she believes were performed.

5. The teacher or other observers discuss those tasks that they believe were performed.

6. The learner discusses those tasks that, in his or her opinion, were not completed, and makes recommendations on how those tasks might have been performed.

7. The teacher or other observers discuss those tasks that they judge were not completed and make their recommendations.

8. Disagreements are discussed and, if possible, resolved.

TABLE 10.2   Map of an Interview

Nature and History of a Problem
Etiology
Patient's Ideas
Patient's Concerns
Patient's Expectations
Effects of Problem(s)
Continuing Problems
Risk Factors
Choosing Action Taken
Sharing Understanding
Involving in Management

9. The learner is left with a clear summary of his or her strengths, and specific changes that might lead to improvement.

As innovators we were seen to some extent as social deviants and had to establish our credibility by example. We also had to present the

TABLE 10.3   Rating Scale for an Interview

1.   Nature and history of problems adequately defined.

2.   Etiology of problems adequately defined.

3.   Patient's ideas explored adequately and appropriately.

4.   Patient's concerns explored adequately and appropriately.

5.   Patient's expectations explored adequately and appropriately.

6.   Effects of problems explored adequately and appropriately.

7.   Continuing problems considered.

8.   Risk factors considered.

9.   Appropriate action chosen for each problem.

10.   Appropriate shared understanding of problems achieved.

11.   Patient involved in management adequately and appropriately.

12.   Appropriate use of time and resources.

13.   Appropriate use of time and resources in long-term management.

14.   Helpful relationship with patient established or maintained.

innovation in a way that was acceptable, manageable, and reduced the risk of failure. We were helped by Everett Rogers's (1983) work on diffusion of innovations; by the availability of portable video recorders and by the clear framework for teaching already described.

We also sought to minimize the risk by insisting on adherence to our rules for feedback and by giving both trainers and trainees the opportunity to encounter these methods for the first time in the relative safety of a course using simulated patients.

ADVANTAGE OF THE NEW APPROACH

Phillip Ley (1980) described the unsatisfactory retention of information and compliance following many patients' visits to the doctor. David Tuckett et al. (1985) described the lack of active exploration of patients' ideas and the limited nature of explanations given to patients. Byrne and Long (1984) described the wide range of styles in the group of doctors they studied, but also individuals' lack of flexibility and often inappropriate styles. They speculated on the reasons for doctors developing and maintaining a particular style. Apart from hospital training and the constraints of time, they also argued that doctor-centered styles were self-reinforcing. They concluded that "When a doctor develops his style there is a possibility that it is a sort of prison within which the doctor will be forced to work." By providing an educational opportunity on a new approach to communications, we were offering many doctors a key to that prison.

DESIGN OF THE COURSE

The aims of the course are

1. to present a rationale from which consultation tasks may be derived;

2. to present a series of seven tasks that may be used to practice and teach effective consulting;

3. to demonstrate the use of video-recording techniques in the office and to discuss the ethical implications;

4. to demonstrate how a consultation's effectiveness can be evaluated;

5. to demonstrate giving feedback without threatening the learner's willingness to be evaluated;

6. to provide an opportunity to practice using the recommended techniques for observing consultation, evaluation, and feedback;

7. to demonstrate identification of strengths and weaknesses in interviewing, and appropriate skills training;

8. to motivate course members to analyze their interviewing style for their own continuing education;

9. to motivate general practice teachers to use the techniques in their own teaching.

The courses last three days and are attended by 20 to 30 general practitioner teachers, working in groups of 6 members and 1 course tutor.

The first day starts with a small-group discussion of members' previous experiences of observing and teaching consultations. Several anxieties are common, particularly uncertainties about what to look for when observing consultations, and fears of giving destructive feedback.

The rationale for the tasks in the consultation is then described and discussed.

Next, the sequence of teaching and teaching tools is described and rehearsed, using recordings made in the group leaders' own practices.

Finally the practical and ethical issues involved in recording consultations in practice are discussed.

The second day is spent entirely in small groups where each member role-plays an interview with a simulated patient. The group then discusses and evaluates the interview.

The patients are played by a group of actors, who are told to react to the way that the interview develops rather than follow a predetermined script. The actors remain in role for part of the subsequent discussion, which provides a unique opportunity for the doctor and the rest of the group to check their perceptions of events in the interview against those of the patient. This is particularly important because of the patient-centered nature of the tasks.

The aim of this day is to help members evaluate the degree to which tasks have been completed in the interviews they have observed, identify the range of skills and strategies that have been employed, and learn to provide effective and supportive feedback.

During the first half of the third day, attention is focused on each member's individual teaching skills and the ways in which observing and teaching interviewing can be integrated into the learner's curriculum.

The last afternoon of the course is spent looking outward again to the teachers' own settings to consider the ways this approach can be integrated into their own curriculum and teaching.

EVALUATION

In the last four years we have held ten courses in the United Kingdom, attended by over 250 teachers. The first two were exclusively for trainers in our own region. The second two included teachers from other regions, and five of the last six workshops have been in other regions, two of which are now running their own workshops.

The courses have been evaluated in several ways. The first was to ask each member at the end of the course to rate the degree of achievement for each of our aims. Second, each member completed an attitude scale at the beginning and end of the course, the items on the scale being related to its aims and content. In the early courses the shift in attitude was highly significant, but it has been less marked recently, due to the ceiling effect produced by a shift in the pre-course attitudes. Our approach is becoming more generally accepted in the culture of general practice. Third, we show a recorded consultation at the beginning and end of each course, with the instructions, "You have just watched a consultation by your trainee or close colleague who has asked for your comments. What comments would you make? Please write up to a maximum of five in the order that you would make them."

Their replies or comments were completely randomized, typed out, and given to four assessors, who were blind to whether these comments were made before or after the workshop, or the order in which they were made. Each comment was scored on whether it related to one of the interview tasks or whether it referred to a desirable or undesirable aspect of the interview in question. The reliability of these ratings was established.

The assessors then rated whether the participants were using the tasks in their feedback by the number of tasks referred to before and after the course or whether they were making positive comments first. In both cases there was a highly significant shift in the desired direction.

The other method of evaluating the courses was to invite three experienced behavioral scientists, Mary Boulton, Anthony Williams, and Paul Arntson, as observers of two of the courses. Their comments have given us many valuable insights into two main areas: course members' reactions to our approach to interviewing and their acceptance and use of the proposed teaching methods.

They observed that some doctors had considerable resistance to our model of an effective interview. They felt that our approach added to the doctors' difficulties. For example, exploring some issues, such as the patients' concerns could be time-consuming and raised the doctors' own anxieties, particularly if they lacked the skills to resolve them.

Completing some of the tasks required quite major shifts in some doctors' established patterns of behavior. Some doctors saw sharing information and reducing the use of their authority as reducing their effectiveness as healers.

Another source of this resistance was that some doctors, particularly those who were Balint trained, felt that this approach ignored the doctors' feelings and, by itemizing the tasks in the interview, ran the risk of trivializing it.

Together these reactions emphasize the value of the parallel process in the course, which starts by exploring the doctors' own ideas about the nature and purpose of their interviews. Many doctors reported at the outset of the course that they had previously encountered difficulties due to lack of a framework to know what to look for in an interview and lack of a clear sense of how visits in general practice differed from those conducted in a hospital. Many doctors have found the process of giving and receiving feedback about consultations painful and welcomed the imposition of our rules.

Both the map and the rating scale were well accepted, though some doctors appeared to prefer the map, perhaps because it is nonthreatening and avoids the need to evaluate the effectiveness of an interview. Some doctors had an initial difficulty in relating their judgments to evidence observed during consultations.

Some teachers' major problem was lack of a repertoire of alternative strategies and skills to offer to their learners, which may lead some to fall back on their own interview style. The ability to consider a variety of approaches is an important attribute of an effective teacher, but it is also necessary to teach effective strategies.

STUDY OF RESIDENT/TEACHER RELATIONSHIPS

There is little systematic research on the resident-teacher relationship. The purpose of the research reported here was to assess this relationship based on three interrelated assumptions.

1. Both participants in the relationship enter with different sets of tasks and expectations.

2. For the resident to develop self-directed learning skills, the relationship must become one of joint problem solving rather than dependency on the teacher.

3. Both the teacher and the resident will be flexible and responsive to needed changes if they are aware of each other's expectations and assessments of the relationship and training year.

These assumptions provided the logic for analyzing the resident-teacher relationship in this research project, which attempted to answer the following research questions.

1. What differences are there between teachers' and residents' expectations and assessments of the training year?

2. What differences are there between teachers' and residents' descriptions of their ideal and actual joint communication and educational behaviors?

METHOD

This study attempted to analyze the entire population of teacher-resident pairs in the Oxford Health Authority Region.

Survey Distribution

A survey was mailed out to each teacher and resident in the Oxford Regional Health Authority. Confidentiality was assured in the cover letter to elicit the most honest answers possible. In six of the eight health districts, the survey was discussed with the residents before the mailing. Two follow-up letters were sent to nonresponders. The course organizers also encouraged doctors in their districts to return the surveys.

Subjects

The survey was sent to 72 teacher-resident pairs; 50 pairs returned the questionnaire. Four teachers returned the questionnaire without their residents doing so, and two residents returned their questionnaires without their teachers doing so. Of the eight districts, only one was underrepresented.

The Questionnaire

The various parts of the questionnaire were developed by talking with course organizers, teachers, and residents at district postgraduate centers. Patterns that emerged from the open-ended questions used in the residential courses were also incorporated into the questionnaire.

Section I lists all the educational activities suggested by teachers and residents. In I A, both groups were asked to evaluate the 14 educational activities. In I B, they were asked to indicate how they thought the training partner had evaluated the 14 activities.

Section II lists 20 educational objectives modified from a regional document on priority objectives in general practice training. The 20 objectives were grouped into five general objectives: medical skills, patient-relationship skills, communication skills, practice management skills, and self-directed learning skills. These objectives were familiar to most of the teachers and many of the residents because the region spent over a year deciding their priority objectives in GP training. Again both groups were asked to indicate their own ratings and to predict their partners' ratings.

Section III examines aspects of the teacher-resident relationship. In III A, both groups were asked to indicate how often they and their partners enacted 14 behaviors, which primarily concerned the amount of initiative and control exhibited in the tutorials.

In Section IV, teachers and residents were asked to describe their own and each other's communication styles on Norton's (1978) communicator style measure. In a study involving 68 general practitioners, Pendleton and Arntson (1985) found the nine indices to be normally distributed—unusual for most self-report instruments. By asking them to describe both their own and each other's styles, we could compute a perceived style similarity score for teacher and resident.

In the last section of the survey, we asked both groups what they would change in order to improve the relationship and what their partner should change.

RESULTS

While no statistical tests were run on the data, patterns of differences will be noted. We will focus on the results in Section II, the educational objectives, and Section III, the teacher-resident relationship.

TABLE 10.4   Teachers' and Residents' Perceptions of the Importance
              of Different Educational Objectives (Average Ratings on
              a Scale of 0 to 10)

Objectives	How Important to Accomplish		Actual Accomplishment	
	Teachers	Residents	Teachers	Residents
Medical Skills	9.0	9.2	7.3	6.8
Patient Relationship Skills	8.4	8.6	6.5	6.3
Communication Skills	9.0	9.1	7.1	7.2
Practice Management Skills	8.2	8.2	6.1	5.6
Self-Directed Learning Skills	8.5	8.0	6.9	6.2

1. What differences are there between the teachers' and residents' expectations and assessments of the educational and relational dimensions of the training year?

Table 10.4 shows teachers' and residents' mean ratings (on a scale
of zero to ten) of the items relevant to the educational objectives. At
least three patterns are noticeable. First, for three of the five skills the
teachers rated their actual accomplishment higher than did the residents. There may be a slight perceptual difference here in how well the
training is going. Second, teachers rated both the importance of self-directed learning skills and their accomplishment higher than the residents did. The third pattern concerns the relative importance and actual
accomplishment of the five skills. The medical skills are again rated

highest and, surprisingly, the practice management skills rated lowest, especially in actual accomplishment.

2. **What differences are there between the teachers' and residents' descriptions of their ideal and actual joint communication and educational behaviors?**

Table 10.5 shows the teachers' and residents' different estimates for themselves and each other in improving tutorial behaviors. In the case of first behavior, determining the content of the tutorials, the residents think the teachers are doing too much of it. The teachers think they could do more and that the residents could improve twice as much as the residents think they could. Another behavior, interrupts the other, has similar differences. The teachers think both they and the residents could do more interrupting. The residents think that both tutorial participants are doing too much interrupting. For four other behaviors—sharing limits of personal knowledge, drawing out principles of general practice, asking open-ended questions, and challenging the other's ideas—the teachers think the residents could improve at least twice as much as the residents think they could improve. The residents have more passive expectations for their tutorial behaviors than the teachers have for the residents' behaviors.

DISCUSSION

Both teachers and residents highly rank learning about the doctor-patient relationship and in particular, communication skills. The program was actually accomplishing that objective with a score of seven out of ten.

The relationship between the clinical teacher and the resident is taken as central to the learning and teaching that occur during the year-long residency program. The relationship begins with two individuals, each with their own expectations of the educational opportunity and perceptions of their appropriate roles.

We present some suggestions for enhancing the growth of the resident by encouraging a joint approach to a problem-solving relationship rather than a dependent relationship.

TABLE 10.5   Teachers' and Residents' Perceptions of Ideal and Actual Behaviors

	Teachers' perceptions (mean differences between teachers' ideal expectations and the actual behaviors		Residents' perceptions (mean differences between residents' ideal expectations and the actual behaviors	
	Self	Resident	Teacher	Self
Determines content of tutorials	0.5	1.4	−0.7	0.7
Shares limits of personal knowledge	0.9	1.1	0.4	0.4
Draws out principles for general practice	0.9	1.8	0.9	0.9
Asks open-ended questions	0.8	1.2	0.6	0.0
Refers to relevant research	1.8	2.0	1.7	1.8
Disagrees with the other	1.2	1.6	1.1	1.5
Makes practical suggestions	0.8	1.0	0.5	1.1
Interrupts the other	0.6	0.9	−0.4	−0.3
Talks about how tutorial is going	1.8	2.2	1.3	1.5
Challenges other's ideas	1.1	2.2	0.8	0.8
Suggests follow-up plans	1.2	1.9	1.8	1.9
Prepares when necessary	1.6	1.4	0.7	1.5
Summarizes what has been said	1.4	1.9	1.3	2.2
Follows through with appropriate action	1.6	1.8	1.4	2.0

It can be argued that a joint approach better prepares young physicians for their professional role in general, and, in particular, for their future doctor-patient relationships.

11

Curriculum Structuring to Enhance Communication Skill Development

Suzanne M. Kurtz

INTRODUCTION

Most United States medical schools currently require formal communication training (Kahn et al., 1979), many in Canada are developing such courses, and several institutions in Britain, Australia, and elsewhere are headed in the same direction. However, despite this substantial progress regarding communication training in medicine, researchers and educators continue to identify several unresolved issues.

1. What communication skills and other content should we include?

2. How do we expand present programs with their emphasis on information gathering so as to include information giving (Boreham and Gibson, 1978; Carroll and Monroe, 1978; Kurtz, 1983; Maguire et al., 1986; Tuckett et al., 1985)?

3. How do we ensure that students not only master skills but also retain and use them in practice (Engler et al., 1981; Helfer, 1970; Maguire et al., 1986)?

4. How do we integrate communication with other clinical skills and the rest of the medical school program (Flaherty, 1985; Poole and Sanson-Fisher, 1979)?

5. Where can we find adequate time for communication training in an already overburdened medical school curriculum (AAMC Project, 1983)?

6. How can communication skills be assessed more effectively and efficiently (Carroll and Monroe, 1980; Flaherty, 1985)?

7. How can the status of communication be secured as a bona fide clinical skill, important not only to primary care or psychiatry where most courses are offered, but also to the other specialties (Flaherty, 1985; Kahn et al., 1979)?

The problems implicit in these questions stem partly from our general tendency to structure communication training into a single, self-contained course offered entirely in the preclinical or early clinical years and concluded with one evaluation of what students have learned about communication in isolation from other clinical skills. The development of independent communication courses and evaluations has been an appropriate beginning point, and I am definitely not suggesting that we do away with self-contained components. But in order to resolve the persistent questions above, we must now turn our efforts toward structuring communication *curriculum*, which extends beyond the initial, self-contained course and examination and actively integrates communication with other parts of the medical school program.

This chapter describes one approach for developing such a communication curriculum. From this description, several strategies emerge for structuring curriculum to address the issues raised in the above questions. The approach is based on a communication curriculum that has evolved over the past 12 years in the Faculty of Medicine at the University of Calgary, Canada.

Helical Model

The helix, pictured as a bedspring wider at the top than at the bottom, is the model on which Calgary bases its curriculum. The model explains how communication skills are learned, developed and, by implication, taught (Bruner, 1966; Dance, 1967). Building on skills already attained, learning follows a helical (as opposed to linear) progression in which repetition and review are essential for maximum development of skills. The well-planned curriculum continuously builds on existing skills, moves toward their application in medical practice, adds new skills, and continuously reviews and refines, each time coming around the spiral of learning at a higher level. The helical model partially explains why students forget or fail to apply mastered communication skills beyond the training period: too few opportunities for reiteration, refinement, and integration, coupled with failure to offer communication training at intervals throughout medical training.

Underlying Assumptions

Five assumptions underlie Calgary's communication curriculum and form a working definition of effective physician-patient communication. Such basic assumptions are essential to curriculum design because they inform subsequent decisions about what to teach, how to teach it, and even how to assess it. The first assumption follows logically from the helical model.

1. *Communication is a series of learned skills.* Communication is learned behavior, so it can be improved through experience, personal effort, and formal training. However, because communication is not a single skill, the goal of "learning to communicate better" is too global to be useful. The curriculum provides a way to break apart, organize, and recall the numerous components of effective communication.

2. *Effective communication is an interaction rather than a direct transmission process* (Dance and Larson, 1972). If communication is viewed as a direct transmission process, the senders of messages can assume that their responsibilities as communicators are fulfilled once they have formulated and sent the message. But if communication is viewed as an interactive process, the interaction is complete only if the sender receives feedback about how the message is interpreted, whether it is understood, or what impact it has on the receiver. Emphasis moves to the interdependence of sender and receiver; the contributions and initiatives of both parties become equally important. Unfortunately, patients and physicians often rely on the direct transmission approach and reap misunderstanding (Tuckett et al., 1985).

3. *Effective communication reduces uncertainty.* Patients and physicians are obviously concerned about reducing uncertainty about health problems, but reducing other kinds of uncertainty is often just as important. For example, patients or physicians may be uncertain about what to expect during a given interview or from a particular member of a health care team,

about the attitudes and values the other person holds, or about the appropriateness of trusting a particular individual. One way to gauge effectiveness in any interaction is to examine how successfully participants identify and reduce uncertainties.

4. *Effective communication is dynamic.* What is appropriate for one situation is inappropriate for another. What the patient understood so clearly yesterday seems beyond comprehension today. The blunders and inadequacies of yesterday's consultation give way to some excellent communication today. We cannot rely on cookbook recipes for good communication, nor can we assume that once we reach a peak, we will stay there indefinitely.

5. *Effective communication requires planning and goal setting.* The best way to determine effectiveness is to think in terms of outcomes and consequences. If I want to express anger and the outcome I seek is to vent my emotion, I proceed in one way. If I want to clear up the misunderstanding that caused my anger, I must proceed in a different way to be effective.

Table 11.1 summarizes the outcomes clinicians seek in terms of communication goals, tasks, kinds of interaction, and skills pertinent to the health care setting. The table provides an easily remembered framework around which we organize curriculum content and assessment procedures.

OVERVIEW OF CALGARY'S COMMUNICATION CURRICULUM

Calgary's communication curriculum is contained in a three-year, systems-based medical school program that exposes students to patients in the first year. We adapt and expand the curriculum continuously according to a growing body of literature (Carroll and Monroe, 1978, 1980; Cassata, 1978; Flaherty, 1985; Kahn et al., 1979; Riccardi and Kurtz, 1983; Tuckett et al., 1985); feedback from preceptors, medical educators, health communication specialists, patients, and students; and personal experience with communication training in medicine, nursing, law, and education.

The communication curriculum includes a four-phase Communication Unit, three certifying evaluations, and overlays of communication

TABLE 11.1   **(Riccardi and Kurtz, 1983) Considerations for Effective Clinical Communication With Patients**

1. BROAD GOALS
   Accuracy
   Efficiency
   Supportiveness (compassion)
2. TASKS
   Initiating the interaction
   Gathering information
   Building relationship
   Giving information/counsel
   Closing the interaction
3. TYPES OF INTERACTION
   Evaluation (history taking)
   Preliminary counseling (tentative conclusions, explanation of diagnostic procedures)
   Definitive counseling
     Informative counseling (providing factual data and explanations, how to do)
     Directive counseling (giving advice, what to do)
     Advocacy counseling (promoting option[s] to expand patient's freedom of choice)
     Supportive counseling (helping patient cope or put things in perspective)
4. SKILLS REQUIRED
   Conceptual skills
   Content skills (what is communicated)
   Process skills (how it is communicated)

content in other courses. In keeping with the helical model, we have organized the curriculum into several components spaced across the preclerkship years as follows (overlays are not included here).

1st Year: Phase I coursework. September to December, 24 hours.
        Phase II coursework. April/May, 8 hours.
        Coordinated Clinical Skills Evaluation 1. May, 90 minutes.

2nd Year: Coordinated Clinical Skills Evaluation 2. November, 99 minutes.
        Phase III coursework. March, 4 hours.
        Coordinated Clinical Skills Evaluation 3. March, 85 minutes.
        Integrative Course (Phase IV). March/April, 1 month.

This design retains the benefits of focused, self-contained communication coursework (Phases I, II, and III). However, spacing coursework components over two years and interspersing them with multiple evaluations ensure reiteration and reinforcement of developing communication skills and content. Moreover, our helical approach permits systematic integration of students' communication skills with their expanding medical knowledge, physical examination skills, and medical problem-solving abilities (Integrative Course and the three evaluations). Table 11.2 summarizes the format and primary focus for the four coursework components of the Communication Unit. For more detailed explanation of course content and methods, see Riccardi and Kurtz (1983).

The curriculum deals with various aspects of consultation between one physician and one patient (we discuss third-party interviews and team care only incidentally). With the exception of four large-group lecture/demonstrations, the format for the Unit is assigned small groups of six students with one MD preceptor. While the group observes, individual students practice interviewing with real patients who are invited from the preceptors' practices and present their own histories, or with simulated patients who are trained to portray specific, actual case histories. After each interview the group gives feedback, discussing issues and difficulties as they arise.

In Phases I and II preceptors tend to be family physicians or psychiatrists; in the Integrative Course they come from internal medicine and other specialties. This fortuitous circumstance gives communication training wide recognition and acceptance within the Faculty. The Unit codirectors—a communication specialist (the author) and a family practice physician—lead the large group lectures and precept for each small group at least once.

Communication Unit Content

Phases I, II, and III are independent parts of a larger Clinical Skills Course, which also teaches physical examination and clinical correlations for each body system. Organized around the schema in Table 11.1, Phases I and II introduce students to the traditional medical history, including everything from presenting problem(s) to functional inquiry. In Phase I students do not attempt to take a complete history all at once. Instead, for the first two small group sessions, they focus on initiating the interview and eliciting information about presenting complaints and history of present illness from patients invited from their preceptors' practices. During the next two sessions the group continues practicing these skills, but includes past and family histories along with a focus on questioning techniques and building relationship. This add-on pro-

TABLE 11.2   Format and Focus of Communication Units

Phase I Format	Primary Focus
• Twelve 2-hour sessions	• Introduction and overview of clinical communication • Conducting a medical interview, especially initiating the interview, gathering information, building relationship (process skills)
• 1 lecture/demo and 11 small group sessions with videotape recording	• Contents of the traditional history
• Actual patients and student role play	• Peer and self assessment

Phase II Format	Primary Focus
• Four 2-hour sessions	• Review and refinement of Phase I process and content skills • Dealing with psychosocial issues • Handling "difficult situations"
• Small groups with videotape recording	• Giving preliminary information to patients • Terminating the interview • Generating and refining hypotheses
• Professional actor patients	• Writing medical records

Phase III Format	Primary Focus
• Two 2-hour sessions	• Review and refinement of Phases I & II process and content skills • Giving information to patients— Preliminary counseling Definitive counseling (i.e., Directive, Advocacy, Informative, and Supportive Counseling)
• Lecture, discussion, and videotape demonstration	• Using supportive counseling in specific "difficult situations" • Preparatory to integrative course

Communication Component of Integrative Course Format	Primary Focus
• Part of Integrative Course (Phase IV) 4 weeks	• Review and refinement of Phases I-III, process and content skills— application to medical problem-solving and decision making
• 1 lecture, all other sessions small groups with videotape recording	• Giving information to patients (definitive counseling) • Integrating communication skills, physical examination, medical problem solving, and knowledge gained in systems courses.
• "Matched" simulated patients	

From Riccardi V. M. and Kurtz S. M. (1983) Communication and Counseling in Health Care. Courtesy of Charles C. Thomas, Publisher, Springfield, Illinois.

cess is followed until all the history-taking and associated skills are introduced.

Phase II continues the review and refinement but adds a "difficult" situation, such as an angry patient or one who is in pain or has a nonspecific complaint. The professional actors who simulate these patients are often excellent at giving feedback and immediately replaying parts of the interview, thus allowing students to try alternative approaches or improve weak spots. Through lecture, videotape demonstrations, and discussion, Phase III introduces skills and content relevant to giving information and counsel to patients. Students then try giving information and counsel to simulated patients in Phase IV, which is part of the Integrative Course.

The Integrative Course consists of a four-week, problem-based, learning experience. It is designed to help students synthesize knowledge gained in their body systems courses, apply that knowledge in clinical settings, and integrate it with communication, physical examination, and medical problem-solving skills. Small groups with preceptors work through ten to twelve patient problems presented in one of three formats: source book, computer simulation, or simulated patient.

Communication skills are particularly emphasized in the third format, which gives students opportunity to carry out all aspects of clinical care, including history-taking and physical examination, explanation of diagnostic tests and procedures (actual physical findings, lab results, etc., are provided in print and on slides), making the diagnosis, considering treatment and management alternatives, and giving information and counsel to the patient. After each interaction with the patient, students receive feedback about communication process, content, and conceptual skills (Kurtz, 1983).

At this stage we seek only to *introduce* students to information giving, encouraging them to experiment with their skills in a simulated patient setting where mistakes have no dire consequences. Further development of information-giving skills can occur during clerkship (and we plan to move in this direction), but refinement of this area is probably more appropriate during residency and continuing education.

Communication Unit Methods

We use several kinds of simulated patients in the Unit's small group sessions: "real" patients who present their own problems and are brought in from preceptors' practices and hospital wards, small-group members who role-play their own past or present problems, professional actors who work from protocols of real cases, and "matched" patients (Barrows and Tamblyn, 1980) who are selected because they have experienced problems or symptoms similar to those of the cases they will portray. As participants of Phase IV, the matched patients receive substantial training so that they can respond appropriately, not only during history-taking parts of the interview but also when students do physical examination procedures, give information and counsel, and discuss treatment alternatives.

Students are videotaped during every interview. Small groups meet in a series of paired rooms, one of which is furnished with stationary microphone, fixed-lens camera, and examining room furniture, while the other contains video-recording equipment, chairs, and blackboard. A large one-way mirror is built into the wall separating the rooms so the small group can observe, tape, and even discuss the interview in progress without interrupting it. With six paired rooms, several groups meet simultaneously; this allows the same patient to be interviewed by several groups in one morning.

Generally, one student conducts an interview and receives immediate feedback. Group members write out feedback as they observe, with some members focusing on content and others on process skills. Although portions of the videotape may be replayed during the feedback session, students are encouraged to review their tapes outside of class and consult their written feedback sheets again at that time. Students first assess their own performance and then receive feedback from patient, peers, and preceptor.

Because feedback (aided by videotape replay) is such a significant part of the learning and evaluation process, we have developed three feedback forms that are used repeatedly throughout the course. The first focuses on content of the history-taking interview. It simply lists the parts of the traditional medical history (e.g., presenting problems, history of present illness, past history, etc.) and provides room for observers to write down details as they are elicited. The second lists communication process skills associated with history-taking interviews. These behaviors are organized under the headings identified in the schema in Table 11.1: Initiating the Interaction, Gathering Information, Building Relationship, Giving Information, and Closing the Interaction. The third guide pertains to giving information and counsel to patients and organizes appropriate communication behaviors under headings such as Strategies to Aid Accuracy and Recall, Negotiating Treatment Goals, Preparing Patient for Diagnostic Procedures, Determining Patient's Beliefs, and Ending the Session.

These forms, which we call Observation Guides, fulfill several purposes. They help ensure that feedback is consistently comprehensive, structured, and descriptive rather than evaluative (i.e., it describes student behavior in detail rather than commenting on whether it is good or bad). They provide students and preceptors with a concise summary of course content for easy reference and review—a vital function, given the number of small-group preceptors involved. Finally, with spaces added for checking each item as satisfactory or unsatisfactory, the first two guides become evaluation forms in the three certifying evaluations described below. (The third guide, which describes definitive counseling, is excluded from the certifying evaluations since the course only introduces it.)

Evaluations

Although students receive detailed descriptive feedback about each interview they perform, they are given ratings along with such feedback only in the three certifying evaluations that determine whether students have mastered the required content. We call these *Coordinated* Clinical Skills Examinations (CCSE 1, 2, and 3) because they evaluate both physical examination and communication skills and because they are designed to work together, in helical fashion, as integral parts of the clinical skills curriculum.

Table 11.3 provides a synopsis of the three examinations. (For a detailed explanation see Heaton and Kurtz, 1988.) In keeping with the helical model, each examination is deliberately scheduled to take place some weeks after the end of the course-work components it assesses. Furthermore, the examinations have two important objectives besides evaluation.

1. They require students to integrate communication with physical examination and medical problem solving skills while applying skills in the context of actual patient problems.

2. They double as effective individualized learning exercises that teach (and/or reinforce) even as they assess.

Students receive considerable descriptive feedback along with ratings of satisfactory, "see me," or unsatisfactory, on the various parts of each examination. Feedback sheets include detailed checklists on com-

TABLE 11.3   Focus and Format for Coordinated Clinical Skills Examinations

Coordinated Clinical Skills Examination 1 (CCSE1)

Focus: To put the parts learned in separate clinical skills units into a coherent whole, centered around a standardized patient problem. Simulated patient/examiner; cardiovascular or respiratory problem.

CCSE2

Focus: To use a multiple stations approach that incorporates aspects of CCSE1 integration but isolates more clinical skills to permit sampling of a broader spectrum of patient problems and physical examination techniques. Simulated patient/examiner; neurological or musculo-skeletal problem.

CCSE3

Focus: To demonstrate ability to apply clinical skills in the context of a non-standardized, real patient in an actual clinical setting. Multisystem problem.

munication and physical examination skills/content as well as space for written comments. Overall ratings of unsatisfactory require individual-ized remedial work and a retake of the examination, while "see me" means the student has done well on most of the examination but must see the course codirectors to discuss and correct significant perfor-mance deficiencies.

Overlays

Overlaying communication content in other medical school courses—such as bioethics, gerontology, and the clinical correlation part of each body systems course—is another strategy that permits reinforcement, integration, and development of communication skills and concepts without requiring that time be found for another separate communica-

TABLE 11.4   Strategies for Designing Communication Curriculum

Organizational Strategies

> Helical model
>
> Identified assumptions
>
> Spaced components
>
> Consistent schema
>
> Consistent assessment instruments
>
> Small group format
>
> Evaluation and course overlays

Assessment Strategies

> Descriptive feedback
>
> Structured by observation guide
>
> Videotape review
>
> Repeated feedback
>
> Self and peer assessment
>
> Same instrument for informal and certifying evaluation

Miscellaneous Strategies

> Simulate clinical setting for learning and evaluation
>
> Apply the literature, make it accessible
>
> Integrate communication with other clinical skills and knowledge
>
> Involve faculty across specialties

tion component. The overlays can take many forms. For example, instructors try to use common language and make explicit reference to each other's course wherever possible in print materials, lectures, and small-group sessions. Gerontology provides practical experience in communicating with the elderly and encourages use of the same self/peer assessment forms that we use in the communication unit. Clinical correlations teaches specific history content relevant to each body system. Plans are underway for extending overlays into clerkship rotations and evaluations.

SUMMARY OF STRATEGIES

From this communication curriculum several strategies emerge for addressing the issues raised in the seven questions at the beginning of the paper. Table 11.4 summarizes these strategies.

The particular strategies in resolving each issue (numbered accordingly) are as follows.

1. In *selecting and organizing content*, the first strategy is to commit to paper underlying assumptions that help define effective physician-patient communication; the second is to develop a one-page schema (as in Table 11.1) on which the content can be organized. Using assumptions and schema as a conceptual framework, the growing body of literature on physician-patient communication begins to become more manageable and useful. From the literature and discussion with interested parties, add skills to flesh out the framework. Finally, structured on the schema and reflecting the literature, develop instruments like our observation guides (and like the checklist proposed by Kraan et al., in Chapter 12) to summarize the skills and provide a format for systematic, descriptive feedback. Such instruments are invaluable in providing continuity and consistency for both students and preceptors, especially where content is taught across time in a number of different courses and by many different teachers.

2. *Extending the curriculum to include information giving* necessitates a schema to determine how information-giving fits into the whole process and where students might best learn about it. Thinking in terms of a helical model, which encourages overlaying communication content on other curricular offerings, provides one means for finding time to teach information given appropriately late in the medical school program. A next step is to devise assessment or feedback instruments focused on this aspect of care that are based on underlying assumptions, the literature, and discussion with interested parties. Working with other faculty responsible for clerkship and residency programs is yet another idea.

3. A number of strategies emerge for *ensuring that students retain and use the skills* they master early in the program. Using the helical model, as the base for curriculum design is perhaps the most potent. It is useful to divide the communication block into segments to be offered at intervals spaced across medical training, rather than all at one time. Intentionally integrating communication with other clinical skills and with students' expanding knowledge also helps students retain and apply skills. Using the same schema and similar assessment instruments throughout the curriculum

helps students more readily conceptualize and remember the components of effective communication. Several other strategies include adding overlays of communication content to other courses and evaluations, using evaluations as learning exercises, teaching students effective self and peer assessment, and providing many opportunities to observe and give feedback based on the very instruments that will be used for certifying evaluations. Descriptive feedback is essential and videotape recording and review are recommended. Educating faculty across disciplines by inviting them to be preceptors for communication units or exposing them to overlays of communication content in other courses and evaluations is helpful, too, because faculty are then more likely to reinforce communication content.

4. These strategies also apply to *integrating communication with other clinical skills and factual knowledge*. In addition, it is useful to design evaluations and learning exercises as close as possible to actual clinical settings wherein students must integrate communication with other skills in order to solve patient problems.

5. The issue of *where to find time* in a crowded medical training program is best addressed by the overlay strategy. Devising more integrated clinical skills exams is also useful.

6. The exam format is in itself a useful strategy for *making assessment more effective and efficient*. Practical exams are so time intensive for faculty that they should double as learning exercises. In any case, providing instruments that give students detailed descriptive feedback, as opposed to more general evaluation ratings, is essential.

7. Finally, all the strategies summarized above contribute toward *securing the status of communication training* and gaining wider recognition for it across medical disciplines and specialties.

The way we structure curriculum can significantly enhance development of communication skill. By more effectively designing communication curriculum, as opposed to isolated courses, we can improve the quality of communication education in medicine.

12

Evaluating Undergraduate Training— A Checklist for Medical Interviewing Skills

Herro Kraan
Alfons Crijnen
Jaap Zuidweg
Cees van der Vleuten
Tjaard Imbos

INTRODUCTION

Medical consultations in primary health care are characterized by un-differentiated clinical problems with a mixture of somatic and psycho-social complaints, often strongly interwoven with the life circum-stances of the patient. The presented problems range from acute, severe disorders and chronic disabilities to nonserious and self-limiting dis-ease or nonmedical problems of life.

In the initial interview the patient presents what he believes to be a new problem. Being relatively uniform in content, such interviews are generally chosen for educational purposes. Moreover, in our setting of Dutch primary care, such interviews comprise about 60% of the consultations.

How can interviewing skill be reliably measured? Our research group has developed and tested an observation instrument for evaluat-ing medical interviewing skills. A common definition of medical inter-viewing skills in Dutch medical schools covers the physicians' skills needed to exchange information (cognitive as well as emotional) with the patient to establish diagnosis and initiate treatment. This rather restrictive definition excludes clinical reasoning and medical problem solving (Schouten et al., 1982).

The research group had objectives in constructing an evaluation instrument. First, the checklist had to be acceptable for use in evaluating training in medical interviewing given to students, residents, and primary care practitioners.

Second, the checklist had to be suitable for use in more fundamental research about the relationship between physicians' interviewing skills and outcome, measured by patient satisfaction, anxiety reduction, detection of minor psychiatric syndromes, comprehension, and insight.

From these objectives, several criteria were developed that determined the instrument's content and format.

1. It must focus on skill measurement during initial interviews in primary health care.

2. It must focus on "trainable" interviewing skills. This restriction has two consequences. First, the content will be dominated by verbal interviewing behaviors. Second, the focus is mainly on process aspects of the interview, as shaped by the physician. However, the patient's contribution during the interview can also be evaluated by the checklist.

3. It must focus on instrumental utility. Groot (1962) maintained that instrumental utility is high when a balance is achieved between practicality and validity. Practicality depends on the ease of scoring, length of observer training, test length, and comprehensiveness of the observer's manual. The instrumental utility decreases when the content validity is heightened by increasing the scope of the content.

After reviewing the existing instruments measuring behavioral aspects of medical interviewing, we established our units of analysis. The criterion, "measuring skills in initial interviews in primary health care," calls for assessment of specific medical content, whereas the criterion "trainable interviewing skills," demands concrete description of interviewing skills. The third criterion of practicality and validity encourages the choice of broad units of analysis. This results in three item formats in the checklist.

1. Items describing interviewing skills as single-act behaviors.
   Example: "Uses closed questions properly."

2. Items combining simple interviewing behavior with aspects of medical content.
   Example: "Asks for the location of the complaint."

3. Items describing more complex interviewing skills.
   Example: "When necessary, makes proper confrontations."

DESCRIPTION OF CHECKLIST

From criteria, we constructed a 68-item checklist, which is divided into six segments or subscales (see Table 12.1). The first three subscales are exploration of the reasons for encounter, history-taking, and presenting solutions. They contain interviewing skills the physician may display during the three typical phases of the initial interview (Kraan and Crijnen, 1987). This type of initial interview follows the primary care consultation model described by several authors (Katon and Kleinman, 1980; Pendleton et al., 1984). These models incorporate the biopsychosocial model (Engel, 1977) and are characterized by patient-centeredness, attention to illness behavior, and negotiation between physician and patient about major conflicting issues.

The fourth to sixth subscales—structuring the interview, interpersonal skills, and communicative skills—represent the physicians' process skills to perform an initial interview.

Exploration of the Reasons for Encounter

This phase of the interview collects information about the patient's frame of reference (Freidson, 1970). The physician gives the patient the opportunity to express his complaints and symptoms in his own words and to expand on the causes and consequences of the complaints and the events that triggered the visit to the physician. This condition has been shown to be important to patient satisfaction (Stiles et al., 1979b). Further questions may be asked about attempted solutions.

The appropriate skills during this phase of the interview are open questions, probes within the patient's frame of reference, active listening, emotional reflections, stimulating summarizations. These process skills are assessed in the subscale "Exploration of the Reason for Encounter" (see Table 12.1).

The skill is scored on a two-point scale (present or absent).

TABLE 12.1   The Maastricht History-Taking and Advice Checklist

I. EXPLORATION OF THE REASON FOR ENCOUNTER
   * 1. Asks for the reason for encounter.
   * 2. Explores the emotional impact of the complaint/problem.
   * 3. Asks the patient to clarify why he is presenting this problem at this particular moment.
   * 4. Asks the patient to give his opinion on the causes of the problem.
     5. Asks how the complaint or problem is discussed within the family or primary group.
   * 6. Asks the patient to state what help (s)he desires.
   * 7. Asks how the patient has tried to solve the problem by him/herself.
   * 8. Explores the influence of the complaint on daily life.

II. HISTORY-TAKING
   * 9. Asks the patient to describe the complaint.
   *10. Explores the intensity of the complaint.
   *11. Asks about the location of the complaint.
   *12. Asks about shifts/radiations of the complaint.
    13. Asks about the course of the complaint during the day.
    14. Asks about the history of the complaint.
    15. Asks which factors or situations triggered the complaint.
    16. Asks which factors or situations increase the complaint.
    17. Asks which factors/situations maintain the complaint.
   *18. Asks which factors/situations decrease and/or eliminate the complaint.
    19. Asks which life circumstances or problems accompany the complaint.
    20. Explores the gains of the complaint.
   *21. Explores both somatic and psychological determinants of the complaint.
    22. Explores the quality of the relationships within the family/primary group.
    23. Explores current professional functioning.
   *24. Explores functioning during leisure time.
    25. Explores risk and vulnerability factors in the patient's biography.
   *26. Asks about illnesses and mental health problems in the past.
   *27. Asks about professional treatment and its effects in the past.
    28. Asks about other current professional consultations.
   *29. Asks about (ab)use of medication and substances.
    30. Asks about hereditary or family aspects of the complaint.
    31. Reviews the system pertaining to the main complaint.

III. PRESENTING SOLUTIONS
   *32. Explains diagnosis or problem-definition understandably.
   *33. Explains causes of the complaint.
   *34. Gives information on prognosis of the complaint.
   *35. Explores the patient's expectations concerning solutions.
   *36. Proposes solutions.

(continued)

TABLE 12.1 Continued

*37. Explains how the solution is appropriate to the problem.

*38. Discusses the pros and cons of the proposed solutions.

39. Explores whether the patient has a different point of view on problem-definition and/or proposed solutions and discusses any different opinion.

*40. Asks whether the patient is intending to comply.

*41. Explains in concrete terms how the advice given should be carried out.

*42. Checks whether the patient has understood the advice given.

*43. Makes appointments for follow-up.

IV. STRUCTURING THE INTERVIEW

*44. Introduces him/herself at the beginning of the interview and clarifies his functional relationship with the patient.

*45. Offers an agenda for the consultation.

*46. Concludes the exploration of the reason for encounter with a summary.

*47. Concludes the history-taking" with an ordering of the main results.

*48. Explores the reason for encounter before history-taking.

*49. Completes the exploration of the reason for encounter and the history-taking sufficiently before presenting solutions.

50. Begins presenting solutions with an explanation of the problem-definition.

51. Asks at the end of the interview if the main problems have been discussed satisfactorily.

V. INTERPERSONAL SKILLS

*52. Facilitates the communication.

*53. Reflects emotions properly.

54. Reacts properly to emotions which are directed towards him/herself as a physician.

*55. Asks the patient about his or her feelings during the interview.

*56. Makes, when necessary, meta-communicative comments.

*57. Performs the history-taking and the review of systems properly.

*58. Puts the patient at ease when necessary.

*59. Sets the proper pace during the interview.

*60. Physicians's non-verbal behavior agrees with his/her verbal behavior.

61. Makes proper eye-contact with the patient.

VI. COMMUNICATIVE SKILLS

62. Uses closed-ended questions properly.

*63. Concretizes at the proper moment.

*64. Makes proper summaries.

*65. Provides information in small amounts.

*66. Checks whether the patient has understood the information.

*67. When necessary, makes proper confrontations.

*68. Uses comprehensible language.

---

*The 49 starred items meet the criterion of homogeneity in their respective subscale.

History-Taking

During this phase the patient is questioned from a medical frame of reference. Questions are about the character of the complaints, location, course and intensity, past illnesses and treatments, medication, etc. Further items pertain to the search for factors that trigger, aggravate, maintain, and alleviate the complaints, and form part of the physician's clinical reasoning process (Elstein et al., 1978).

This subscale also contains items about psychosocial issues: interpersonal relations, family life, professional and leisure time functioning, important life events, vulnerability, and risk factors.

The appropriate skill during this phase is typically the open-to-closed-cone style of questioning (Goldberg et al., 1980). Some important cue is raised during the interview, leading the physician to more open-ended probing, then directive questions, ending with closed questions to acquire accurate factual information.

This subscale contains 23 items, scored on a two-point scale (present or absent).

Presenting Solutions

This phase follows both previous phases and the physical examination if one is performed. The physician informs the patient about his condition, its causes, and the prognosis. He then explores the patients' feelings evoked by this information. Physician and patient may then negotiate about the problem definition. Next, the physician makes a proposal for further follow-up, which may also be negotiated. Finally, the physician gives concrete advice based on the outcome of the negotiation. This negotiation for consensus has been shown to affect outcome measures like satisfaction, compliance, and therapeutic outcome (Stimson and Webb, 1975; Eisenthal et al., 1983). The physician concludes with appointments for follow-up.

The scoring is on a two-point scale (present or absent).

Structuring the Interview

This eight-item subscale measures the skills by which the physician opens and closes the interview and links the previously mentioned three phases, for example, "Begins the 'presenting solutions' phase by providing information about the problem or diagnosis."

The scoring is on a two-point scale (present or absent).

Interpersonal Skills

According to Hess (1969), basic interviewing skills can be divided into interpersonal and communicative skills.

Interpersonal skills refer to interviewing behavior that establishes patient rapport, trust, and acceptance, which are found to be important for patient compliance and satisfaction (Hulka et al., 1976; Korsch et al., 1968). These effects are attributed to several interviewing skills: showing empathy, warmth and concern, active listening, facilitative behavior, instillation of positive expectations, and self-disclosure.

The ten items of this subscale are scored on a three-point scale (yes, indifferent, no), allowing a qualitative rating (according to the criteria of the observers manual, Kraan and Crijnen, 1987).

Communicative Skills

Communicative skills promote the flow of information between physician and patient. These skills relate to appropriate techniques of questioning, providing information and giving advice (Ley, 1983), for example, "Explores patient's feelings during interview."

As with the interpersonal skills the seven items of this subscale are scored on a three-point scale (yes, indifferent, no), allowing a qualitative rating (according to the criteria of the observers manual, Kraan and Crijnen, 1987).

The Patient's Contribution to the Interview

In the first two subscales, the physician collects information from the patient. Two subscales called "obtained information" have been constructed, reflecting the same content aspects as the physicians' subscales. For example, the physician asks how the patient attempted to solve the problem. In the "obtained information" subscale this becomes "Patient expresses his attempted solutions." These subscales can be used in evaluating the quantity and quality of the information obtained, according to the outcome.

Use of the Checklist

This version of the checklist has been used after preliminary testing during the last two years in medical education and research.

Reasonable reliability is attained only after substantial training of observers.

The initial training consists of reading the manual, which contains an introduction to the checklist, definitions of interviewing skills, and criteria for scoring each individual item. Two training sessions, each of two- to three-hours duration, are devoted to step-by-step scoring of test videotapes. The observers' training group discusses the score on each item, especially differences from appropriate scores, in order to learn the criteria for scoring.

Refresher training sessions of one- to two-hours duration are necessary when observers have not scored the checklist for several months.

In education the checklist is used as a guideline or taxonomy of interviewing skills for staff and students, to provide individual feedback during training sessions.

When the checklist is used as a test, for instance in summative evaluation, there should be some preamble.

Judging the quality of the physician's interviewing skills has to encompass both the physician's interviewing behavior and the patient's contribution to interview. To accomplish this, both process and outcome have to be measured.

RELIABILITY AND SCALABILITY

Rigorous reliability testing has been conducted on the items in the checklist under test conditions with moderately trained observers. The test consisted of 20 videotaped interviews of family physicians with five simulated patients. Six observers scored the 100 videotapes. The percentage agreement between two observers was acceptable for all items, ranging from 0.70 to 0.90.

In situations where the process of measurement is heavily dependent on human observers, major problems with regard to the standardization of measurement are likely to occur. Because of this we decided to study inter-observer variation in greater depth. In the following paragraphs, we report on the inter-observer reliability of the individual items determined by means of generalizability studies (Cohen, 1960; Cronbach et al., 1972; Guilford et al., 1981; Shrout et al., 1979).

Observers are usually regarded as potential sources of error in the measurement of observational data. Psychometricians have therefore developed a variety of indices that all purport to reflect inter-observer agreement and reliability (Mitchell, 1979; Tinsley et al., 1975).

Three types of generalizability coefficients were calculated using the formulae described by Thorndike (1982).

Items in the scale "exploring reasons for encounter" display moderate generalizability coefficients (.15-.60). Appending a second observer significantly diminishes unreliability due to observer influences (.49-.80).

Items in the scale "history-taking" show moderate to high levels of inter-observer reliability (.18-.89). Appending a second observer has a considerable impact on the reliability of items with moderate generalizability coefficients (.31-.98).

Items in the scale "presenting solutions" show low to moderate levels of inter-observer reliability (.05-.54). Appending a second observer considerably enhances reliability (.10-.60).

Items in the scale "structuring the interview" show low to moderate levels of inter-observer reliability (.10-.60). Adding a second observer enhances reliability, although still only moderate levels of reliability are achieved (.18-.77).

Items in the scale "interpersonal skills" show low generalizability coefficients (.00-.33). Adding a second observer almost doubles the size of the coefficients, although still only low to moderate levels are achieved (.00-.50).

The scale "communicative skills" displays low levels of inter-observer reliability with the exception of the item on the quality of summaries (.00-.29). Increasing the number of observers has very little impact on reliability (.00-.44).

We have analyzed and discussed here the inter-observer reliability for each of the checklist items separately. High levels of reliability are seen when items are worded in behavioral terms. Low reliability is reported in items that require interpretation by the observers. Similar results were found when the five scale scores were tested for reliability. The central issue during the process of scale construction is to bring together a set of items, all of which measure to a satisfactory degree the trait of interest and which collectively reflect different levels of possession of this trait.

Scale construction is guided scientifically by scaling models that formalize the relation between a subject's responses on items and indices representing a subject's ability in the intended dimension. In the literature, two scaling models are known that are based on either the latent trait models or the classical test theory. In our work, we rely heavily on the Rasch-model, a one-parameter logistic model, which is the most demanding but also the most attractive latent trait model.

To provide data for Rasch analyses, 100 interviews between physicians/medical students and simulated patients who presented complaints accompanying a myocardial infarction were observed and scored on the checklist by experienced observers. Since Rasch analyses require dichotomized data variables in the scales, basic interviewing skills were dichotomized according to predetermined criteria.

The scale "exploring reasons for encounter" fits in the Rasch-model after elimination of one item. The eliminated item is, unfortunately, very important, as it addresses the issue of a patient's interpersonal relations and social support system.

The scale "history-taking" fits in the Rasch-model, and the items use a broad range of item difficulties. The scale thus displays adequate measurement properties. To increase the fit of the scale in the Rasch-model, the number of items was reduced significantly from 23 to 11.

The scale "presenting solutions" fits in the model after exclusion of one item. The items display a wide range of item difficulties. The scale thus has attractive measurement properties.

The scale "structuring the interview" corresponds well to the Rasch model, although two items had to be eliminated.

The scale "interpersonal skills" fits well in the Rasch-model and the items appear to display a broad range of item difficulties, which enhances their measurement properties. During the process of scale construction, two items were excluded pertaining to the physician's ability to handle negative emotions directed at himself and to the quality of eye contact.

The scale "communication skills" fits only marginally in the Rasch model, and it is interesting to note that the item referring to the quality of closed-ended questions, which is generally regarded as essential, is eliminated from this scale.

In summary, the reliability of items and the six subscales is adequate with the exception of the subscale regarding communicative skills, which involves judgments about physicians' behavior. Furthermore, a shorter checklist of 49 items has been developed for research situations in which the investigator needs homogeneous subscales for scoring and analysis (see the 49 starred items in Table 12.1).

VALIDITY STUDIES

The convergent and divergent validity of the checklist has been studied by comparing scores on each subscale with scores on medical knowledge tests, global expert ratings of interpersonal skills, tests of medical problem solving, and self-ratings of attitudes towards patient care. These studies have been performed with recently graduated students and residents in general practice interviewing simulated patients. The results are published in more detail elsewhere (Kraan and Crijnen, 1987).

In the multitrait-multimethod matrix, several dimensions in medical interviewing skills are measured with several methods. The resulting correlation matrix is scrutinized by means of four criteria that were developed by Campbell and Fiske.

For the History-taking and Advice Checklist, the convergent validity of "history-taking," "presenting solutions," "structuring the interview," and "interpersonal skills" is clearly supported by the strength of the correlations, whereas the "exploration of reasons for encounter" and "communication skills" fail to provide evidence of convergent validity.

Divergent validity of dimensions in medical interviewing skills is established for "history-taking," "presenting solutions," "structuring the interview," and "interpersonal skills." Again, difficulties arose in distinguishing dimensions referring to the "exploration of reasons for encounter" and "communication skills." Furthermore, the checklist appears to demonstrate better divergent validity than the self-rating scale or global rating scales.

SUMMARY

The checklist is an important addition to the literature on evaluating communication skills because it has been rigorously tested for content, reliability, scalability, and validity.

PART IV

Research Issues

We have brought together some unique perspectives of the research literature on doctor-patient communication. These appraisals reflect where we have been, analyze why we were there, and suggest the directions for the future. To arrive at these insights, we commissioned several very different kinds of reviews, designated to balance one another and, together, to provide a synthesis stronger than any one on its own.

At the broadest level of abstraction, Roter analyzes the empirically-based literature on doctor-patient communication over the past 25 years. Her meta-analysis contributes in four main ways. First, the literature is characterized in terms of study design, sample composition and size, setting, instrumentation, and analytic strategy. Second, while over 200 different independent variables descriptive of communication were reported in this body of literature, most of them can be placed in one of six conceptual groupings, which formed the basis of the meta-analysis. The analysis provides more statistical power to identify true effects than is possible in most individual studies. Finally, Roter tentatively suggests a hypothesis of reciprocity between the doctor-patient interaction and subsequent patient behavior that explains the results of the meta-analysis and provides a basis for future inquiry into the dynamics of interaction.

Inui and Carter challenge the investigator to consider research design more seriously. These authors take an interesting and quite unorthodox approach to their critical review of the literature. They polled the faculty of the International Conference on Doctor-Patient Communication, whom they considered knowledgable, active consumers of the literature, for the most important contributions to the scientific understanding of doctor-patient communication.

Of 37 articles thus identified, three kinds of studies emerge: developmental/descriptive studies, which included both conceptual papers and empirical investigations and comprised about half of the literature cited; sub-experimental etiological research, which examined both general process-outcome relationships and specific hypotheses and was present in about one-third of the papers; and intervention studies, which are relatively infrequent. Each of these types of studies brings with it particular strengths, but also a litany of methodological and utility challenges. The authors present a matrix to help investigators select a study type by outlining the relevant design issues and their potential usefulness to the clinical, educational, and research audience.

Stiles and Putnam present a five-way classification of coding strategies to measure doctor-patient communication, including 1) content categories, generally based on topics of interest; 2) speech acts or instrumental categories, such as questions, statements, or compliments; 3) nonverbal communication, such as tone of voice, gaze, body posture; 4) activity counts of behaviors, like chart reading and interruptions for telephone calls; and 5) affective ratings reflecting the intensity of a particular emotional tone, such as the amount of anger, anxiety, or friendliness.

While these categories improve our understanding of the relevant measurement issues, the complexity of human interaction renders any one approach inadequate. In fact, many investigators mix classification modes and conduct detailed multidimensional analyses of doctor-patient communication in an attempt to fill the obvious gaps of single methods. The authors conclude that despite increasing sophistication in the development of coding systems, no one system has yet provided a totally satisfactory approach to interaction analysis. They document the variety of challenges still to be met in this field.

Investigators of doctor-patient communication are intent on doing more than merely describing communication patterns; they want to evaluate the end result of doctor-patient communication. Beckman,

Kaplan, and Frankel note that the end result of most interest has changed over the past several decades; we now recognize that, in addition to patient satisfaction and compliance, an increase in the patient's assertiveness and a reduction in the patient's anxiety are relevant. Beckman et al. organize outcomes into four broad categories, according to the time of measurement: process outcomes, short-term outcomes, intermediate outcomes, and long-term outcomes. The choice of which outcome to assess in any given study implies a judgment about the usefulness of the doctor-patient encounter.

The ultimate question about the usefulness of doctor-patient communication is "does it change patients' health status?" This bottom-line question about health status has only recently begun to receive the attention it deserves.

In exploring the impact of physician-patient interaction on the functional and physiological outcomes of patients with chronic disease, Kaplan, Greenfield, and Ware present the results of three separate randomized, controlled trials of an intervention to increase patient participation in the doctor-patient interaction. The three trials include patients with ulcer disease attending a local VA Hospital, hypertensive patients at a local free clinic, and diabetic patients being seen at the endocrinology clinic of a university hospital. The populations and care settings could not be more diverse, yet there was a common response to the intervention. The authors found at follow-up that patients receiving the experimental intervention demonstrated lower blood glucose (among the diabetic group) and lower diastolic blood pressure (among the hypertensives). The mechanism for this achievement appears to be through effective information seeking and active participation in the medical interaction on the part of patients. Further, the experimental intervention explained the greatest proportion of the variance (28%) in functional limitations.

The authors suggest that doctors may influence outcomes not only directly through the technical medical care that they deliver, but also by shaping how patients behave and their ability to control their health.

A volume such as this is incomplete without a look backward to our research traditions; we therefore end our volume with the reflections of pioneer researcher Barbara Korsch. The studies Dr. Korsch and her colleagues conducted in the late 1960s have withstood the test of time and created paradigms for research still used today. Her studies are among the best cited works in the field and have inspired a whole generation of researchers.

In looking back and projecting forward, Korsch cautions her readers that while microanalytic procedures may be necessary in detailed interaction analysis—she was responsible for the widespread adoption of Bales' Interaction Analysis Scheme in medical settings—they need to be balanced by an appreciation of how the parts become a whole. Further, Dr. Korsch stresses that research must not only pass the test of scientific rigor, but also pass the test of relevance and usefulness to doctors and patients.

13

Which Facets of Communication Have Strong Effects on Outcome—A Meta-Analysis

Debra Roter

Summaries of the literature on doctor-patient communication (Inui and Carter, 1985; Pendleton, 1983; Wasserman and Inui, 1983) reveal the exploratory nature of this research. In fact, the results appear so disparate that a reviewer of this literature characterized his results as a "Rorschach test" in which overall interpretations are apt to reveal as much about the reader as about the results themselves (Inui and Carter, 1985).

My colleagues and I have analyzed the literature by quantitative summary of research findings, or meta-analysis (Glass et al., 1981; Green and Hall, 1984; Rosenthal, 1984). This chapter is an overview of our analysis and the theoretical framework derived from it for viewing doctor-patient communication (Hall et al., 1988; Roter et al., 1988).

There are several reasons for presenting data in this manner.

1. To evaluate the state of the art of measuring doctor-patient communication, focusing on design and sample characteristics.

2. To facilitate a synthesis of research findings across studies through meta grouping of individual variables.

3. To add to the body of research findings by aggregating and comparing study results to commonly defined outcome measures and by common sample and setting characteristics.

METHOD

Search Procedure and Sample Selection

We reviewed 80 articles published from 1962 to 1986. Criteria for inclusion were

1. to be published in an English-language journal or book;

2. to involve either student or graduate doctors;

3. to deal with nonpsychiatric encounters between doctor and patient;

4. to record interaction using neutral observers, audiotape, or videotape;

5. to present quantifiable descriptive or correlational results relating the doctor's behavior to outcome. In five studies the patients were trained simulators or role-playing subjects.

Procedures for finding suitable studies consisted of Medline (on-line database) searches, searching references in published papers, searching an unpublished bibliography of around 700 references provided by the Society for Research and Education in Primary Care Internal Medicine, hand-searching ten key journals, and scrutinizing our own reprint files.

These search procedures produced 80 articles describing 61 separate studies. A coding form listed issues of study design and sample characteristics for each study reviewed. For the 47 coded attributes, the median agreement rate between two coders who independently co-scored 15 of the studies was 87%.

Conceptual Groupings of Communication Variables

The first phase of our meta-analysis identified 247 different communication variables addressed in the studies. Variables were grouped together in six mutually exclusive categories: information-giving, information-seeking, social conversation, positive talk, negative talk, and partnership-building. The last category applied to physicians' communication only.

Physicians' communication was studied about twice as often as patients' communication, and many more physician than patient vari-

TABLE 13.1   Specific Variables Included in Patient Categories

I. Information-giving:	Presents symptoms, answers questions, responds to instructions, gives problem related experience, suggestion, opinion, orientation, information.
II. Information-seeking:	Asks for orientation, opinion, instruction, suggestion, asks questions (general), asks questions about medication, treatment, lifestyle, prevention, self-care.
III. Social conversation:	Social exchange, social remarks, introductory phrases, nonmedical social conversation, family/social conversation (not psychosocial exchanges).
IV. Positive talk:	Laughter, friendliness, shows solidarity, tension release, agrees, shows approval.
V. Negative talk:	Shows antagonism, disagrees, shows tension.

ables were identified (Hall et al., 1988). For instance, the category of physician information-giving includes 32 different variables while patient information-giving includes only eight variables. Examples of specific variables and their assignments within categories are shown in Tables 13.1 and 13.2 for patient and physician interaction, respectively.

RESULTS

Design and Sample Characteristics

The mean number of patient encounters was 174 (median = 81), with a range from 4 to 2500. Patient age groups were 63% adult, 22% pedi-

TABLE 13.2   Specific Variables Included in Physician Categories

Information giving	Gives information, opinion, suggestion, instruction, counsels or persuades, tries to motivate patient, give directions, instructs or teaches, % communication which is teaching, % communication which is educational, verbal explanation, gives information and orientation, problem related expressions, explains, discusses problem resolution, descriptive communication, edification, disclosure, advertisement, answers patient questions, volunteers explanation, volunteers information, gives medical information, discloses, gives information on or discusses: patient condition, nature of illness, cause, symptoms, diagnosis, current health treatment, drugs, non-medical treatment, medical treatment, self care, prevention, prognosis, seriousness of condition, physical activity, diet, health promotion, lifestyle, mentions exam findings, discusses physical exam.
Information seeking	Asks questions, asks for information, asks for instructions, takes medical history, asks about compliance (open and closed questions), non directive history taking, % of communication which is questions, time devoted to history-taking.
Social Conversation	Greetings, shows courtesy, introduces self, nonmedical statements, personal remarks, social remarks, casual conversation, discusses social/family matters.
Positive Talk	Agrees/shows understanding, shows approval, laughs, uses humor, tension release, shows solidarity, gives reassurance, offers support, encourages, shows empathy, calms patient, shows simple attention, % communication with positive affective content, socioemotional cluster (personal remarks, laughs, agrees, approves), doctor-patient friendly rapport.
Negative Talk	Disagrees/criticizes, confronts, shows antagonism or hostility, shows tension, negative affect, tension build up, anxiety/nervousness, speech errors, negative errors, negative interaction, bored.
Partnership building	Asks for patient's opinion, understanding, suggestions, questions, ideas, makes interpretation, reflects patients statements, facilitates patient response.

atric, 5% mixed (adult and pediatric), and 10% not stated. Ethnicity was reported in only 38% of the studies, representing a population that is 18% white, 5% black or Hispanic, and 15% mixed. Predominant social class was 15% low, 15% middle, 19% mixed. The remaining 51% of the studies did not report social class. The mean number of male patients was 64 (median = 40) and females patients was 84 (median = 58). However, patient sex was noted in only half the studies.

The mean number of physicians was 20 (median = 14), with a range from 1 to 143. Of the studies, 6% were on medical students, 28% on residents, interns, or fellows, 46% on graduate physicians, and 5% on a combination of all three. Physician experience was not stated in 15% of studies. Specialties studied were internal, family, or general medicine (57%), pediatrics (18%), subspecialties (16%), and 9% of the studies did not specify speciality. Physician sex was reported in 21% of the studies; the mean number of male physicians was 14 (median = 10) with a range of one to 43, and the mean number of female physicians was four (median = four) with a range of one to ten.

Settings for the studies were in clinics (57%), private practice (23%), and private and prepaid practice (10%). The remainder could not be ascertained. Chronic disease was the diagnosis in 22% of studies, undifferentiated chronic and acute diagnosis in 37%, well visits in 7%, acute visits in 3%, and diagnosis was not stated in 31%. The patient and physician were previously acquainted in 17% of studies, not known to one another in 30%, mixed in 11%, and prior acquaintance was not recorded in 42%.

A patient questionnaire was administered in two-thirds of the studies, usually following the visit, and most commonly immediately afterwards. These questionnaires measured satisfaction in 26 studies. Patient recall of medical information was measured in 18 studies and compliance in 10 studies. When compliance was assessed, drug measures were the most common, with assessment by objective means reported as often as self-report.

Methods of Interaction Analysis

Half the studies used audiotape as their primary method of observation; the remaining studies were equally likely to use videotape or impartial observers.

The choice of video or audiotape as the method of observation was closely associated with the kind of research undertaken. Research directly related to physician training favored the use of videotape for both evaluation and intervention. Audiotape was the frequent choice in more general research. Use of the same system of analysis in more than two studies was unusual: the 61 studies employed 28 different analysis schemes.

Most unique systems attempted to abstract and categorize the factual information physicians communicated during the encounter. These approaches were generally limited to the one coded category of information-giving and did not attempt to put information-giving within the broader context of physician and patient communication, although they generally related the communicated information to patient recall.

The most commonly used process analysis systems were those of Bales (1950), Roter (1977), and Stiles (1978-1979), but even these were used in only 5 to 7 studies each. One study included all three systems in an attempt to compare these approaches and draw some conclusions about their relative practical and predictive value (Inui et al., 1982), and another study attempted to validate one approach through its comparison with another system (Wolraich et al., 1986).

Twenty studies included measures of both verbal and nonverbal aspects of participants' behavior; but only 11 separated the two. Most often these assessments were based on videotape.

Reliability of coding across coders was reported for roughly two-thirds of the studies in terms of percent agreement or correlations; in two studies a reliability coefficient was based on an analysis of variance of repeated measures. Eight studies reported "adequate" reliability, but did not quantify this assessment. For the remaining studies, 13 reported reliabilities above .90 (or 90% agreement) and 18 reported reliabilities in the .50 to .90 (50% to 90% agreement) range.

Overview of Interaction Profiles

We calculated grand means of proportions of communication from all studies reporting results for any of the six categories we constituted. Because of the wide range in sample size, the grand means were weighted for the number of participants. Tables 13.3 and 13.4 show an overview of communication derived from these calculations for both patients and physicians. The means represent *proportions*, that is the amount of communication a speaker devoted to a particular category, divided by all interaction contributed by that speaker.

Reviewing physician communication, we found that information-giving is most frequent: 35.3% of all interaction (See Table 13.3). The forms by which information is communicated may reflect quite different intent, such as information, persuasion, or control. Some studies do indeed separate these in analysis but not so often as to allow summary here.

Question-asking by physicians accounts for 23% of the visit; this is usually done during history-taking and mostly consists of closed-ended questions: those for which a yes/no answer is expected. Questions that allow the patient some discretion in the direction he may take in answering are open-ended questions, for example, "Tell me about your

TABLE 13.3   Profile of Physician Interaction

Variable	# Studies	Range	Mean	Median	Weighted Mean	S.D.
Information Giving	12	4–60%	35.3%	38.5%	24.8%	16.90
Information Seeking	12	6–40%	22.6%	22.5%	20.1%	9.61
Social Conversation	6	5–10%	6.0%	5.0%	5.4%	1.83
Positive Talk	10	1–31%	15.0%	14.5%	11.9%	9.27
Negative Talk	3	.5–2.5%	1.3%	1.0%	2.3%	0.94
Partnership Building	7	3–25%	10.6%	10.0%	8.8%	6.52

leg pain, what seems to be the problem?" Unfortunately, this summary does not distinguish question types.

Positive talk comprises 15.0% of visits and serves two functions: approval and signalling that the speaker can continue. Often included are communications more aptly described as noises, such as, hm, uh-huh, ahh.

Partnership-building is a more heterogeneous category of process variables, occurring when the physician attempts to engage the patient in the medical dialogue, either by directly enlisting the patient's input (asks for opinion, asks for understanding, facilitates response) or by interpreting or reflecting patient statements. Social, nonmedical conversation comprises some 6% of interaction, including greetings, casual

TABLE 13.4   Profile of Patient Interaction

Variable	# Studies	Range	Mean	Median	Weighted Mean	S.D.
Information Giving	9	28–67%	46.9%	54.0%	43.5%	14.50
Question Asking	9	2.6–14.5%	7.0%	6.0%	6.1%	3.53
Social Conversation	5	4–42%	13.4%	7.0%	5.7%	14.40
Positive Talk	4	11–23%	18.7%	20.5%	20.11%	4.92
Negative Talk	3	5–13%	8.3%	7.0%	9.5%	3.40

remarks, and niceties. To some extent, both partnership-building and social talk develop a sense of solidarity between patient and physician.

Finally, negative talk is quite rare. It includes disagreements, confrontations, and antagonisms, such as, "You've gained weight since your last visit, I am disappointed in you." While physicians do not often express negative statements, negative emotional messages are nonetheless conveyed through nonverbal messages, such as voice tone or facial and body expressions.

More than half of patient talk is information-giving, much of it in response to physicians' questions (see Table 13.4). Only 6% of the interaction involves patient question-asking.

TABLE 13.5   **Summary of Correlations Between Physician Communication and Outcomes**

PHYSICIAN COMMUNI- CATION	SATISFACTION		COMPLIANCE		RECALL	
	Maximum r	Combined Z*	Maximum r	Combined Z*	Maximum r	Combined Z*
Information Giving	.33	6.31	.16	3.63	.40	5.71
Question Asking	−.08	.91	−.24	3.68	−.18	2.14
Partnership Building	.27	4.19	−.06	1.19	.29	3.50
Positive Talk	.26	3.65	.08	1.26	.05	1.84
Negative Talk	.012	1.40	−.05	2.88	INS**	
Social Talk	.17	2.84	INS**		INS**	

*Z = 1.96 is statistically significant
**INS: insufficient data for calculation

Social conversation is largely reciprocal; patients' and physicians' contributions were about equal. Patients contributed seven times as much negative talk as did physicians. Patients may be more direct than their physicians because they have fewer communication options; they cannot easily express their disagreements through lecture, counseling, or imperatives. However, they also engage in more positive talk than physicians. The patient is likely to have a far more emotional investment in the proceedings of the visit than the physician, and this is expressed in both positive and negative terms.

Physicians almost always talk more than patients do during medical visits. This is something of a surprise to physicians, who almost always overestimate the amount of patient talk, and underestimate their own talk. The average amount of physician contribution to the medical dialogue is 60% (range 51-77%). Patients, on the other hand, contribute 40% to the dialogue (range from 23-49%).

Correlational Findings

A subset of 41 of the studies reviewed reported correlates of physician communication with outcome variables—patient satisfaction, recall, and compliance. Several of these outcome variables were reported frequently enough to permit aggregation of correlations and combined significance levels for each combination.

The statistical methods used to derive the average correlations and combined significance levels are described elsewhere (Hall et al., 1988). They are consistent with accepted methods of meta-analysis (Rosenthal, 1984). Our primary findings are summarized in Table 13.5, which shows significant relations between the outcome variables and almost all of the physician communication groupings.

Satisfaction was most consistently related to physician communication, and this was positively associated with all variables except question-asking. Compliance showed a comparatively weak relation to physician behavior. In terms of combined probabilities, however, some of the aggregate results were significant, showing that compliance was associated with more information-giving and positive talk, but negatively related to question-asking and negative talk. As one would expect, recall was best predicted by information-giving, but was also related to less question-asking, which elsewhere has been shown to be negatively related to information-giving (Roter et al., 1987).

The table does not include correlations for ratings of physician competence, since an appreciable number of results were available only for patient satisfaction. Competence, defined by the original investigators, involved either multi-item checklists or global ratings of competence, based on direct observations. We considered them process variables, classifying them as either interpersonal or technical. Both were related to satisfaction. Technical competence was correlated with satisfaction at .22 (combined $Z = 3.73$) and interpersonal competence at .33 (combined $Z = 6.80$).

Comparison of Results Within the Task and Socioemotional Domains

The process we undertook to identify the meta groupings represents a consensual validation, and we can defend our results on the basis of content and face validity. The groupings represent the most common categories of behaviors addressed in interviewing guides and manuals

(Morgan and Engel, 1969). They are also behavioral reflections of the primary functions of the medical visit, including history-taking, patient education, therapeutic management, and counseling. The groupings are also consistent with prior conceptual work in the field, particularly that of Parsons (1951), Bales (1950), Bloom (1983), and Ben-Sira (1980).

One might conceptualize information-giving, information-seeking, and technical competence as serving the medically relevant task goals of the visit and partnership-building, social conversation, interpersonal competence, and positive and negative talk as within the socioemotional domain. From the patient's perspective, compliance and recall may be considered behaviors relevant to the task-focused aspects of the visit, whereas satisfaction is relevant to the socioemotional or affective aspects of the visit. The purpose of such a conceptualization is heuristic; its two dimensions are: medically task relevant goals versus socioemotional goals.

Using our framework, we found the strongest relationships between corresponding domains of communication (Hall et al., 1988). As reflected in Table 13.6, the median absolute correlation between physician task behaviors (information-giving and question-asking) and patient task behaviors (compliance and recall) was .21; the median correlation between physician socioemotional behaviors (positive, social, and negative talk, interpersonal competence, and partnership building) and patient socioemotional reaction (satisfaction) was .26.

For correlations between domains, we found an asymmetrical pattern. The median correlation between physician task behaviors (information-giving, question-asking, and technical competence) and patient satisfaction was .22, but the correlation between physician socioemotional behaviors (partnership-building, positive and negative talk) and patient task behaviors (compliance and recall) was only .10.

TOWARD A THEORY OF RECIPROCITY
IN THE MEDICAL ENCOUNTER

We believe that an explanatory mechanism for this pattern of results may be provided through the broad concept of reciprocity. The concept of reciprocity is regarded as critically important to the understanding of social relations, yet remains ambiguous, with few theorists posing an operational definition. For a history of the concept and attendant diffi-

TABLE 13.6   Median Correlations Between Physicians and Patient Behavior Categories (Absolute Values)[a]

Physician Domain	Patient Domain	Median Absolute Correlation
TASK	TASK	
Information giving	Compliance	.24
Question-Asking	Recall	
TASK	SOCIOEMOTIONAL	
Information giving	Satisfaction	.22
Question-Asking		
Technical competence		
SOCIOEMOTIONAL	TASK	
Partnership-Building	Compliance	.10
Positive talk	Recall	
Negative talk		
SOCIOEMOTIONAL	SOCIOEMOTIONAL	
Partnership-building	Satisfaction	.26
Positive talk		
Negative talk		
Interpersonal competence		
Social conversation		

[a]Table taken from Hall, J. A., Roter, D. L., Katz, N. R. (1988) "Meta-analysis of correlates of provider behavior in medical encounters." *Medical Care.* Used by permission.

culties in definition, see Gouldner's extensive discussion (Gouldner, 1960). For insight into social psychological elaboration of the concept in terms of equity theory, see Berkowitz and Walster (1976). Simply put, behaviors generate reciprocal, or like, behaviors. Physician task behaviors and patient task behaviors reciprocate one another as do physician and patient socioemotional behaviors.

We suggest, however, that such reciprocated exchange is not equally operative between different domains of communication. We believe that physicians' task behaviors carry socioemotional significance for patients, and that because of this, one may expect to see correlations between physician task behaviors and patient socioemotional behaviors. Task behavior can take on socioemotional meaning in two ways: through conveyance (voice quality, for example) and through interpretation, as defined above. As examples, physicians who provide more medical information have been found to speak with an interested voice quality (Hall et al., 1987); or a physician who is proficient or otherwise active in the task domain may be interpreted as interested and caring regardless of what he or she expresses through specifically socioemotional behaviors (Roter et al., 1987) because the patient makes a positive inference about the physician's motivation for engaging in the task behaviors.

This view is consistent with a growing literature demonstrating the efficacy of information-giving for a variety of therapeutic effects, including shortened hospital stays, decreased use of analgesics, and reduced patient anxiety (Mumford et al., 1982). We suggest that the mechanism by which information achieves its therapeutic effects is through the interpreted message of interest and caring. Because of the generalization of positive affect from the task domain, a socioemotional response by the patient, expressed in satisfaction or other affective behaviors, can be expected.

In contrast, the weaker relation between physicians' socioemotional behaviors and patients' task behaviors, found in the meta-analysis, can be seen as a lack of reciprocity between these domains. In our view, physicians' socioemotional behaviors do not have sufficient task or technical significance to lead strongly or frequently to reciprocal task-relevant responses in patients. Consistent with the simulation study of Willson and McNamara (1982), patients may not typically make task attributions (e.g., competence) on the basis of socioemotional behavior. The physician who is positive may inspire friendliness or liking in the patient, but no, or only weak, task responses, such as attending to information, modifying lifestyle, or adhering to a therapeutic regimen.

Further, we suggest that information-giving may be viewed as enhancing patient power and increasing the patient's ability to participate actively in the therapeutic process. Question-asking, while an important problem-solving activity for the physician may have little intrinsic value to the patient (Waitzkin, 1985).

This is also supported by the meta-results. Question-asking was negatively correlated with both patient compliance and recall and unrelated to patient satisfaction, while information-giving was quite strongly related to satisfaction, compliance, and recall.

CONCLUSIONS

In conclusion, our analysis of the literature suggests that in order for the area to flourish, investigators must attend to both the conceptual nature of the work and its application in order to improve medical practice. Furthermore, we were struck by the fact that so many authors devised their own schemes to analyze interactions rather than use previously developed schemes. Therefore, our second recommendation is that investigators build on each others' work. Finally, we do not suggest that this review of the literature constitutes a final test of our hypotheses on reciprocity in patient and physician communication. It does, however, offer suggestive evidence and we look forward to greater debate and research in these matters.

14

Design Issues in Research on Doctor-Patient Communication

Thomas S. Inui
and
William B. Carter

Our intent is to review and discuss the methodologic architecture of doctor-patient communication research. In attempting to classify research types, objectives, design issues, and other special problems in research on the doctor-patient relationship, we asked 20 experienced investigators to select the studies they felt had made "the most important contributions to the scientific understanding of doctor-patient communication." Our citation sample included 37 papers, which represent a cross-section of the topics and methods covered in the study of doctor-patient communication.

STUDY TYPES

The studies cited were of three types, which we have characterized as "developmental/descriptive" (18 out of 37, or 49%), "sub-experimental/etiologic" (14 or 38%), and "interventional" (5 or 13%).

Developmental/Descriptive Research

The purpose of this research is to expand the repertoire of theories, measures, and experience available to serve as a basis for empirical research on doctor-patient communication. We sub-classified this group into conceptual and empirical investigations (Table 14.1).

TABLE 14.1   Developmental/Descriptive Studies

	Cox, Hopkinson and Rutter '81	Goldberg et al. '84	Hopkinson et al. '81	Maguire et al. '76	Marks et al. '79	Rutter and Cox '81	Stewart et al. '86
DESIGN							
Cross-sectional	X		X	X	X	X	
Longitudinal		X					X
Cohort							
Case-control							
Experimental							
Quasi-experimental							
SETTING/OCCASION							
First visit	X	X	X	X	X	X	
Outpatient	X	X	X	X		X	X
ER/walk in clinic							
SAMPLING (N)	36	100	36	50	2098	12	49
Representative	X	X	X	X	X	X	X
Retrospective/Prospective	P	P	P	P	P	P	P
PROCESS MEASURES							
Patient	X		X			X	X
Physician	X	X	X	X	X	X	X
METHOD OF OBSERVATION							
Direct observation					X		
Audiotape/Videotape	X	X	X	X		X	X
CODING SYSTEM							
Interactional analysis content categories (study specific)	X	X	X	X	X	X	X
RELIABILITY MEASURES	X		X			X	

Eleven of the 18 articles were conceptual, including two literature reviews (Cresswell, 1983, with comments by Sackett et al.; Wasserman and Inui, 1983), descriptions of a new theoretical approach and taxonomy for discourse analysis (Stiles, 1978-1979), and seven presentations of alternative approaches to doctor-patient interactions supported by literature reviews and case studies (Brown et al., 1986; Engel, 1980; Kleinman et al., 1978; Levenstein et al., 1986; McWhinney, 1985; Pendleton, 1981; and Quill, 1983). These seven papers were directed principally to clinicians, although they offer a number of important insights and testable hypotheses for researchers. One study (Marks et al., 1979) empirically examined interviewing style and identification of psychiatric cases in a variety of general practice settings. The remaining six empirical studies focused on process related to clinical training. These studies evaluated new process measures (Rutter and Cox, 1981), described effects of training (Stewart et al., 1986), described problems in history-taking (Maguire and Rutter, 1976a), and examined different interviewing styles among psychiatric trainees (Cox et al., 1981; Goldberg et al., 1984; Hopkinson et al., 1981). With one exception (Goldberg et al., 1984), the results of these descriptive studies were used to design randomized, controlled trials to evaluate new methods for teaching history-taking (Rutter and Maguire, 1976), assess systematically different interviewing styles (Rutter et al., 1981), and characterize their impact on eliciting factual information (Cox et al., 1981) or feelings (Cox et al., 1981).

Most of these studies employed cross-sectional designs, but two (Goldberg et al., 1984; Stewart et al., 1986) followed a cohort of training physicians and described process changes. The settings for such studies are very diverse and seem to have been chosen most often for convenience. Sampling methods have been aimed at collecting a "representative" set of cases, whether an unbiased sample of particular problem cases or of a particular clinical area. Quantitative developmental/descriptive studies have employed a variety of measures to characterize the "substrate" sample and to describe process. Analyses are relatively simple counts, proportions, and descriptions of sequence to provide a new description of encounter events.

The significance of these developmental/descriptive studies is to be judged in terms of their validity, reliability, and feasibility. Several different forms of validation can be considered. If an alternative, descriptive technique is available (external to the new system being tested) construct validation can be attempted. We believe that there is insufficient attention to the "face validity" of proposed descriptive techniques and the products of such developmental/descriptive work. This kind of validation might be best characterized as a serious attempt to resolve the question: Does all of this make sense to clinicians, patients, and/or clinician educators? Unless the descriptive method is reliable, two observers might disagree about the content of a single event or one observer might describe the same encounter in different ways at two different times. Both kinds of reliability are important preconditions for research and training applications. Feasibility of new techniques for capturing and describing events depends partly on the setting of care, but may also be judged in terms of obtrusiveness, acceptability, work burden, and other aspects of cost.

Subexperimental Etiologic Research

There is a plethora of cause-and-effect theories linking clinical communication to certain global or more selective outcomes of care, but inadequate empirical support. We subdivided the subexperimental/etiologic category into two subcategories to differentiate studies that examine general process-outcome relationships from studies that examine specific questions or hypotheses resulting from either a theoretical prediction or an observed problem (see Table 14.2).

Studies in the former subcategory have employed interaction analysis systems to characterize the communication process and have attempted to identify elements of the encounter related to important patient outcomes, such as patient knowledge, compliance, satisfaction. Several studies (Freemon et al., 1971; Korsch et al., 1968; Stewart, 1984; Stiles et al., 1982) have incorporated several outcome measures in their assessments, but only one study has examined multiple interaction analysis systems (Inui et al., 1982). More recent studies have either further subdivided the units of the encounter into very small linguistic events (Stiles et al., 1982) or attempted to define larger "exchange" units or "interacts" (Wasserman et al., 1983). Finally, it is sometimes possible to conduct a study within a larger study to explore further or to clarify the etiology of some communication outcomes. For example, we employed a case-control design (Carter et al., 1982) to develop causal hypotheses from a general process-outcome study (Inui et al., 1982). These analyses provided some insight into the face validity of our interaction analyses.

TABLE 14.2   Subexperimental Etiologic Studies

	Bass et al. '86	Carter et al. '82	Davis '68; '71	Freemon et al. '71	Headache Study Group '86	Inui et al. '82	Korsch et al. '82	Starfield et al. '81	Stewart '84	Stiles et al. '82	Svarstad '76	Waitzkin '85	Wasserman et al. '83
DESIGN													
Cross-sectional	X	X	X	X	X	X	X	X	X	X	X	X	X
Longitudinal													
Cohort													
Case-control		X											
Experimental													
Quasi-experimental													
SETTING/ OCCASION													
First visit		X	X		X	X					X		X
Outpatient	X	X	X			X		X	X		X	X	X
ER/walk in clinic				X			X			X			
SAMPLING (N)	193	101	154	285	265	101	800	135	140	115	153	336	40
Representative	X	X	X	X	X	X	X	X	X	X	X	X	X
Retrospective/ Prospective	P	P	P	P	P	P	P	P	P	P	P	P	P
PROCESS MEASURES													
Patient		X	X	X		X	X		X	X		X	X
Physician		X	X	X		X	X		X	X	X	X	X
METHOD OF OBSERVATION													
Direct observation											X		
Audiotape/ Videotape		X	X	X		X	X		X	X		X	X
CODING SYSTEM													
Interactional analysis		X	X	X		X			X	X			X
Content categories (study specific)							X	X			X	X	
RELIABILITY MEASURES		X	X	X					X	X		X	X
MEDICAL CARE OUTCOMES													
Single measure	X		X					X			X		
Multiple measure		X		X	X	X	X		X				X

Several studies examined specific questions rather than the entire encounter. Starfield et al. (1979, 1981) and Bass et al. (1986) studied the relationship between provider-patient agreement and the outcome of care. A second approach focused on information transmittal and tested theoretically grounded hypotheses about provider information-giving (Waitzkin, 1985). A third approach measured patient perceptions of the encounter and assessed their relationship to outcome (Headache Study Group, 1986).

The majority of these subexperimental studies are cross-sectional. Other potential designs include the case series, but this design is so subject to bias that we do not recommend it. Alternative designs include case-control and retrospective or prospective cohort studies. Both are applicable to the examination of cause-and-effect hypotheses, but have different advantages and disadvantages. The case-control study is relatively more subject to bias, but is generally less expensive to conduct. The cohort study is more appropriate in examining relatively common outcomes of care related to doctor-patient communication, for example, the patient who leaves without a complete understanding of his/her drug regimen. The case-control study design, on the other hand, may be the only feasible approach to examining the communication causes of relatively rare outcomes of care, such as patients' requests to transfer their care to other physicians, doctors' acknowledgments of anger at particular patients, or departures from hospital against medical advice.

The settings for such subexperimental etiologic studies deserve special comment. Case-control studies require a monitoring process or a central registry. Cohort studies should take place in an environment where the outcome-of-interest is common. Cohort studies on relatively rare outcomes are prohibitively expensive. Sampling for case-control studies is, of course, retrospective, but may be prospective or retrospective for cohort studies. Analyses may be statistically complicated, but are intended to estimate relative risks or odds ratios. The product of such studies is a supported or rejected causal mechanism. The significance of the conclusion is judged on the strength of the association demonstrated (or the power of the demonstration of nonassociation), its plausibility, demonstrations of like associations in other work, and other epidemiologic causal criteria.

Intervention Research

The *intervention study* is undertaken because there is a promising suggestion on how to improve the results of doctor-patient communication, but there is no evidence for the efficacy of such a suggestion. While interventions have been successfully utilized in training settings, few have been attempted in a practice setting. Of the five intervention studies in our database (Table 14.3), only one directly involved patients, attempted to change the nature of the interactive communication process, and evaluated this change for its impact on patient outcomes (Greenfield et al., 1985).

All of these studies were randomized trials. Other possible intervention designs include before-and-after time series, quasiexperimental work (for example, contrasting behaviors and communication effectiveness among medical student experimental and control groups). The appropriate settings for such work are diverse, but presumably would have in common the existence of a demonstrated problem in communication process or communication-related outcomes. Sampling approaches may be helpful: within any setting it is usually possible to identify certain clinicians or clinician-patient pairs who have problems communicating. The "problem pairs" become the target for the intervention.

Intervention study measures are intended to characterize the subject sample, compare treatment and control groups, characterize those behaviors that we hope to alter through our intervention, and to demonstrate effect on outcome of communication. Analyses are conducted to estimate effect size. Such work supports or rejects the suggested intervention. The significance of the product is judged on statistical grounds, but must also be appraised on its clinical importance (often a matter of cost/benefit ratio), clinical acceptability, and generalizability. These last two may be particularly difficult to judge in doctor-patient communication experiments, which are often undertaken by innovator-enthusiasts with attitudes and organizational clout that may be difficult to replicate elsewhere.

APPROACHES TO SPECIAL PROBLEMS

Special problems exist within each of these three categories of research in doctor-patient communication. In the *developmental/descriptive* category, basic theory and measures have often been devel-

TABLE 14.3   Intervention Studies

	Cox, Holbrook, and Rutter '81	Cox, Holbrook, and Rutter '81	Greenfield et al. '85	Rutter et al. '86	Rutter et al. '81
DESIGN					
Cross-sectional					
Longitudinal					
Cohort					
Case-control					
Experimental	X	X	X	X	X
Quasi-experimental					
SETTING/OCCASION					
First visit	X	X		X	X
Outpatient	X	X	X	X	X
ER/walk in clinic					
SAMPLING (N)	24	24	45	24/28	24
Representative	X	X	X	X	X
Retrospective/Prospective	P	P	P	P	P
PROCESS MEASURES					
Patient	X	X	X		X
Physician	X	X	X	X	X
METHOD OF OBSERVATION					
Direct observation					
Audiotape/Videotape	X	X	X	X	X
CODING SYSTEM					
Interactional analysis					
Content categories (study specific)	X	X	X	X	X
RELIABILITY ANALYSIS	X	X	X		
MEDICAL CARE OUTCOMES					
Single measure					
Multiple measure			X		

oped in other disciplines and are therefore remote from clinical practice (Inui and Carter, 1985; Wasserman and Inui, 1983). Some approaches with particular promise include

1. development of tailored, explicitly clinical descriptive systems;

2. efforts to ground theory in the events of clinical practice;

3. adaptation of clinical rating scales for interaction analysis instruments;

4. scrutiny of "meta-events," such as doctor-patient negotiations or clinicians' communication styles.

Any of the first three might produce descriptive systems more appropriate to clinical process (and, for that matter, outcomes of greater relevance to clinical objectives than knowledge, satisfaction, and compliance). For example, the "resource exchange" interaction analysis necessitates that the available resources—information, reassurance, medications, appointments, etc.—most germane to the clinical event be listed. A prelude to such work, therefore, should include qualitative consideration of the clinical encounters to which such measures are to be applied. It may even include physician and patient review of these events (possibly aided by audiotapes, videotapes, or transcripts) to identify "remarkable events" and to explain what happened. Patients, for example, can give their views on the agenda for a doctor-patient visit, on the appropriateness and effectiveness of the physician's behavior, and how they would evaluate the outcomes of medical care. Qualitative research, in our view, would go a long way toward making our descriptive measures more appropriate.

Clinical rating scales have been developed for evaluating the performance of clinicians or clinician-students in the diagnostic interview (see Chapters 11 and 12). They express reasonably succinctly the prevailing "clinical wisdom" about affective behaviors. If one or more of these might be adapted as a descriptive system for interaction research, the product of such research would probably be more accessible to clinicians. Identification of events within the clinician-patient interview (such as an expression of disagreement and attempts to arrive at a negotiated consensus) would permit selection of events with greater instrumental importance. Describing the many clinician behaviors that might identify competing habitual approaches to talking with patients ("styles") would focus attention on sequential behaviors and patterns of events.

Subexperimental etiologic research in doctor-patient communication also faces special difficulties: multifactorial causal models are likely to be most appropriate for the outcomes of interest; communication is dominated by *interaction*, with physician and patient behaviors arising in response to one another's actions or states in an explicit but sometimes fruitless effort to achieve the outcome of interest; and there is a major potential for patient and physician bias in retrospective reporting of communication after an outcome has been achieved.

We suggest several approaches to these problems. First, meta-analyses (such as Chapter 13) conducted on data from several etiologic studies might produce common findings, though such information syntheses do pose methodologic problems of their own (including a heterogeneity of clinical settings, subject types, and process and outcome measures). Etiologic research might be cleaner and more powerful if settings or occasions were more carefully selected so that the communication process is more likely to be responsible for the outcomes of interest. Examples might include informed consent encounters, introduction of a new therapy, discussion of a new diagnostic finding of uncertain significance (for example, the abnormal chest Xray in a smoker), or genetic counseling sessions in which the question of a therapeutic abortion must be addressed. These events might place a greater premium on physician effectiveness in communication and, therefore, highlight the causal relationships, or differences in the consequences of effective and ineffective styles.

In this work, it will be important to make *prior* hypotheses explicit to avoid false-positive associations that emerge by chance. It will also be important to choose targeted measures for process and outcome most likely to demonstrate the relationships hypothesized. Where possible in prospective work, it may be particularly helpful to employ "change variables" for outcomes of interest (for example, perceived health status, knowledge states, or self-assurance before *and* after the doctor encounter) to deal more effectively with recall bias and reactive behaviors. Change variables would also make it possible to describe the marginal gains (or losses), which are feasible in the settings we are using for research, and the variability to be expected in such outcomes.

This latter information will be invaluable in estimating appropriate sample sizes for future experimental evaluations of interventions.

Finally, case-control and cohort research on causal relationships between process and outcome will best be implemented in a "laboratory" that permits prospective capture of process and outcomes. Routine procedures would have to be implemented for capture of pre-encounter states, clinical process (for example, by audio or videotaping) and selected outcomes of care. In a case-control study format, encounters with adverse outcomes would constitute cases, and a certain proportion of other encounters would be the controls. Pre-encounter characteristics of patients or clinicians would serve as prior states for change variables of outcome, or as potential confounders and effect modifiers in subsequent analyses. Audio or videotapes of cases and controls could be analyzed to describe the frequency and intensity of the putative causes.

Interventional studies in doctor-patient communication are especially subject to several other problems: "moving targets," multiple influences on the outcomes of interest, subject-subject contamination, and difficulty in assessing the clinical importance of such work. Many such experiments have been conducted with clinicians-in-training, for whom the natural history of communication effectiveness is to improve. The intervention therefore competes with accumulating experience and teaching in producing greater communication competence.

It is also difficult and/or inappropriate to isolate such subjects from one another, virtually guaranteeing that experimental contamination will occur. There are several approaches to these difficulties. First, we recommend true experiments, since before-and-after studies do not control for historical change produced by conditions external to the experiment. This enhances the need, mentioned above, for descriptive work as a prelude to experiments. Powerful, salient interventions are preferable, possibly conducted simultaneously at similar institutions, to avoid contamination and to check generalizability.

Sensitive, tailored measures of effect will also be advantageous. Trained patient surrogates may be particularly able to comment on differences among clinician communicators, but some of the more important outcomes of interest (for example, problem resolution, anxiety alleviation, and changes in functional abilities) may be unattainable from such individuals.

Finally, we need to supplement our outcomes of interest with other "clinically meaningful" observations. We are often asked whether the suggested style of communication takes longer than a regular visit would take and whether these approaches are likely to result in better diagnoses, more appropriate therapy, or more favorable end results. These are reasonable questions, but not easily addressed on the basis of information from most research being done in doctor-patient communication today. We can begin to respond to some of these concerns by expanding *our* outcome measures to include several dimensions clinicians consider relevant, when they evaluate the results of medical care: request fulfillment, improvement of physiologic state, alleviation of distress, improvement of function (physical or psychosocial), and cost. This emphasis on broad outcome measurement may seem a particularly onerous one for communications researchers, but it will be important to the credibility of our work and the likelihood of its exerting any impact on practice (see Chapter 16 for more on outcome measures).

Such work will have an important, useful impact on medical education and medical practice in the end. In most primary care settings, technical issues are the least important determinant of outcomes; the effectiveness of the clinician in understanding a patient's illness and in arriving at a joint plan for managing the distress are the key skills and true causes of a better result. Even in tertiary care settings, cure is rare and coping is the norm. Research in provider-patient communication, then, should contribute to our basic understanding of what is truly accomplished in medical care and may be more likely to show clinically important impacts than most standard biomedical research.

CONCLUSION

The final assessment of research in this domain, as in others, is on the basis of usefulness. About developmental/descriptive studies, one asks whether the outcomes are translatable into suggestions for descriptive system improvement, new theory, and/or new clinical cause-and-effect hypotheses. To the extent that such descriptive work results in simple affirmation of common wisdom, we may have validated the descriptive system used, but we have not provided new substrate for etiologic work.

Of subexperimental etiologic studies, one asks whether the inferences drawn are subject to verification by clinical trial. If it would be unethical to conduct such a trial, the etiologic work has focused on a

TABLE 14.4   Doctor-Patient Communication Study Types

	Developmental/ Descriptive	Sub-Experimental Etiologic	Interventional
Problem	Limited repertoire of measures and experience	Large universe of hypotheses, limited empirical support	Lots of clinical wisdom, little efficacy evidence
Design	Cross-sectional, cohort	Case-control, cohort	Before-and-after, quasi-experimental, randomized controlled trial
Setting	Any	Outcome registry available or outcome-enriched environment	Problems demonstrated
Sampling	Representative	Prospective or retrospective	Prospective
Measures	Any needed to characterize sample, describe process	Any needed to characterize: sample, confounders, effect modifiers, putative causes, putative effects	Any needed to characterize: sample, treatment and control groups, target behaviors, and intended effects
Analyses	Counts, proportions, sequence	Estimate relative risk, odds ratio, or equivalent	Estimate effect size
Product	Description of events	Supported or rejected causal mechanism	Support or rejection of the suggested intervention
Significance	Validity, reliability feasibility	Strength of association, plausibility, etc. (epidemiologic causal criteria	Statistical and clinical importance, acceptability, generalizability
Special problems for doctor-patient communication research	Basic theory and measures remote from clinical practice; descriptions atomistic, non-sequential; "multi-channel" events	Multi-factorial causes, interaction process, measure potential for recall bias with retrospective studies	Moving targets, multiple influences, contamination, difficulty in assessing importance
Approaches to special problems	Tailored descriptive systems, grounded theory, adaptation of clinical rating scales, scales, scrutiny of "meta-events" (e.g. negotiations, clinical styles)	Meta-analyses, selected setting/occasions—"pure culture" of critical events, prior hypotheses, targeted measures, change variables for outcomes, laboratory which allows prospective record of process and outcome	True experiments, careful choice of targets and timing, powerful interventions, sensitive measures of effect, clinically meaningful outcomes
Usefulness	Are the outcomes translatable into suggestions for descriptive system improvement, new theory, clinical cause-and-effect hypotheses?	Are inferences subject to verification by clinical trial?	Can the results be used to improve practice or teaching?

domain in which change would be unacceptable. If, on the other hand, a clinical trial cannot be formulated because the results of the etiologic research cannot be "translated" into a clinical strategy, then the sample was inadequate or the descriptive system employed for putative causes was too arcane.

Finally, about interventional studies, one asks if the results can be used to improve practice or teaching. If this question cannot be answered, any of several matters may yet be unresolved: the extent to which the problems prevail in that setting, the actual content of the interventional strategy employed, the acceptability or feasibility of the intervention in that setting, or the cost/benefit ratio of the intervention. Table 14.4 summarizes our findings about the three types of studies.

The works cited in our poll of communications researchers range from developmental to interventional research. Sample sizes are respectable, there is careful attention to standard measures of process and outcome (usually with new checks on reliability), and more than one outcome of care is included (often limited, however, to two). We need to pay increasing attention to prior hypotheses, causal models, the theoretical underpinning of our hypotheses, the need to experiment with interventions outside of training programs, the need for cohort studies with a longer follow-up, the continued heterogeneity of clinical settings and occasions used as "substrate" for such work, and the increasing importance of concluding each piece of research with a statement of what should be done next.

It is encouraging to have the opportunity for cross-fertilization among the social scientists, educators, and practitioners that this book represents. Our informal sample of important research suggests that this dynamic young field is producing research with considerable promise and a continuing need for collaborative efforts involving all these parties.

15

Analysis of Verbal and Nonverbal Behavior in Doctor-Patient Encounters

William B. Stiles
and
Samuel M. Putnam

Verbal communication between patients and physicians has many aspects and levels. Just as a patient's cardiac function cannot be fully characterized by a single measure, the communication between two people cannot be fully described by a single coding. Investigators must choose their measures based on what they want to know about a medical encounter.

This paper reviews some of the measures that have been used to characterize medical interactions. To organize the enormous variety of coding systems into an understandable framework, we have developed a "meta-classification scheme" of interactions between patients and physicians. Our goal in this paper is to recommend a conceptual framework for understanding measurement of patient-physician communication, not to review this area comprehensively. Readers are referred to the thoughtful articles by Pendleton (1983), Wasserman and Inui (1983), and Inui and Carter (1985) for recent overviews.

Our meta-classification is based on an earlier classification of language in psychotherapy (Russell and Stiles, 1979) that contained three main categories: a) *content* categories: the denotative or connotative semantic content of what is said; b) *speech act* (or instrumental) categories: what is done when someone says something; and c) *nonverbal communication* categories: communication outside strictly linguistic channels. In addition to these three categories, we consider d) *activity counts*, which measure behaviors occurring during the interview but are not direct communications; and e) *affective ratings*: emotional tone of an interaction.

These five categories, which we call "meta-classes," are distinct. They may all be used to characterize a particular interaction. Sometimes, as we discuss below, investigators use several meta-classes. For example, studies have looked at content *and* speech act categories. Within a meta-class, investigators may develop mutually exclusive categories. Coding schemes developed from a theoretical base can do this through rules of logic that allow a coder to classify any unit of communication in one and only one category. Other coding schemes are based on verbal descriptions that are usually accompanied by examples that serve as standards for each category. Coders must compare specific utterances with these examples in order to determine the correct coding category.

CONTENT CATEGORIES

Content categories concern the denotative or connotative semantic meaning of the utterance. Content analysis has long been widely used in the social sciences (Bertakis, 1977; Holsti, 1969; Sprunger, 1983).

Because meanings vary, the variety of possible content categories is enormous. After all, a thesaurus is a content-based classification system. To reduce this to manageable proportions, investigators have limited the classification to particular topics of interest (e.g., topics relating to illnesses or to medications) or grouped topics into more general categories. For example, we have studied the transcripts of visits to a medical walk-in clinic and categorized each patient's symptom as a separate unit (e.g., nausea and vomiting were coded as two topics). Later, we combined individual topics into broader categories representing the different systems in a traditional medical review of systems (e.g., nausea and vomiting were combined into gastrointestinal system).

The choice of content categories obviously depends on what topics are of interest. A study that focuses on too many categories quickly becomes unwieldy. On the other hand, categories as broad as biomedical, socioemotional or chit-chat may provide too little information. Finding that 78% of an interview concerned biomedical topics gives only a vague idea of what was said.

SPEECH ACT CATEGORIES

Speech act categories are instrumental; they concern what is *done* when someone says something, as opposed to what is said. For example, "How long have you been out of work?" is about the patient's employment, but what the speaker has done is ask a question. *Question* is an example of a speech act category. Linguists and philosophers call questions and the other categories we consider under this heading *illocutionary acts* (Austin, 1975; Searle, 1969; Stiles, 1981).

Most of the best-known coding systems of medical interactions use speech act categories. Bales's (1950) Interaction Process Analysis has been adapted by many investigators for studying medical interviews (Brownbridge et al., 1986; Carter et al., 1982; Davis, 1971; Freemon et al., 1971; Roter, 1977; Stewart, 1983, 1984). Another coding system for medical interviews is Stiles's (1978) Verbal Response Modes (Brownbridge et al., 1986; Carter et al., 1982; Inui et al., 1982; Meeuwesen, 1986; Orth et al., 1987; Putnam et al., 1985; Stiles et al., 1979a, 1979b, 1979c, 1982, 1984).

Other examples of schemes composed mainly of speech act categories are a) Byrne and Long's (1976) classification system (Brownbridge et al., 1986; Buijs et al., 1984); b) Bain's scheme (1976, 1979); c) a scheme by Greenfield et al. (1985); and d) a scheme by Heszen-Klemens and Lapinska (1984).

Speech act categories, unlike content categories, imply an intended audience (Russell and Stiles, 1979; Stiles, 1981). One asks *another person* a question, gives an opinion to *another person*, offers advice to *another person*. Because the speaker is *doing* something to another person, each category characterizes the relationships between people. Each act can be considered as a *microrelationship* between the speaker and the intended audience. This added dimension of speech act coding schemes is recognized explicitly in the theoretical concepts used to construct some speech act coding systems (Heszen-Klemens and Lapinska, 1984; Stiles, 1978).

Since the categories are acts rather than content areas, they can be used in different settings (Bales and Hare, 1965; Stiles, 1986). For example, they have been applied to counseling and psychotherapeutic sessions (Elliott et al., 1982; Stiles and Sultan, 1979), interactions of teachers and students (Cansler and Stiles, 1981; Stiles et al., 1979d), interactions of parents and children (Stiles and White, 1981), interactions of husbands and wives (Fitzpatrick et al., 1984; Premo and Stiles, 1983), interactions of nursing home caregivers (Caporael and Culbertson, 1986), courtroom interrogations (McGaughey and Stiles, 1983), and even political speeches (Miller and Stiles, 1986; Stiles et al., 1983).

Whereas content categories seem almost infinitely varied, speech act categories appear very similar across systems (Heszen-Klemens and Lapinska, 1984; Stiles et al., 1979c). A recent comparative study of six speech act classification systems used to study counseling and psychotherapy found six categories that were used similarly (i.e., coders applied them to the same speech units). These six categories (Question, Advisement, Reflection, Interpretation, Disclosure, and Information) accounted for most of the psychotherapists' utterances in the psychotherapy sessions studied (Elliott et al., 1987).

- Some coding systems have subdivided one or more of these major categories. For example, questions have been divided into a) open and closed questions (Putnam et al., 1988); b) direct questions, closed questions, self-answering questions, and correlational questions (Byrne and Long, 1976); or c) asks for opinion, asks for orientation, and asks for suggestion (Bales, 1950). On the other hand, speech act categories can be drastically collapsed, for example, into "statements" and "questions" (Sprunger, 1983).

Although categories are similar across systems, the relationship between these categories and outcomes of care are not (Inui and Carter, 1985; Pendleton, 1983; Stewart, 1984). Expository utterances (measuring provider explanation) have correlated with favorable outcomes in some studies (Orth et al., 1987; Putnam et al., 1985; Smith et al., 1981; Stiles et al., 1979b; Svarstad, 1976), but not in others (Carter et al., 1982; Inui et al., 1982). This inconsistency may be due to an inappropriate statistical criterion used to assess the link between process categories and outcomes (see The Correlation Criterion Problem, p. 219).

NONVERBAL COMMUNICATIVE BEHAVIORS

Not all communicative behavior in medical interviews is verbal. Tone of voice, gaze, posture, hesitations, laughter, facial expressions, touch, and many other nonverbal behaviors may modify the meaning of verbal utterances. These behaviors are believed to convey the emotional tone of interpersonal communication (Argyle, 1975; Ekman et al., 1972). Harrigan and colleagues (1981, 1983) studied physicians' posture, gestures, gaze, and other nonverbal behaviors within interviews in relation to perceived rapport with patients. Hall et al. (1981) used electronically filtered tape recordings of interviews to study voice tone independently of verbal content, in relation to the affective tone of interviews. DiMatteo et al. (1979) used individual difference tests (particularly the Profile of Nonverbal Sensitivity or PONS test [Rosenthal et al., 1979] to study nonverbal sensitivity in medical settings. Although they have not systematically coded nonverbal communication in substantial samples of medical interviews, they suggest that a physician's nonverbal sensitivity can contribute to patients' satisfaction with their interviews.

Laboratory studies have suggested that emotional states are often more clearly expressed nonverbally than verbally (Argyle, 1975; Ekman et al., 1972; Mehrabian, 1969, 1972). In psychotherapeutic interactions, nonverbal categories have been found to be particularly sensitive to clients' transitory emotional states (Russell and Stiles, 1979). For these reasons, affective rating scales (see below) are often based on nonverbal communication.

Despite increased use of videotapes in physicians' training programs, there is little empirical support for the usual admonishments to physicians to use facilitating nonverbal behaviors. An exception to this is the study by Larsen and Smith (1981) in a family practice setting. No doubt the slow progress in this area reflects the difficulty in developing a systematic approach to coding these behaviors (Ekman and Friesen, 1976).

ACTIVITY COUNTS

Activities that occur during the interview but which are not directly involved in the communication between patients and physicians must be distinguished from the nonverbal behaviors described above. For example, to assess the impact of computer-aided medical history-taking, Brownbridge et al. (1986) coded the doctor's focus of attention as being on the patient, the computer, paper records, or various combinations, with and without a microcomputer present and in use in the examining room. Other activities might include telephone interruptions, chart-reading, and departures from the room.

Silence could be coded as a nonverbal communicative behavior or as an activity. Samph and Templeton (1978) coded silence as **uncertain** (physician is uncertain about next step) **attentive** (physician has eye contact with patient), and **nonattentive** (physician is reading or writing). Since the first two behaviors occur as the speakers communicate directly with each other, they might be considered nonverbal communicative behaviors. The last behavior is deliberately noncommunicative, and therefore might be classified as an activity.

RATING SCALES

Rating represents a quantification strategy that is clearly distinct from coding. Coding classifies differences without measuring them; for example, a question is not greater than or less than a disclosure. Rating scales, on the other hand, are attempts to measure behavior on a continuum. Raters are asked to judge the degree or amount of some scalable quantity.

In principle, the range of possible rating scales seems infinite, but in practice two broad types have been used in medical interactions: **evaluative scales**, in which the rater judges how well (how appropriately, how expertly) an activity has been performed, and **affective scales**, in which the rater judges the emotional tone. The restricted range of what is rated may reflect the fact that human observers are better at recognizing and classifying behaviors than at combining and quantifying them (Meehl, 1954).

Even though coders may agree on the criteria for a particular behavior, they have difficulty in agreeing on the threshold for coding the occurrence of the behavior. For example, raters readily agreed on the criteria by which expressions of sympathy should be recognized, but had difficulty in deciding how much sympathy had to be present for sympathy to be coded (Rutter and Cox, 1981: 280).

Evaluative ratings have been widely used (e.g., Barbee et al., 1967; Irwin and Bamber, 1984). Because they presuppose a rater competent to judge the value of the target behavior, they are often carried out by professionals (Hess, 1969). However, nonprofessional raters can be trained to provide accurate evaluations (Helfer, 1970). An example of an evaluative rating scale is provided in Chapter 12 of this book (Kraan, et al.)

One of the major gaps in medical interview teaching is an empirical base for the standards used to evaluate medical interviewing. Many are borrowed from counseling and psychotherapy, but we believe the differences between medical and psychiatric interactions make this inappropriate. We hope the issue of appropriate evaluative standards will be addressed by educators and investigators in the near future.

Affective rating systems have typically included several (3-10) Likert scales that ask raters to judge one or both participants on a set of affective qualities, such as anger/irritation, anxiety/nervousness, dominance/assertiveness, interest/concern, and friendliness/warmth (Roter, 1985). Similar approaches have been used by Brownbridge et al. (1986), Inui et al. (1982), and Carter et al. (1982).

MIXING META-CLASSES

We identify three ways in which investigators can employ more than one meta-class in a single study: constructing conjunctive categories and using mixed systems, both of which are problematic, and using multidimensional coding, which we recommend.

Conjunctive categories combine categories from different meta-classes. For example, the conjunctive category "questions about medications" is a subdivision of the speech act category "questions" restricted to medication related content. Such categories have been used by Byrne and Long (1976) and Terasaki et al. (1984). However, a coding system using conjunctive categories that attempts to be comprehensive quickly becomes unwieldy because there are so many possible combinations.

Mixed systems contain categories from more than one meta-class. For example, the Bales (1950) scheme is composed largely of speech act categories (e.g., "asks for opinion"), but also includes "shows tension," a nonverbal behavior. In mixed systems, mutually exclusive definitions are impossible. For example, a person could "ask for an opinion" and "show tension" at the same time. Resolving such coding conflicts requires rules of priority that tend to distort the frequency of the lower priority categories.

We recommend multidimensional coding—selecting schemes from more than one meta-class and using each scheme independently. This allows a multidimensional view of the interaction without blurring the distinctions between the classes. Examples of multidimensional classifications can be found in Cassell and Skopec (1977), Alroy et al. (1984), Rutter and Cox (1981), Roter (1985), and Diers and Leonard (1966).

SEGMENTS OF THE MEDICAL INTERVIEW

Unlike psychotherapy sessions, medical interactions involve at least three distinct activities: collection of a medical history, physical examination, and negotiation of a therapeutic plan. Since these three components involve different verbal exchanges (Stiles et al., 1979c, Stiles et al., 1982), it is important to clarify which sections of the interview are being recorded, coded, and analyzed. In some of the early studies of medical interactions (Davis, 1971), different segments of the interview were recorded and coded, making it impossible to compare these studies with others. For the same reason, it is important to consider each segment of the interview independently when relating specific codes to outcomes of care. For example, an interview that has a particularly long physical examination segment will probably contain many directives (advisements) as the physician tells the patient to sit up or breathe deeply. Since these utterances might not be appropriate during the conclusion when the physician negotiates a therapeutic plan, the physical exam segment should be excluded if one wants to study exchanges of negotiations between patients and physicians.

WHY ARE THERE SO MANY CODING SCHEMES?

Investigators devise new schemes because they are dissatisfied with old ones. Although the result is confusion in the literature, standardization on a scheme that does not meet investigators needs is clearly worse (Inui and Carter, 1985). Presumably, as better systems are developed (or the merits of existing systems recognized), investigators will naturally gravitate towards these.

However, within meta-classes, there seems to be considerable consensus on some of the categories. Researchers who have done comparative studies of coding systems (e.g., Brownbridge et al., 1986; Inui et al., 1982) could help by reporting the extent to which coders apply apparently similar categories to the same speech units. When investigators do use comparable categories, patients' and physicians' use of these categories is remarkably similar (Heszen-Klemens and Lapinska, 1984; Stiles et al., 1979c). The implication is that patient and physician roles are very stable and robust, and that the verbal components of these roles are well captured by verbal (particularly speech act) coding systems.

THE CORRELATION CRITERION PROBLEM

The standard criterion for judging the value of a coding scheme in medical studies is the degree to which coding categories correlate with outcome measures such as patient satisfaction, compliance, or symptom relief. Although recent reviewers such as Pendleton (1983) and Inui and Carter (1985) have pointed out that correlational designs are limited in their inability to demonstrate causal relationships, and have called for experimental process-outcome research, their recommendations suggest that correlational criteria be used to evaluate systems of process coding. Patients and physicians, like any human being, are highly responsive. They give and receive signals as to what each requires in the interaction. At the very simplest level, people who require information are likely to ask questions. People who are in distress are likely to reveal that distress. Respondents, particularly physicians, are likely to react appropriately.

While physicians' responses to patients will usually be correlated with patients' needs, it is false to assume that the physicians' responses per se will be correlated with the outcome of the visit. For example, information about the relation of sodium to blood pressure is probably causally important to hypertensive patients' adherence to a low-salt diet. Since physicians are an important source of this information, their delivery of it in an interview may contribute to patient compliance. However, physicians realize that not all patients on all visits require the same amount of information; some may remember the information from previous visits or may have obtained it from other sources. Statistically then, there might be variation both in physician information-giving (responsive to patient needs), and in patient adherence (for reasons other than lack of information), but these would not be expected to correlate, even though the information-giving may be crucially and causally important to patient adherence.

We point this out as a limitation of the usual correlational procedure for testing process-outcome relations (Stiles, 1988).

Our dilemma is that we have no clear alternative for assessing the effect of patient-physician interactions on outcomes. Two general approaches, though flawed, may provide partial resolution to the dilemma.

EXPERIMENTAL STUDIES OF PROCESS

As reviewers such as Pendleton (1983) and Inui and Carter (1985) have noted, experimental manipulation of process variables in the interaction, with subsequent measurement of outcomes of interest, would provide the most direct evidence for which processes are important. Cox's studies (in Chapter 7) demonstrated that when psychiatrists alternated between certain interviewing styles, the quality of the information varied with the style of interviewing (Cox et al., 1981). Putnam et al. (1988), however, could demonstrate no difference in patient satisfaction, compliance, or symptom status between physicians trained to elicit expositions from patients and give them explanations about their illnesses. One explanation for the failure to demonstrate any difference was the fact that physicians before training were already providing high levels of explanations.

There are two difficulties with the experimental approach. First, on ethical grounds, it may be very difficult to ask physicians to decrease certain verbal behaviors, yet as shown in the studies just mentioned, it may be necessary to do this in order to show any effect. Carried to extremes, a study may try to prohibit physicians from giving information or allowing patients to give expositions. While this may have a dramatic effect on outcomes, it would clearly be ethically unacceptable. Second, the responsiveness of human interactions may tend to compensate for experimental manipulations. A physician told to decrease explanations may compensate by giving more relevant explanations or by allowing patients to talk more or ask more questions. If undetected, or uncorrected in the analyses, these compensations may confound the main experimental effect.

MICROANALYSIS

Another approach to the study of interviews is the use of microanalytic techniques such as conversation analysis and discourse analysis, sequence analysis, and interpersonal process recall. These techniques have been developed for research in other types of interactions, such as social conversations or psychotherapy, but they also hold promise for studies of medical interactions.

Conversation and discourse analysis are detailed, multidimensional analyses of each utterance or nonverbal act, studied in relation to the context. Developed in studies of everyday social interactions (Goodwin, 1981; Sacks et al., 1974), they have been applied to psychotherapy (Labov and Fanshell, 1977) and medical interviews (Frankel, 1984; West, 1984). The intensity and detail of the analysis make it difficult to apply these techniques to more than brief segments of an interview. The data are often qualitative rather than quantitative.

Sequence analysis is the examination of the transitional probabilities among different scored categories—the study of what follows what. This is a quantitative approach, analyzed using Markov chains or lag correlations. The technique has been widely applied, particularly in the study of marital and family interactions (Allison and Liker, 1982; Bakeman, 1978; Dumas, 1984; Gottman, 1979). There have been a few attempts to apply it to medical interactions (Frankel, 1984; Meeuwesen, 1986; Stiles et al., 1984). Samph and Templeton (1978) have developed a modified sequence analysis whereby a matrix is constructed for an interaction showing the frequency with which codes follow each other. Thus, it is possible to demonstrate how often a physician's question is followed by a patient's response.

Reviewers have strongly recommended sequence analysis (Inui and Carter, 1985; Wasserman and Inui, 1983) as offering a window into the details of the process of the interview not provided by the usual aggregation techniques, an advantage shared by the other microanalytic techniques noted here. One disadvantage of sequence analysis is that it requires large numbers of interviews, coded with exhaustive, mutually exclusive categories, in order to obtain stable estimates of transition probabilities. Furthermore, some early work (Stiles et al., 1984) indicates that the results of sequence analysis often reveal linguistic constraints, such as the tendency for answers to occur more frequently after questions than at other times, rather than phenomena of more immediate medical relevance. Nevertheless, sequence analysis can clearly contribute to the detailed understanding of interviewing processes.

Interpersonal Process Recall, developed by Kagan (1975), consists of playing back segments of videotaped interviews to participants and eliciting reports of their mental processes at the time. This technique can provide startlingly rich accounts of process; interactants have a wide range of thoughts and feelings during an interview, which they can recall when they review their taped interactions (Frankel and Beckman, 1982; Terasaki et al, 1984).

The microanalytic techniques do not directly answer the question of which processes can be causally related to outcomes of medical care. Although we share Inui and Carter's (1985) impatience with research in patient-physician communications, we realize that until we have a better understanding of the process of this communication, it may be impossible to know how to select the right processes and the right outcomes for our research.

We hope that our attempts to construct "meta-classes" for the wide variety of coding schemes that have been developed for patient-physician interactions has helped clarify the need to arrive at some common definitions of the interview process. Our field may be similar to that of oncology before methods of classifying cancers were agreed upon, when oncologists could not agree on treatment protocols, for they had no way of determining who should be treated with what and what difference it made anyway. Once they had agreed on the terminology and criteria for classifying and staging cancers, they could begin to build on each other's clinical experiences. As we have tried to demonstrate above, different coding schemes of patient-physician interactions serve different goals. Therefore, rather than considering developing one common scheme, it might be possible to develop several standard schemes that can be recommended for specific purposes.

16

Outcome Based Research on Doctor-Patient Communication: A Review

Howard Beckman
Sherrie H. Kaplan
Richard Frankel

Sections 2 and 4 of this book describe two parallel processes evolving over the past 20 years: practice theory and research. As research methods became more sophisticated and researchers more experienced in defining behaviors of interest, practice theory also advanced dramatically. Educators encouraged the alliance by focusing physicians' attention on listening to patients' problems, negotiating plans for evaluation and treatment, and incorporating patients' views and beliefs into the therapeutic strategies.

Central to the success of this research and education has been the collaboration of practitioners with experts from such fields as anthropology, linguistics, sociology, and psychology. The medical encounter has been studied from the perspectives of the practitioner, the patient, and society. The interplay between these perspectives, captured by interdisciplinary teams, has resulted in many of the critical advances in our understanding of the factors influencing the process of care and the outcomes of that process.

Such a group met at the International Conference on Doctor-Patient Communication to define and classify outcome variables relevant to research in the field. The purpose of this chapter is to summarize those discussions in a manner that will assist investigators in their selection of the appropriate outcome measure for their particular study.

The term "outcome" in health care is defined as an observable consequence of prior activity occurring after an encounter, or some portion of the encounter, is completed. Outcomes are best categorized by their point of occurrence in the process of health care delivery.

Process outcomes occur within the medical encounter (see Table 16.1). An example of a process outcome is Beckman and Frankel's (1984) work, which demonstrates the effect of interruption on completion of the patient's agenda. This type of research has two major objectives. The first is to recognize successful interactional behavior and improve the quality of interaction, ultimately to improve subsequent longer-term outcomes. This approach can identify behaviors and interaction sequences that produce desired process outcomes such as mutuality, agreement, or empathy. Attention to specific details of the early interaction that have the most significant effects on later process is the first step in designing more effective interventions.

The second use of process outcomes is in demonstrating the cause and effect relationship of an intervention. For example, Greenfield et al. (1985) used process outcomes to demonstrate the success of increasing patient assertiveness. They measured the level of patients' participation, effectiveness of patient information seeking, patients' direction of the discourse, and opinion sharing. These process outcomes demonstrated changes in behavior between pre- and post-intervention encounters, and in comparison to a control group. Increased patient assertiveness in the experimental group was identified as the cause of improvement in the long-term outcome of interest (functional status of patients with peptic ulcer disease). Similar work is described in detail in Chapter 17.

Short-term outcomes can be assessed immediately after the medical encounter is completed (see Table 16.1). The prototype short-term outcomes are patient satisfaction and intention to comply with a medical regimen. As with process outcomes, short-term outcomes have been used to test associations between aspects of the medical interview and their effects. Because some researchers have found associations between satisfaction and compliance, satisfaction has often been substituted for compliance, which is more difficult to assess. The limitation of using short-term outcomes is that the long-term effects are unknown. A patient may be satisfied in the short run but may not comply with medical recommendations in the longer run.

TABLE 16.1   Health Care Outcomes Requiring Study

PROCESS OUTCOMES

1.   Coparticipation/mutuality
2.   Patient assertiveness
3.   Provider empathy/encouragement
4.   Direct evaluation of medication compliance
5.   Agreement on evaluation, treatment options
6.   Solicitation for patients' attribution of concerns
7.   Completed solicitation of patient's concerns
8.   Frequency of interruption
9.   Frequency of open ended questions

SHORT-TERM OUTCOMES

1.   Patient satisfaction
2.   Tension release
3.   Health/disease knowledge acquisition
4.   Doctor satisfaction
5.   Intention to comply
6.   Acceptance of recommended services

INTERMEDIATE OUTCOMES

1.   Adherence/compliance
2.   Accuracy of diagnosis
3.   Anxiety reduction
4.   Health/disease knowledge
5.   Completion of recommended service
6.   Increased self-esteem
7.   Increased self-confidence
8.   Altered locus of control

LONG-TERM OUTCOMES

1.   Symptom resolution
2.   Physiologic status
3.   Behavioral status
4.   Functional status
5.   Anxiety reduction
6.   Quality of life
7.   Global health perception
8.   Costs of care/utilization
9.   Work loss
10.   Cure rate
11.   Survival

Intermediate outcomes indirectly measure a response to evaluation or therapy (see Table 16.1). Compliance is an example, because achievement of the goal may not necessarily result in a significant or even a desirable health outcome. For example, the goal may be to improve medication compliance in patients with high blood pressure, but compliant patients may have no greater reduction in blood pressure than a control group. As the concepts of patient negotiation and assertiveness are developed, our framework for compliance may change dramatically. Physicians may actively encourage patients to criticize their recommendations in the hope of creating more realistic treatment plans and goals.

Until recently few studies looked at *long-term outcomes* (see Table 16.1). Clearly, one of the signs of a maturing field of investigation is the researchers' willingness to submit their hypotheses to more rigorous testing. Inui and Carter, in Chapter 14, categorize these investigations as subexperimental/hypothesis testing and/or interventional, depending on the method. We define long-term outcomes as direct measures of therapeutic or evaluation responses. Examples can come from the biological, psychological, or sociological spheres, and include such effects as reduced blood pressure, improved quality of life, and survival. Two previously cited studies by Starfield et al. (1979, 1981) are examples of subexperimental/hypothesis testing involving long-term outcomes. The long-term outcome was problem resolution as judged by physician and patient. The variable that most positively correlated with problem resolution in both studies was agreement between patient and physician on the problems requiring follow-up.

The next level of investigation involves testing a hypothesis using a randomized, controlled trial. Greenfield et al. (1985) have conducted several randomized controlled trials to test the effect of patient assertiveness training on long-term health outcomes. Their most recent studies are described in Chapter 17.

The menu of important outcomes shown in Table 16.1 contains a wide variety of potential variables. The choice of a variable for any one study is a value-laden decision. For example, outcomes considered important by a health care economist might be viewed quite differently by individual patients; the current emphasis on cost containment might encourage a researcher in health economics to select reduced length of hospital stay as a positive outcome, while consumers of health care might look at the same outcome as a threat to the quality of their care. In another example, physicians and patients might regard quality of life as an important outcome for people with terminal illness, while health care economists and insurers might discount its value.

CONCLUSIONS

The past two decades have been extremely exciting for students and researchers of the medical encounter. From initial, relatively unsophisticated methods, collaborative research has now fostered a more integrated framework and methods for demonstrating the reciprocal effects of physiological and psychosocial functioning. The future of outcome-based research in health services holds great promise, especially as researchers begin to address the long-term outcomes listed in Table 16.1.

Because of research with an integrated theoretical framework, increasingly sophisticated methodology, and interdisciplinary collaboration, interviewing skills are being recognized as an important influence on the outcomes of health care. We look forward to exciting advances in this area in the near future.

17

Impact of the Doctor-Patient Relationship on the Outcomes of Chronic Disease

Sherrie H. Kaplan
Sheldon Greenfield
John E. Ware, Jr.

INTRODUCTION

Researchers must always ask the awkward and difficult to answer questions: "So what? What difference does doctor-patient communication make to health care?" Research in doctor-patient relationships has reached that juncture. Current cost-containment efforts that are changing the manner in which health services are being delivered may be placing the doctor-patient relationship at risk for compromise. Pressured to see more patients and reduce the costs per patient, doctors may be spending less time counseling, educating, and negotiating with patients. So what? Does the manner in which health care services are delivered have any recognizable, meaningful impact on patients' health outcomes? Do changes in elements of the doctor-patient relationship lead to changes in patients' health? It is a critical time for policy makers, medical educators, health care financiers, consumers, and health services researchers to come to terms with these questions.

Health services researchers have focused empirical study on the impact of the doctor-patient relationship on patient satisfaction (Bartlett et al., 1984; Bertakis, 1977; DiMatteo and Hays 1980; DiMatteo et al., 1980; Doyle and Ware, 1977; Hall et al., 1981; Kallen and Stephenson, 1981; Korsch et al., 1968; Ley, 1982; Roter, 1977; Stiles et al.,

1979b; Weinberger et al., 1981; Willson and McNamara, 1982; Woolley et al., 1978). As well, patient compliance has been studied (Bartlett, et al., 1984; Davis, 1968; Francis et al., 1969; Hulka et al., 1976; Roter, 1977; Svarstad, 1976; Willson and McNamara, 1982). There are a number of reasons why these variables are appropriate bench marks for assessing the effectiveness of doctor-patient relationships. Dissatisfied patients are more likely to disenroll from health plans (Davies et al., 1986), "doctor-shop" (Kasteler et al., 1976), initiate malpractice suits (Ware et al., 1978), and ignore medical advice (Hayes-Bautista, 1976; Haynes et al., 1979). As patients become increasingly sophisticated in their demands of medical care and in their abilities to evaluate the performance of doctors, their opinions must be taken into account in evaluating the quality of care, including the doctor-patient relationship (Haug and Lavin, 1979; Report Card, 1985; Vaccarino, 1977). At least one medical society has recognized the importance of patient satisfaction in evaluating the humanistic skills of doctors (Patrick et al., 1983).

Satisfaction alone, however, does not address the patient's health status. As a function of their own values or expectations, patients may be satisfied with inadequate health care (Korsch et al., 1968; Woolley et al., 1978) or suboptimal health outcomes (Patrick et al., 1983). In one of the few studies relating patient satisfaction to patient health status, more satisfied patients were found to be less healthy than dissatisfied patients (Patrick et al., 1983). Patients' evaluations of their health care, especially the interpersonal aspects of that care, may therefore be confounded with the patients' values, needs, and expectations, handicapping patient satisfaction as a comprehensive, objective barometer of doctors' behavior. Nevertheless, because patient satisfaction is an important determinant of other aspects of care that can directly influence outcomes, such as frequent changes in doctors, and because patient satisfaction has shown a consistent relationship to elements of the doctor-patient relationship, it should be included in a comprehensive assessment of the quality of that relationship.

Patient compliance has also been used as an outcome measure for assessing the effectiveness of the doctor-patient relationship. Like satisfaction, however, patient compliance does not provide information about patients' health status. First, in the case of chronic disease, even strict adherence to a medical treatment regimen does not always guarantee a good health outcome for the patient. Second, intuitively, compliance with treatment recommendations should be the natural consequence of a doctor-patient relationship in which information about rationale and options for treatment, side effects of medications, nature and need for follow-up and monitoring is provided persuasively by the doctor. However, this assumption presumes that the patient is solely motivated to comply as a function of the compelling nature of the medical advice provided by the doctor. More probably, patients chose to comply with or ignore medical advice based on a complex set of factors, only a few of which have to do with the doctor-patient relationship. Methodologic variations in both the specific elements of the doctor-patient relationship chosen for study along with the methods for measuring patient compliance, and the atheoretical nature of the majority of research in this area, have made it difficult to synthesize the existing research findings (Inui and Carter, 1985; Pendleton, 1983). Compliance is therefore limited as a measure of the overall quality of the doctor-patient relationship.

Least used in empirical studies of the quality of doctor-patient relationships are measures of patients' health status. The relationship between specific elements of conversation and changes in physical health has been studied more widely in nonmedical situations, such as the effect of conversation between spouses on blood pressure, than in the context of the doctor-patient relationship (Ewart et al., 1983; Marburg et al., 1979; Williams et al., 1972). The few studies relating doctor-patient conversation to patients' health outcomes have favored post-hoc patient reports of that conversation over direct observation, and have focused on patients' reports of symptom status over more generic measures of patients' functioning or physiologic measures of patients' health. Nevertheless, in six of the eight studies relating conversation between doctors and patients to patients' health outcomes, a positive relationship between such conversation and patients' subsequent health status was found (see Table 17.1). Improvement in or resolution of the patient's health problem was found to occur more often when there was agreement between doctors and patients about the nature and severity of the patient's health problem by four separate groups of investigators (Bass et al., 1986; Headache Study Group, 1986; Starfield et al., 1981; Stewart et al., 1979). In studies of the effects of the doctor-patient relationship on physiologic health status of the patient, Orth et al. (1987) found improvements in follow-up blood pressures among patients who were allowed uninterrupted expression of their health concerns by their doctors during office visits.

TABLE 17.1   Studies Relating Doctor-Patient Conversation to Patients' Outcomes

Investigator	Data Source	Health Outcome	Effect
Orth et al. (1987)	Audio tapes	Blood pressure control	Observed
Starfield et al. (1981)	Questionnaire	Problem resolution	Observed
Stewart et al. (1979)	Questionnaire	Perceived recovery	Observed
Bass et al (1986)	Questionnaire	Problem resolution	Observed
Headache Study (1986)	Questionnaire	Problem resolution	Observed
Woolley et al. (1978)	Questionnaire	Functional status	Not observed
Hulka et al. (1975)	Questionnaire	Blood sugar control	Not observed
Kaplan et al. (1985)	Audio tapes	Blood pressure control blood sugar control	Observed

If the ultimate aim of medical care is to produce optimal health outcomes, then the evaluation of the effectiveness of any component of that process, including the doctor-patient relationship, must be subjected to that standard. The ultimate questions for research involving the quality of the doctor-patient relationship are, therefore: Does it change patients' health status? If so, how?

There are several possible ways to approach these questions. Naturally occurring changes in patients' health status over time could be observed in relation to specific communication behaviors, or patterns of those behaviors. Alternatively, interventions designed to change specific aspects of the doctor-patient relationship, such as conversational behavior, could be devised. The impact of changes in the doctor-patient relationship, as a function of these interventions, on patients' health status could then be observed.

We have focused our research efforts on the latter. In three separate randomized controlled trials of an intervention designed to change patient participation in the medical care process, we measured both doctor-patient conversation and patients' health status (using survey reports and physiologic measures) before and after the intervention (a time interval ranging from 6 to 18 months).

METHODS

All three studies described in this chapter were designed as randomized controlled trials, and were conducted among patients with chronic disease, specifically, ulcer disease (Greenfield et al., 1985), hypertension (Kaplan et al., 1985) and diabetes (Greenfield et al., 1988). At enrollment in the study, audiotape recordings of doctor-patient conversation were obtained to provide baseline data. At this same visit, patients were given a self-administered questionnaire that was completed and returned by mail prior to their next office visit. Baseline physiologic measures were also collected at the enrollment visit. At the time of their next regularly scheduled office visit, patients were randomized either to experimental or control group, and the appropriate intervention was administered. Physicians saw both experimental and control group patients, and were blind to group membership. The conversation between doctor and patient was also audiotaped on this visit. Patients were seen again by the research assistant for a second intervention session at the time of their second regularly scheduled office visit following enrollment. This visit was also audiotaped and the physiologic measures that served as outcome measures for the study were collected. From 8 to 12 weeks following this last visit, patients were mailed a second questionnaire that included measures of functional and perceived health status, preference for involvement in medical decision-making, satisfaction with care, and knowledge of disease.

Description of the Study Samples

The patient study groups included patients with ulcer disease who attended a local Veteran's Administration Hospital outpatient clinic, hypertensive patients at a local free clinic, and diabetic patients being seen in the endocrinology clinic of a university teaching hospital. The sociodemographic characteristics of each study sample have been presented in Table 17.2. There were statistically significant differences in years of education completed ($F(1,206)=8.65$, $p < .01$) and in proportions of females. There were also substantial differences in the ethnic composition of the study samples.

TABLE 17.2   Sociodemographic Characteristics of Study Samples[1]

Patient Characteristics	Ulcers (N = 45)	Hypertension (N = 105)	Diabetes (N = 59)
Age (years)	55	54	50
	(12)	(13)	(14)
Education (years)	13	8	13
	(3)	(5)	(3)
Percent female	2	68	49
Percent Spanish speaking[2]	0	62	0

[1]Data in rows 1 and 2 are means with standard deviations in parentheses below.

[2]Exclusively Spanish speaking; patients in the ulcer, diabetes, and breast cancer samples were selected to exclude those who could not speak and read English.

Measurement of Doctor-Patient Conversation

The coding scheme chosen to analyze audiotape recordings of doctor-patient conversation contained a total of 30 conversational codes. These codes were divided among three categories: control, communication, and affect. This scheme, derived from Bales's Interaction Analysis (Adler and Enelow, 1966; Adler et al., 1970), has been described in detail elsewhere (Greenfield et al., 1985). Indicators of the style of doctor-patient conversation from the basic codes in this scheme included doctor control, patient control, information exchange and positive and negative affect expressed by doctors and patients. Each of these indicators was computed as a sum of the conversational codes for doctors and for patients within each of the three categories (control, communication, and affect). In addition, we grouped the conversational codes into empirically derived combinations of doctor and patient conversational behavior including a patient effectiveness index (number of factual statements by doctors divided by the sum of all controlling conversational utterances by the patient); communication ratio (proportion of patient to doctor conversational utterances during the visit); and one of three patterns describing the total encounter: doctor-direction (characterized by questions, interruptions by the doctor and responses by the patient), patient direction (characterized by questions, interruptions by the patient with responses by the doctor), and affect/opinion exchange (combining any display of emotion or statement of personal opinion by doctor or patient).

Measurement of Health Outcome

The measures used to represent patients' health status included physiologic and survey measures (see Table 17.3). Blood sugar control among diabetic patients was measured by level of glycosylated hemoglobin (HbA1); the average of three consecutive sitting diastolic blood pressure readings was used to measure hypertension control. Survey measures of patients' health status included a 13-item shortened version of the RAND Functional Status Questionnaire, measuring patients' abilities to perform usual daily activities.

Statistical Analysis

All multi-item scales, including the derived indicators of doctor-patient conversation, were tested for internal consistency reliability using Cronbach's alpha formula (Cronbach, 1951), and were shown to be satisfactory (alpha > .65) for group comparisons. Pearson product-moment correlations were computed for measures of doctor-patient conversation and measures of patients' health outcomes. For purposes of presentation, scores on the measures of doctor-patient conversation were dicotomized at the mean into high and low scoring groups. Mean scores on the measures of functional limitations and physiologic outcomes were determined for each of these dicotomized groups. Analyses of covariance, controlling for baseline measures of doctor-patient conversation and patient health status, were computed separately for the functional limitations and each physiologic health outcome measure. To facilitate presentation, t-tests for differences in mean scores on health outcome measures for each of the dicotomized doctor-patient conversation groups are presented. To assess the impact of changes in doctor-patient conversation on patients' health outcomes, change scores were computed for each of the conversation indicators and for each of the health outcome measures; correlations between these change scores were computed.

RESULTS

Tables 17.4 and 17.5 present the mean health outcome scores, measured at follow-up, for patients who scored above and below the mean and for patients whose doctors scored above and below the mean for each of the conversational categories, measured at baseline. Separate analyses of covariance performed for each of the conversational categories, controlling for baseline conversational behavior and patient health status, showed results consistent with those presented in Tables 17.4 and 17.5. We observed similar results when this analysis was performed separately for each of the three study samples; accordingly, data presented in these tables represent a combined sample (N=209).

As evident from Table 17.4, the conversational behavior of both patient and doctor showed a relatively consistent relationship to patients' functional limitations at follow-up.

Patients who were more controlling, gave less information, were more effective in eliciting information from the doctor, and showed more emotion during the baseline visit reported fewer functional limitations at follow-up. Patients whose doctors were less controlling gave more information and showed more emotion, especially negative emotion (including tension, anxiety, strain, self-consciousness, frustration, impatience), during the baseline visit reported fewer functional limitations at follow-up. Of the three interaction pattern measures defined in Table 17.3, only the affect/opinion exchange pattern was significantly related to patients' functional limitations and is presented in last row of Table 17.4.

Table 17.5 presents the mean blood glucose and diastolic blood pressures of patients who themselves score above and below the mean and of patients whose doctors score above and below the mean for each of the conversational behaviors. Paralleling the results for functional limitations, patients who were more controlling, expressed more emotion (particularly negative emotion), gave less information, and were more effective in eliciting information from the doctor during the office

TABLE 17.3   Description of Measures

Measure	# of Items	When Measured	Meaning of High Score	Definition	Data Source	Scoring
I. Physician-Patient Interaction Indicators						
Level of patient participation	NA	Baseline	More patient control	Control attempts by patient during interaction	Tapes	Sum of all controlling utterances made by patient (that is, those intended to influence behavior of the physician or to control the nature of the conversation, such as interruptions, suggestions, assertions)
		Baseline	More patient involvement	Ratio of patient to physician utterances	Tapes	Sum of all patient utterances during the encounter divided by all physician utterances, an indicator of patient assertiveness relative to the physician
Effectiveness of patient information seeking	NA	Baseline	More effective information seeking	Ratio of physicians' information-conveying statements to patients' control attempts	Tapes	Sum of all factual statements made by the physician divided by the sum of all patient controlling utterances; an indicator of patients' ability to elicit information effectively from the physician
Interaction pattern	NA	Baseline	More doctor direction	Physician direction of interaction	Tapes	Sum of all physician controlling utterances and all patient factual statements divided by length of encounter in minutes; portion of the encounter directed by the physician
		Baseline	More patient direction	Patient direction of interaction	Tapes	Sum of all patient controlling utterances and all patient factual statements divided by length of encounter in minutes; portion of the encounter directed by the physician

236

		More affect and opinions	Baseline	Affect-opinion sharing between physician and patient	Tapes	Sum of all affect (emotion) expressed by physicians and patients, plus all non-factual opinion statements of physicians and patients divided by length of the encounter in minutes; portion of the encounter; portion of the encounter reflecting personal involvement
II. Physiologic Measures of Health						
Blood sugar	1	Poorer control of diabetes	Baseline	Level of glycosylated hemoglobin, measured using boronate affinity column kit (Endocrine Sciences, Tarzana, CA)	Lab reports	Continuous; range = $6 \leq 15$
Blood pressure	1	Poorer control of hypertension	Baseline	Level of diastolic pressure; average of three consecutive seated readings	Medical record	Continuous; range = $60 \leq 125$
III. Survey Measures of Health						
Functional Limitations Index[.]	13	More limitation	Enrollment and follow-up	Limitations imposed by illness on physical, role, social, mobility	Questionnaire- sample item: "Are you unable to drive a car because of your health?" (Mobility)	1 = yes, 2 = no; range = 0-10

TABLE 17.4   Doctor-Patient Conversation and Patients' Functional Limitations (N = 209)

Conversation Measure[2]	Patient/Doctor		Functional Limitations Index[3]	t[4]
Control	Patient	High	3.7 (1.8)	−2.43*
		Low	4.5 (2.0)	
	Doctor	High	4.4 (2.1)	
		Low	3.8 (1.5)	
Positive Affect	Patient	High	4.3 (2.4)	
		Low	4.3 (3.1)	0
	Doctor	High	4.4 (1.9)	
		Low	3.6 (1.9)	1.62
Negative Affect	Patient	High	3.8 (1.7)	
		Low	4.5 (1.9)	−1.50
	Doctor	High	4.1 (2.1)	
		Low	5.2 (1.4)	−2.37*
Information Giving	Patient	High	4.6 (2.2)	
		Low	2.9 (2.6)	2.71*
	Doctor	High	3.6 (1.6)	
		Low	4.9 (2.1)	−2.67*
Effectiveness Index	Both	High	3.9 (1.8)	
		Low	5.0 (2.0)	−2.20*
Affect-Opinion Exchange	Both	High	4.0 (2.1)	
		Low	5.3 (1.3)	−2.87*

*$p < .05$

[1]Data presented are means with standard deviations in parentheses.
[2]Conversational measures were determined at baseline.
[3]Functional limitations were measured at follow-up.
[4]Based on comparison of group means with pooled variance.

visit had lower blood glucose levels (diabetic patients) and lower diastolic blood pressure levels (hypertensive patients) at follow-up.

TABLE 17.5   Doctor-Patient Conversation and Patients' Physiologic Health Outcomes

Communication Measure	Patient/ Doctor		Blood Glucose[3] (N = 59)		t[4]	Diastolic Blood Pressure[5] (N = 105)		t[4]
Control	Patient	High	8.6	(1.8)		84.7	(7.9)	
		Low	9.8	(2.2)	−2.29*	94.5	(8.6)	−6.06*
	Doctor	High	9.9	(2.1)		100.1	(10.4)	
		Low	8.7	(1.4)	2.59*	91.6	(8.7)	2.32*
Positive Affect	Patient	High	9.2	(2.0)		93.5	(8.6)	
		Low	9.8	(1.6)	−1.28	92.9	(9.3)	.34
	Doctor	High	10.5	(1.3)		96.0	(10.0)	
		Low	9.3)	(2.0)	2.72*	91.3	(9.1)	1.29
Negative Affect	Patient	High	8.8	(1.4)		83.3	(7.6)	−7.37*
		Low	10.0	(1.8)	−2.85*	95.5	(9.2)	
	Doctor	High	9.4	(1.6)		87.1	(8.1)	
		Low	11.1	(2.0)	−3.47*	97.9	(9.9)	−4.78*
Information Giving	Patient	High	10.6	(1.9)		95.6	(10.1)	
		Low	9.0	(1.3)	−3.15*	90.5	(7.8)	2.91*
	Doctor	High	9.2	(1.3)		83.7	(9.1)	
		Low	10.1	(2.1)	−1.97	96.5	(9.5)	−3.64*
Effectiveness Index		High	9.3	(1.6)		83.9	(8.1)	
	Both	Low	11.8	(2.4)	−4.69*	92.5	(9.2)	−5.06*
Affect-Opinion Exchange		High	8.9	(1.7)		84.1	(9.1)	
	Both	Low	10.8	(1.2)	−4.97*	97.4	(10.6)	−6.87*

*p < .05

[1]Data presented in the tables are means with standard deviations in parentheses.
[2]Conversational measures were determined at baseline.
[3]Blood Glucose was measured as hemoglobin A1C; values were obtained at follow-up.
[4]Based on comparison of group means with pooled variance.
[5]Average of three seated diastolic blood pressure readings; values were obtained at follow-up.

TABLE 17.6   Effects of the Interventions on Patients' Functional Limitations

| Study Sample | | Functional Limitations | | t^2 |
		Experimental	Control	
Diabetes (N = 59)	Pre	2.69 (2.14)	3.57 (2.98)	3.19
	Post	1.31 (1.91)	3.30 (3.09)	
Hypertension (N = 102)	Pre	2.91 (2.04)	3.11 (3.01)	4.04*
	Post	1.71 (1.67)	3.40 (2.79)	
Ulcers[2] (N = 44)	Pre	3.11 (2.34)	3.45 (3.68)	2.89*
	Post	1.17 (2.58)	3.71 (3.07)	

*p < .05

[1]Based on differences between groups adjusted for baseline scores in separate analyses of covariance.
[2]Baseline data reflect aggregated health status measure obtained by taking best linear combination of four health status measures from principal components analysis.[41]

Also paralleling the findings for functional limitations, patients whose doctors were less controlling, showed more negative emotion, gave more information during the office visit, and had lower blood glucose and blood pressure levels.

The effect of the interventions on patients' health outcomes is presented in Tables 17.6 and 17.7. Patients in the experimental groups reported fewer functional limitations at follow-up, controlled for baseline functioning, than patients in the control group for all three study samples (see Table 17.6). Similarly, patients in the experimental group had better blood glucose control and better blood pressure control than those in the control group, adjusted for baseline measures (see Table 17.7). The experimental intervention also affected doctor-patient conversation. Patients in the experimental group were more controlling, more

TABLE 17.7   Effects of the Interventions on Physiologic Health Outcomes

		Experimental	*Control*	t^2
	Pre	10.6	10.3	.55
		(2.1)	(2.0)	
Blood Sugar (HbA1) (N = 59)				
	Post	9.1	10.6	2.81*
		(1.9)	(2.2)	
	Pre	95	93	.80
		(11)	(14)	
Diastolic Blood Pressure (N = 44)				
	Post	83	91	−5.00*
		(8)	(8)	

*p < .05

[1]Data presented are means with standard deviations in parentheses.
[2]Based on comparison of group means with pooled variance.

effective in eliciting information from their doctors, showed more emotion, and were more successful in engaging their doctors in discussions involving opinions and emotional exchange than patients in the control group (data presented elsewhere in Greenfield et al., 1985; Greenfield et al., 1988; Kaplan et al., 1985).

Were the effects of the interventions on doctor-patient conversation and patient outcomes related? Table 17.8 shows the relationship between changes in doctor-patient conversation and changes in health outcomes from baseline to follow-up in the three study samples. As evident, there is a consistent relationship between changes in patients' behavior and improvements in patients' health outcomes, both functional and physiologic. Patients who were more controlling, showed more emotion, particularly negative emotion, and improved their effectiveness in eliciting information from their doctors showed improvements in functional limitations, in blood glucose control, and in blood pressure control. Patients of doctors who were more controlling had worse health outcomes at follow-up. Patients and doctors who spent

TABLE 17.8   Relationship of Changes in Doctor-Patient Conversation to Changes in Health Outcomes (n = 209)

Communication Measure[2]	Functional Limitations[3] (Ulcers)	Outcome Measure Blood Glucose[4] (Diabetes)	Diastolic Blood Pressure[5] (Hypertension)
Patient Control	−.27*	−.31*	−.19
Patient Positive Affect	−.05	−.11	−.18
Patient Negative Affect	−.25*	−.27*	−.39*
Patient Information Giving	.07	.04	.22*
Doctor Control	.31	.25*	.36*
Doctor Positive Affect	.17	.07	.11
Doctor Negative Affect	−.37*	−.39*	−.49*
Doctor Information Giving	−.20	−.22	−.26*
Effectiveness Index	−.39*	−.43*	−.29*
Communication Ratio	−.26*	−.29*	−.41*
Doctor-Directed Pattern	.01	.03	.11
Patient-Directed Pattern	−.17	−.09	−.20
Affect-Opinion Exchange Pattern	−.34*	−.37*	−.42*

*p < .05

[1]Data in the table are Pearson product-moment correlations for differences between baseline and follow-up measures of doctor-patient conversation and baseline and follow-up measures of health outcomes.
[2]DYAD indices are computed as indicated in Table 3.
[3]Functional Limitations were measured using the RAND Functional Status Questionnaire (see Table 3).
[4]Hemoglobin A1 was used to measure blood glucose.
[5]Average of three seated diastolic blood pressure readings; values were obtained at follow-up.

proportionally more of their conversation in the affect-opinion exchange conversational pattern had improved health outcomes, both functional and physiologic.

DISCUSSION

Our findings underscore the importance of the specific aspects of the conversation between doctors and patients for patients' health outcomes. We observed, for example, that more patient control (in the form of questions and interruptions) expressed during office visits was associated with improvements in blood sugar and blood pressure control as well as with improvements in functional limitations. Conversely, we observed that more control expressed by doctors was associated with elevated subsequent blood glucose and blood pressure levels, and more functional limitations reported at follow-up. That control expressed during doctor-patient conversations might influence health outcomes is consistent with other studies showing a relationship between the exercise of control in specific situations, even in limited amounts, on improvements in health status (Langer and Rodin, 1976; Rodin, 1983; Schulz, 1976). Current training programs designed to change doctors' interpersonal manner during office visits, although effective in changing other conversational behaviors of doctors, do not emphasize patient involvement in care as it was defined in our studies (Barbee and Feldman, 1970; Inui et al., 1976; Kauss et al., 1980; Lipkin et al., 1984; Werner and Schneider, 1974). Specifically, these programs do not teach doctors to train patients in effective negotiation, in eliciting and weighing options for care, in choosing between competing options, and in stating their (i.e., the patients') preferences. Our studies indicate that these very skills may have important implications for patients' health outcomes.

The type and quality of information exchanged between doctors and patients has long been recognized as an important aspect of the doctor-patient relationship. In studies of and policy surrounding informed consent, the quality of the doctor-patient relationship is evaluated in terms of the information transferred from doctor to patient. Evaluations of the success of informed consent programs have used patients' understanding of the information provided as the outcome measure (Wu and Pearlman, 1988). Little is known about the impact of such information on patients' health outcomes. Data from our studies do not inform the question regarding the content of information that influences patients' health status. However, we have shown that less information supplied by doctors is associated with poorer patient health outcomes. It is possible that doctors are more controlling with (i.e., ask more questions of, interrupt more often, are more directive with), and therefore less prone to provide information to, sicker patients. The clinical agenda with such patients is more complex and the conversational behavior we observed may reflect the doctors' more aggressive pursuit of the diagnosis and work-up of complications. Inconsistent with this interpretation are our findings that experimentally manipulated changes in patients' effectiveness in eliciting more information from their doctors was related to substantial improvements in health outcomes. It is possible that greater information supplied by the doctor, in the form of instruction, education, or explanation, may contribute to patients' understanding, sense of well-being, and/or confidence regarding the management of their disease. Doctors may in fact influence the outcomes of patients with chronic illness, not only by competent medical care, but also by shaping how patients feel about the disease, their sense of commitment to the treatment process, and their ability to control or contain its impact on their lives.

The relationship that we observed between affect or emotion expressed in doctor-patient conversations has been found by other investigators (Hall et al., 1981). It should be noted that in ours and other coding schemes (Roter, 1977; Stewart, 1984), "negative emotion" is defined broadly covering such conversational behaviors as tension, apprehension, impatience, strain, misgivings, stammering, nervous laughter, frustration, anxiety, and self-consciousness. The positive relationship between negative emotion and improved health outcomes may therefore reflect some normal tension between doctors and patients, reflecting a shift in the roles of both. Patients who are more successful in engaging doctors in negotiation may disrupt their usual relationship with the doctor in ways consistent with a healthier posture toward management of their disease. Further research is needed to clarify the nature of the influence of emotion in the context of the doctor-patient relationship and health outcomes, particularly in an era in which researchers (Cope et al., 1986), educators (Kahn et al., 1979), and policy makers (Report Card, 1985) are defining humanism as an important dimension of the quality of doctor-patient relationships.

The manner in which health services are delivered is undergoing rapid and basic changes. Some of these changes will affect doctor-patient relationships, some will not. Longitudinal studies tracking the impacts of these organizational changes on the styles of doctor-patient relationships and, simultaneously, on patients' health outcomes, such as the National Study of Medical Outcomes (Stewart et al., 1988), are needed to address the "so what" of doctor-patient relationships. Our studies suggest that these relationships may be an important bond, with implications for patients' health outcomes. Defining the boundaries of responsibility for care in the context of this relationship and identifying the specific elements of it that must be preserved in order to maximize patient outcomes without compromising the quality of technical care or the doctor-patient relationship is an important ethical, policy, and research direction in the assessment of health care.

18

The Past and the Future of Research in Doctor-Patient Relations

Barbara M. Korsch

There is little need to impress upon patients the importance to medicine of doctor-patient communication; they have long valued this aspect of the caring and curing process. Resistance, however, to the notion that communication skills are critical to good doctoring has come from the medical side of the equation. The traditional model of medicine simply does not regard communication skills as central to the practice of medicine. While sole commitment to the traditional model has lessened over the years, with increasing attention to issues of communication and the ascendancy of biopsychosocial and patient-centered models, medicine is still far from a consensus in this regard.

Having been both witness and participant to this struggle for the past many years, my aim here will not be to give a fully representative account of past and present research—other authors have done that in previous chapters of this book—but rather I will take the luxury of a personal historical perspective.

HISTORICAL PERSPECTIVE

In the late 1940s and early 1950s, there was a general increase in awareness of psychiatric and psychologic concepts, which were increasingly incorporated into education, child rearing, and medical practice. In pediatrics the very successful family-centered child guidance movement began. Through its teamwork—dealing with the child and family as a team on the one hand and incorporating psychiatry, psychology, and social work on the other—it was very valuable to a great many children and families in trouble.

A statement by the Group for the Advancement of Psychiatry dealing with the relationship between pediatrics and child psychiatry was published in 1951. Many of the topics that are of vital concern today were listed then as being essential for study and incorporation into medical practice. Under the heading "knowledge of interviewing techniques," the effective use of time, dealing with anxious argumentative patients, expressing respect for patients, the art of listening, control of the interview, ending the interview, recognition of verbal and nonverbal communication, and the importance of attitudes were all highlighted much as we would today. Moreover, an appreciation for the dynamics and importance of the doctor-patient relationship itself was very much in evidence.

The answers offered in those years tended to consist mostly of incorporating principles and practices from psychiatry or social work into the practice of pediatrics. Pediatricians were enjoined to be better, kinder, and more tolerant. They were asked to adopt psychiatric techniques in their interviews, to listen more, to be more patient, and to use open-ended questions, but it was all done on a "how to" basis, which led to a great deal of intellectual and other dissatisfactions. While the value of psychiatry's contribution was recognized, its importation into pediatrics was not wholly successful. Psychiatric strategies and skills could not be simplistically incorporated into another discipline's framework, and much of the advice missed its mark. They were simply not appropriate for the problems of daily pediatric practice. Pediatricians needed strategies and skills relevant to a pediatric frame of reference.

The effort to provide more scientific and quantitative investigation into doctor-patient communication began to be developed shortly thereafter. My own first collaboration was with Dr. David Levy. Under his tutelage we developed a number of very specific studies of communication between pediatricians and parents and came up with some technical, and very practical, pointers on how to communicate with patients. My own group at the Children's Hospital of Los Angeles and Milton Davis at Cornell Medical Center went on to do some of the best-known work in this area. Our efforts were enthusiastically received by pediatricians because, I believe, they spoke so directly to the clinical problems of their daily practice.

WHAT IS GOOD COMMUNICATION?

One of the problems was then, as it still is now, to find a gold standard by which one could measure effective communication. There were no models, no established norms with which to compare the communication process. During my lifetime there have been many attempts to come up with good outcome variables for doctor-patient communication. As reflected in the important work of Kaplan and associates (Chapter 17) and Beckman and colleagues (Chapter 16), we have become quite sophisticated in the identification and validation of meaningful process and outcome measures for this research. While it is clear that much more needs to be done in this area, the diversity of measures is impressive. The distinction within outcome measures of short-term, intermediate, and long-term variables is helpful in clarifying anticipated results for particular processes. For example, satisfaction (both patient and physician) is conceived as a short-term outcome of the medical interaction and, as such, may be measured immediately following an encounter. Compliance, anxiety reduction, or increased self-esteem and confidence can be considered intermediate outcomes, and it may take some time before effects are evident. Finally, symptom resolution and changes in functional status and quality of life, as well as decreases in morbidity and mortality are long-term outcomes that may need a relatively longer period of follow-up and careful monitoring before their effects are evident.

Our progress is less clear in terms of the actual measurement of the communication process.

There has been a focus on specific units of interaction, specific interaction content, the sequence, the relative degree of structure, and the kinds of questions used (interruptions, etc.). As in many other scientific endeavors, easily measurable aspects of the interaction tend to be measured, to the exclusion of more challenging features. For instance, the task that is addressed in a particular encounter, such as history-taking or patient-education, will sometimes give direction to the analysis, overlooking perhaps a more meaningful process that is common across many tasks. Besides the task, the attributes of the two persons involved in the interaction obviously make a tremendous difference. For example, a videotape of a young white female physician sitting at a desk talking to a dignified older black man who is in the process of tucking his shirt into his trousers, portrays how some very highly charged medical advice is given in a rather paternalistic way. Do our usual techniques of analysis deal with this problem? The setting, the context, and other contributing state variables for the interaction have sometimes been ignored for the sake of purer methodology but should now be given more attention, need to be controlled for, and need sometimes to be treated as important independent variables.

We may be at the same early stage that the field of physiology was when they used crude enzyme measurements based on grinding up whole tissues for analysis. This is like studying a fine Swiss watch by stomping on it and reducing it to its metallic fragments to be weighed and measured in various ways. At times, this approach is necessary; one may need to know how much metal and crystal there needs to be in the interaction. At other times, the pattern of the whole needs to be preserved in order for the analysis to make any sense.

DOCTOR-PATIENT RELATIONSHIP

Perhaps more than anything else, this issue relates to the subject of the therapeutic potential of the physician and of the doctor-patient relationship itself. When considering nonmeasurable, highly significant features of the doctor-patient interaction, obviously the underlying relationship is the essential feature. Following my increased knowledge of and involvement in doctor-patient communication, the most helpful insights I gleaned in understanding what went on between doctors and patients were from clinician-teachers, not scientists. They had tremendous insight and intuition into clinical practice and were interested in the impact of the physicians' own attitudes and feelings on their relationships with patients and on the medical care offered. Many authors such as Balint (1964) and Engel (1980) advanced our understanding of the importance of the physician's personal attitudes about pain, dependence, hostility, noncompliance, poverty, obesity, drugs, homosexuality, and, most of all, about death and dying. We understand how these attitudes influence physicians working with patients and how they can become significant barriers if not understood and dealt with. Traditional medical education does *not* foster the most adaptive attitudes in many of these areas; the process of medical education could be modified to help professionals in training deal with some of the critical issues they encounter.

THE FUTURE

Doctor-patient communication and improved doctor-patient relationships are teachable, learnable skills. Knowledge of this area will provide a foundation as well as an inspiration to the teaching and practice of the highest level of doctor-patient interaction. Our inquiry, however, needs to be a dynamic and changing one. Our patients have shown us that they want more knowledge about health and a more active part in doctor-patient communication. Thus, the doctor-patient relationship is shifting more and more in the direction of interaction and egalitarian participation, centering on the patient as a person, taking into account his individuality and cultural strengths and weaknesses.

These trends give a very different flavor to the kind of communication patterns and relationships that will be formed and will be a subject for investigation. We will have to transform the current biomedical model to a new model of medical practice. This will not be easy or without controversy. It will tax our knowledge, skills, traditions, and even personal integrity, but it is necessary. As technology burgeons and we add new technical competencies to our armamentarium in order to keep people alive (often with distressing consequences for the family and for the patient's quality of life), we will need to find new resources to meet the needs of survivors and their families. In this context, ethics will become an increasingly important part of our thinking (e.g., the way in which messages are given and the way in which questions are asked may often imply a value system that will have an important impact on the patient). Thus, being aware of the judgmental and ethical implications of the communication process will be another important dimension for study.

We now have more sophisticated insight into the problems for which physicians are consulted. Morbidity is more frequently identified in the psychosocial and behavioral areas, either directly or indirectly. Thus, more and more attention has to be focused on the doctor-patient interactions than when we were narrowly limited to the more traditional medical tasks and settings, and we are doing what is commonly referred to as "shooting at a moving target from a moving platform." The very process of health care is changing, communications are changing, and we are simultaneously trying to improve and adapt our methods of observation and scrutiny so that we will have increased understanding and insight.

Clearly the ultimate goal will be to arrive at a body of knowledge that deals with the essential features of what goes on between physicians and patients, and that applies to clinical practice.

As knowledge about the doctor-patient relationship and communication with patients within this relationship improves, and as medical education is modified to deal with physicians' growth and development as human beings, medical practice will be more effective and also increasingly gratifying to both physician and patient.

Conclusions

Moira Stewart
and
Debra Roter

The quality of the relationship of two persons, patient and doctor, is central to the task of medicine. "To bring discipline to those decisions that involve persons as well as disease, to relieve that face of human suffering—that would be new, that would be a revolution in medicine. The search for such rigor is at the edge of a truly new frontier in medicine, where the moral and the technical, when person and body come together" (Cassell, 1976, p.121). The work in this book is a contribution to that search for rigor.

To date, studies on doctor-patient communication have been deficient for one or more of the following reasons. They have researched what is measurable, whether or not it was central (it may even have been trivial). The studies have generally not been informed by theoretical models of excellent communication. Until very recently, researchers have worked in single disciplines rather than on interdisciplinary teams. Finally, research findings have had a dubious relevance to educators seeking guidance about what, let alone how, to teach concerning communications.

This book, in addition to its stress on scientific rigor, provides frameworks or models of communication relevant to clinical practice. Such models are essential to focus research on the crucial questions and to guide educators in planning curricula. The models both reflect and help provide answers to the important questions asked by physicians, educators and investigators, such as:

- What are the tasks of the interviews?
- How can interviews be carried out effectively, humanely and efficiently?
- How can both process and outcome be measured?
- How can the necessary knowledge, skills, and attitudes be taught and learned?

THE MODELS

This book presents a model, which McWhinney describes as the transformed clinical method, or the patient-centered approach. It stresses understanding the meaning of the illness for each patient.

What does this model and the research based on its principles have to say to the clinicians? First, we do not think it would be overstating the case to conclude that attaining excellent communication will be a clinician's lifelong effort; it might be better described as a quest or journey rather than a course of study. One key to satisfactory relationships with patients is the physician's self-awareness. The influence of doctors' interaction with patients on the healing process cannot be overestimated. However, the research methods represented in this book are not adequate to understand fully either the doctors' inner world or the healing process.

A second major point is that the winds of change are blowing through medicine. New clinical methods are stressing that understanding patients' subjective experience of their illnesses is a key to comprehensive assessment and management. In the same vein, patients' answers to questions such as "Why me?" and "Why now?" can be very important to the clinical problems.

What does this book have to say to the educators who are implementing programs to teach undergraduate and graduate physicians about communication issues? The main point is that the writers think expertise in communication rises from much more than skills training. One component of excellent communication is a set of attitudes in student-physicians, life skills and experience, and, to some extent, personality change such as the Balint Groups encourage. Teaching has to be tailored to individual students' needs. They are going through developmental stages not only in their learning but also in their lives. We believe that, just as communication with patients must incorporate the patients' world and world view, so must teaching of communication embrace the students' world view.

Effective skills training programs include as a minimum, videotaping and individual feedback. One drawback of this kind of training is that it demands so much faculty time. Furthermore, it sometimes encourages defensive reactions among those who have not had a positive experience with this sort of peer review. We hope that the enduring results of Maguire and his colleagues will convince the skeptics of the long-term worth of such training programs.

The book provides examples of first-class teaching programs in medical education at the undergraduate, postgraduate, and faculty levels. The variety of successful approaches include curriculum structuring in undergraduate education (Kurtz), videotape and feedback in undergraduate teaching (Maguire, Fairbairn, and Fletcher), and Balint Group process over a two-year postgraduate residency training program (Frenette and Blondeau).

Each approach is informed by a model of doctor-patient communication, either explicit or implicit. We recommend that the model be clearly stated, that it should be reflected in the content of the teaching on communication and in the evaluation tools used. Several such tools or checklists are presented in the book, all of which are derived from an explicit model and one of which has been rigorously tested for reliability and validity (Kraan et al.).

What conclusions can be drawn from this book relevant to the investigator of doctor-patient interactions? In future studies, investigators can use the overviews of Stiles and Putnam and Beckman et al. to frame their thoughts when choosing measures of doctor-patient interaction and outcome. We recommend that investigators consider their selection of measures carefully and especially, that they choose more than one measure to assess important variables. Such a strategy would permit comparison among various facets of communication and perhaps tease out the relative importance of each to patient outcomes. Also, use of multiple outcomes provides information for many different groups. For example, physicians and nurses are most interested in the patient's recovery, health educators are predominantly interested in patient behavior change, and health economists and administrators are interested in efficient decision-making.

In general, we suggest three directions for the future. First, in our view the main flaw of studies conducted to date is that they are difficult to interpret to the student and the practising clinician. This is partly because many studies do not test a particular well-described model of communication, but rather seek to correlate conceptually discrete verbal behaviors to outcomes. Far better to start with a teachable model and derive the research questions from that model. Many studies incorporate all parts of the interaction, a lumping phenomenon (remember the smashed Swiss watch analogy) that does not permit recommendations about a particular problem in a particular facet of the interview. We suggest a new generation of studies, analyzing interactions using the models described in this book and testing the hypotheses that these approaches are associated with improved patient outcomes. Even better, in Inui and Carter's taxonomy of research designs would be studies assessing outcomes from two groups of physicians, one trained in communications and one not.

We also recommend studies of specific problems or challenges in communication between patients and doctors that would be likely to result in a set of instructions for that problem in that setting.

For excellent communication between patients and doctors to become reality, studies need to be conducted on what may seem at first glance to be peripheral issues. For example, we need to know which problems, rising from poor communication, practicing physicians deem to be serious. Does the physician believe the models, such as the patient-centered method presented in this book, are time-efficient enough for the resultant benefits?

Next, researchers need to be as stringent as those who evaluate drugs in terms of assessing the potential negative effects from various styles of doctor-patient communication. Just as drug studies are considered unsophisticated if they do not consider drug side effects, so our work ought to consider and measure what we think may be potential negative effects of communication, such as a patient's overdependence on the physician.

Finally, a more concerted effort to combine the quantitative kinds of analyses presented in this book with qualitative methods, best represented here by Frankel and Beckman, would overcome some of these problems and move the field forward toward the overall goal of better communication between patients and their doctors.

References

AAMC Project. (1983). Emerging perspectives on the general professional education of the physician. *Association of American Medical Colleges.*

ABIM. (1983). *Annals of Internal Medicine, 99,* 720-724.

Adler, L.M., & Enelow, A.J. (1966). Instrument to Measure Skill in Diagnostic Interviewing: A Teaching and Evaluation Tool. *Journal of Medical Education, 41,* 281.

Adler, L.M., Ware, J.E., Jr., & Enelow, A.J. (1970). Changes in Medical Interviewing Style after Instruction with Two Closed-Circuit Television Techniques. *Journal of Medical Education, 45,* 21.

Allison, P.D., & Liker, J.K. (1982). Analyzing sequential categorical data on dyadic interaction: A comment on Gottman. *Psychological Bulletin, 91,* 393-403.

Alroy, G., Ber, R., & Kramer, D. (1984). An evaluation of the short-term effects of an interpersonal skills course. *Medical Education, 18,* 85-89.

Argyle, M. (1975). *Bodily communication.* New York: International Universities Press.

Austin, J.L. (1975). *How to do things with words* (2nd ed.). Oxford, England: Clarendon Press.

Bacal, H.A. (1972). Balint's group: Training or treatment? *Psychiatry and Medicine, 3,* 373-377.

Bain, D.J.G. (1979). The content of physician/patient communication in family practice. *Journal of Family Practices, 8,* 745-753.

Bain, D.J.G. (1976). Doctor-patient communication in general practice consultations. *Medical Education, 10,* 125-131.

Bakeman, R. (1978). Untangling streams of behavior: Sequential analysis of observation data. In G.P. Sackett (Ed.), *Observing behavior: Vol 2. Data collection and analysis methods* (pp.63-78). Baltimore, MD: University Park Press.

Baker, S.S. (1984). *Information decisionmaking and the relationship between client and health care professional in published personal narratives.* Unpublished doctoral dissertation. University of Texas.

Bales, R.F. (1950). *Interaction process analysis: A method for the study of small groups.* Cambridge, MA: Addison-Wesley.

Bales, R.F., & Hare, A.P. (1965). Diagnostic use of the interaction profile. *Journal of Social Psychology, 67*, 239-258.

Balint, E. (1986, May). Proceedings of the International Balint Memorial Congress, Budapest, Hungary.

Balint, M. (1966). Psychoanalysis and Medical Practice. *International Journal of Psychoanalysis. 47, 54.*

Balint, M. (1964). *The doctor, his patient and the illness.* London: Pitman Medical Publishing.

Balint, M. (1961). The other part of medicine. *Lancet. 1*, 40-42.

Balint, M. (1957). *The doctor, his patient and the illness,* London: Pitman.

Balint, M., Hunt, J., Joyce, D., Marinker, M., Woodcock, J., (1970). *Treatment or diagnosis: A study of repeat prescriptions in general practice.* Toronto: J.B. Lippincott.

Balint, E., & Norell, J.S. (1976) *Six minutes per patient.* London: Nethuen.

Barbee, R.A., & Feldman, S.E. (1970). A three-year longitudinal study of the medical interview and its relationship to student performance in clinical medicine. *Journal of Medical Education, 45*, 770-776.

Barbee, R.A., Feldman, S., & Chosy, L.W. (1967). The quantitative evaluation of student performance in the medical interview. *Journal of Medical Education, 42*, 238-243

Barrows, H.S., & Tamblyn, R.M. (1980). *Problem based learning: An approach to medical education.* New York: Springer.

Barsky, A.J.3rd (1981). Hidden reasons why some patients visit doctors. *Annal of Internal Medicine, 94*, 492-498.

Bartlett, E.E., Grayson, M., Barker, R. (1984). The effects of physician communication skills on patient satisfaction, recall and adherence. *Journal of Chronic Diseases, 37*, 755-764.

Bass, M.J., Buck, C., Turner, L., Dickie, G., Pratt, G., & Robinson, H.C. (1986). The physician's actions and the outcome of illness in family practice. *Journal of Family Practice. 23*(1), 43-47.

Bass, L.W., Cohen, R.L. (1982). Ostensible versus actual reasons for seeking pediatric attention: another look at the parental ticket of admission. *Pediatrics, 6*, 870-874.

Becker, E. (1975). *The denial of death.* New York: Free Press.

Becker, M.H., & Rosenstock, I.M. (1984). Compliance with medical advice. In A. Steptoe, & A. Matthews (Eds.). *Health care and human behaviour.* (pp. 153-178) London: Academic Press.

Beckman, H.B., & Frankel, R.M. (1984). The effect of physician behavior on the collection of data. *Annals of Internal Medicine, 101*, 692-696.

Beckman, H.B., Frankel, R.M., & Darnley, J. (1985). Soliciting the patients complete agenda: A relationship to the distribution of concerns. *Clinical Research, 33*, 714A.

Beecher, H. K. (1956). Relationship of significance of wound to the pain experienced. *Journal of the American Medical Association, 161*, 1609-1613.

Belenky, M.F., Clinchy, B.M., Goldberger, N.R., & Tarule, J.M. (1986). *Women's ways of knowing—The development of self, voice and mind.* New York: Basic Books.

Ben-Sira, Z. (1980). The function of the professional's affective behavior in client satisfaction: A revised approach to social interaction theory. *Journal of Health and Social Behavior, 21*, 170.

Benarde, M.A., & Mayerson, E.W. (1978). Patient-physician negotiation. *Journal of the American Medical Association, 239*, 1413-1415.

Bernatchez, J.P., Blondeau, F., Brunet, F., Bury, J., & Gervais, S. (1975). *Aspects psychologiques et sociaux de la pratique medicale, guied de l'etudiant.* Quebec: Universite Laval.

Berkowitz, L., Walster, E., (Eds.) (1976). *Equity theory: Toward a general theory of social interaction. advances in experimental social psychology* (Vol. 9). New York: Academic Press.

Bertakis, K.D. (1977). The communication of information from physician to patient: A method for increasing patient retention and satisfaction. *The Journal of Family Practice, 5,* 217-222.

Blacklock, S. M. (1977). The symptom of chest pain in family practice. *Journal of Family Practice, 4,* 429-433.

Bloom, S. (1983). *The doctor and his patient: a sociological interpretation.* New York: Russel Sage.

Boreham, P., & Gibson, D. (1978). The informative process in private medical consultation: A preliminary investigation. *Social Science and Medicine, 12,* 409.

Brent, D. A. (1981). The residency as a developmental process. *Journal of Medical Education, 56,* 417-422.

Bridges, K., & Goldberg, D. (1984). Psychiatric illness in patients with neurological disorder: Patients' views on discussion of emotional problems with neurologists. *British Medical Journal, 289,* 656-658, 917-920, 1226.

Brody, D. S. (1980). The patient's role in clinical decision-making. *Annals of Internal Medicine, 93,* 718-722.

Brody, H. (1980). *Placebos and the philosophy of medicine: Clinical, conceptual and ethical issues* (pp. 115-130). Chicago: University of Chicago Press.

Brody, D. S., & Miller, S. M. (1986). Illness concerns and recovery from a URI. *Medical Care, 24,* 742-748.

Brown, J. B., Stewart, M. A., McCracken, E., McWhinney, I. R., & Levenstein, J. H. (1986). The patient-centred clinical method. 2. Definition and application. *Family Practice- An International Journal, 3,* 75-79.

Brownbridge, G., Fitter, M., & Wall, T. (1986). *Doctor-patient communications and the consulting room use of computers in general practice.* DHSS Supported Research Project Final Report, MRC/ESRC Social and Applied Psychology Unit, University of Sheffield.

Bruner, J. (1966). *Toward a theory of instruction.* Cambridge, MA: Bilknays.

Buijs, R., Sluijs, E.M., & Verhak, P.F.M. (1984). Byrne and Long: A classification for rating the interview style of doctors. *Social Science and Medicine, 19,* 683-690.

Burack, R.C., & Carpenter, R.R. (1983). The predictive value of the presenting complaint. *Journal of Family Practice. 16,* 749-754.

Byrne, P.S., & Long, B.E.L. (1984). *Doctors talking to patients.* London: Royal College of General Practitioners.

Cansler, D.C., & Stiles, W.B. (1981). Relative status and interpersonal presumptuousness. *Journal of Experimental Social Psychology, 17,* 459-471.

Caporael, L.R., & Culbertson, G.H. (1986). Verbal response modes of baby talk and other speech at institutions for the aged. *Language & Communication, 6,* 99-112.

Carmichael, L.P. (1980). The relational model: A paradigm of family medicine. *Journal of the Florida Medical Association, 67,* 860-862.

Carroll, J.G., & Monroe, J. (1980). Teaching clinical interviewing in the health professions: A review of empirical research. *Evaluation Health Profession, 3,* 21.

Carroll, J.G., & Monroe, J. (1979). Teaching medical interviewing: a critique of educational research and practice. *Journal of Medical Education, 54,* 498-500.

Carroll, J.G., & Monroe, J. (1978). *Teaching the interpersonal skills of medical interviewing: A review of the literature.* Paper presented at the Conference on Research in Medical Education, Association of American Medical Colleges, New Orleans.

Carter, W.B., Inui, T.S., Kukull, W., & Haigh, V. (1982). Outcome-based doctor-patient interaction analysis: II. Identifying effective provider and patient behavior. *Medical Care, 20,* 550-566.

Cassata, D.M. (1978). Health communication theory and research: An overview of the communication specialist interface. In B.B. Ruben (Ed.), *Communication Yearbook.* New Brunswick, NY: Transaction Books.

Cassell, E. J. (1985). *Talking with patients: Volume 2 Clinical technique.* Cambridge, MA: MIT Press.

Cassell, E.J. (1976). *The healer's art.* Cambridge, MA: MIT Press.

Cassell, E.J., & Skopec, L. (1977). Language as a tool in medicine: Methodology and theoretical framework. *Journal of Medical Education, 52,* 197-203.

Chickering, A. W. & Associates. (1981). *The Modern American College.* San Francisco: Jossey-Bass.

Cohen, S. J. (1985). An educational psychologist goes to medical school. In Eisner, E. W. *The educational imagination: On the design and evaluation of school programs* (pp. 324-338) (2nd ed.). New York: Macmillan.

Cohen, J. (1960). A coefficient of agreement for nominal scales. *Psychological Medicine, 2,* 37-43.

Coombs, R. H. (1978). *Mastering medicine—Professional socialization in medical school.* New York: Free Press.

Cope, D.W., Linn, L.S., Leake, B.D., et al. (1986). Modification of residents' behavior by preceptor feedback of patient satisfaction. *Journal of General Internal Medicine, 3*(1), 9-20.

Cox, A., Hopkinson, K., & Rutter, M. (1981a). Psychiatric interviewing techniques: II. Naturalistic study: Eliciting factual information. *British Journal of Psychiatry, 138,* 283-291.

Cox, A., Holbrook, D., & Rutter, M. (1981b). Psychiatric interviewing techniques VI. Experimental study: Eliciting feelings. *British Journal of Psychiatry, 139,* 29-37.

Cox, A., Rutter, M., & Holbrook, D. (1981c). Psychiatric interviewing techniques: V. Experimental study: Eliciting factual information. *British Journal of Psychiatry, 139,* 144-152.

Cox, A., Rutter, M., & Holbrook, D. (1988). Psychiatric interviewing techniques—A second experimental study: Eliciting feelings. *British Journal of Psychiatry, 152,* 64-72.

Cresswell, S. (1983). Doctor/patient communication: A review of the literature (with commentary from D.L. Sackett et al.) *Ontario Medical Review* (November), 559-567.

Cronbach, L.J. (1951). Coefficient alpha and the internal structure of tests. *Psychometrika, 16,*297-334.

Cronbach, L.J., Gleser, G.C., Nanda, H., & Rajaratnam, N. (1972). *The dependability of behavioral measurements: Theory of generalizability for scores and profiles.* New York: John Wiley.

Crookshank, F.G. (1926). The theory of diagnosis. *Lancet, 2,* 939-942, 995-999.

Daloz, l.A. (1986). *Effective teaching and mentoring.* San Francisco: Jossey-Bass.

Dance, F.E.X. (1967). Toward a theory of human communication. In F.E.X. Dance (Ed.) *Human communication theory: Original essays*. New York: Holt, Rinehart & Winston.

Dance, F.E.X., & Larson, C.E. (1972). *Speech communication: concepts and behavior*. New York: Holt, Rinehart & Winston.

Davis, M.S. (1968). Variations in patients' compliance with doctors' advice: an empirical analysis of patterns of communication. *American Journal of Public Health, 58*(2), 274-288.

Davis, M.S. (1971). Variation in patient compliance with doctors' orders: Medical practice and doctor-patient interaction. *Psychiatry in Medicine, 2*, 31-54.

Davies, A.R., Ware, J.E. Jr., & Brook, R.H. (1986). Consumer acceptance of prepaid and fee-for service medical care: Results from a randomized controlled trial. *Health Service Research, 21*, 429-452.

DeVries, M. (1985). Healing and the process of healing. *Humane Medicine, 1*(2). 53-61.

Diers, D., & Leonard, R.C. (1966). Interaction analysis in nursing research. *Nursing Research, 15*, 225-228.

DiMatteo, R., & Hays, R. (1980). The significance of patients' perceptions of physician conduct: A study of patient satisfaction in a family practice center. *Community Health, 6*, 18.

DiMatteo, M.R., Prince, L.M., & Taranta, A. (1979). Patients' perceptions of physicians' behavior: Determinants of patient commitment to the therapeutic relationship. *Journal of Community Health, 4*, 280-290.

DiMatteo, M.R., Taranta, A., Friedman, S., & Prince, L.M. (1980). Predicting patient satisfaction from physicians' nonverbal communication skills. *Medical Care. 18*, 376-387.

Doyle, B.J., & Ware, J.E., Jr. (1977). Physician Conduct and other factors that affect consumer satisfaction with medical care. *Journal of Medical Education, 52*, 793-801.

Duffy, D.L., Hammerman, D., & Cohen, M.A. (1980). Communication skills of house officers. *Annals Internal Medicine, 93*, 354-357.

Dumas, J.E. (1984). Interactional correlates of treatment outcome in behavioral parent training. *Journal of Consulting and Clinical Psychology, 52*, 946-954.

Eisenberg, L., & Kleinman, A. (1981). *The relevance of social science for medicine* (pp. 165-196). Boston: D. Reidel.

Eisenthal, S., Koopman, C., & Lazare, A. (1983). Process analysis of two dimensions of the negotiated approach in relation to satisfaction in the initial interview. *Journal of Nervous and Mental Disease. 171*(1), 49-54.

Ekman, P., & Friesen, W.V. (1976). Measuring facial movement. *Environmental Psychology and Nonverbal Behavior, 1*, 56-75.

Ekman, P., Friesen, W.V., & Ellsworth, P. (1972). *Emotions in the human face: Guidelines for research and a review of findings*. New York: Fergamon.

Elliott, R., Hill, C. E., Stiles, W. B., Friedlander, M., L., Mahrer, A. R., & Margison, F. R., (1987). Primary therapist response modes: Comparison of six rating systems. *Journal of Consulting and Clinical Psychology. 55*, 218-223.

Elliott, R., Stiles, W.B., Shiffman, W., Barker, C.B., Burstein, B., & Goodman, G. (1982). The empirical analysis of help-intended communications: Conceptual framework and recent research. In T.A. Wills (Ed.), *Basic processes in helping relationships* (pp. 333-356). New York: Academic Press.

Elstein, A.S., Shulman, L.S., & Sprafka, S.A. (1978). *Medical problem solving*. Cambridge, MA: Harvard University Press.

Engel G.L. (1980). The clinical application of the biopsychosocial model. *American Journal of Psychiatry, 137*(5), 535-544.

Engel, G.L. (1977). The need for a new medical model: A challenge for biomedicine. *Science, 196,* 129-136.

Engler, C.M., Salzman, G.A., Walker, M.A., & Wolf, F.M. (1981). Medical students' acquisition and retention of communication and interviewing skills. *Journal of Medical Education, 56,* 572-579.

Erikson, E. H. (1980). *Identity and the life cycle*. New York: Norton.

Erikson, E. H. (1963). *Childhood and society* (2nd ed.) New York: Norton.

Ewart, C.K., Burnett, K.F., & Taylor, C.B. (1983). Communication behaviors that affect blood pressure: An A-B-A-B analysis of marital interaction. *Behaviour Module, 7*(3), 331-344.

Faulkner, A., & Maguire, P. (1986). Training ward nurses to monitor cancer patients. *Clinical Oncology, 10,* 383-389.

Feinstein, A.R. (1967). *Clinical judgement*. Baltimore: Williams and Wilkins.

Fitzpatrick, M.A., Vance, L., & Witteman, H. (1984). Interpersonal communication in the casual interaction of married partners. *Journal of Language and Social Psychology, 3,* 81-95.

Flaherty, J.A. (1985). Education and evaluation of interpersonal skills. In A.G. Rezler and J.A. Flaherty *The Interpersonal Dimension in Medical Education*. New York: Springer.

Foucault, M. (1975). The birth of the clinic. An archaeology of medical perception (A.M. Sheridan Smith, Trans.). New York: Vintage.

Francis, V., Korsch B.M., & Morris, M.J. (1969). Gaps in doctor-patient communication: Patients' response to medical advice. *New England Journal of Medicine, 280,* 535-540.

Frankel, R.M. (1987). Talking in interviews: A dispreference for patient initiated questions in physician-patient encounters. In G. Psathas (Eds.) *Interactional Competence*. New York: Irvington

Frankel, R.M. (1984). From sentence to sequence: Understanding the medical encounter through microinteractional analysis. *Discourse Process, 7,* 135-170.

Frankl, V.E. (1973). The doctor and the soul from psychotherapy to logotherapy (2nd ed.). New York: Vintage.

Frankel, R.M., & Beckman, H.B. (1982). An interaction-based method for preserving and analyzing clinical transactions. In L.S. Pettegrew, P. Arntson, D. Bush, & K. Zoppi (Eds.), *Straight talk: Explorations in provider and patient interaction*. Austin, TX: International Communication Association.

Freemon, B., Negrete, V.F., Davis, M., & Korsch, B.M. (1971). Gaps in doctor-patient communication: Doctor-patient interaction analysis. *Pediatric Research, 5,* 298-311.

Freer, C. B. (1980). Self-care: A health diary study. *Medical Care, 18,* 853-861.

Freidson, E. (1970). Professional dominance: The social structure of medical care. New York: Atherton.

Gerber, L. (1983). *Married to their careers*. New York: Tavistock.

Glass. G.V., McGaw, B., & Smith, M.L. (1981). Meta-analysis in social research. Beverly Hills, CA: Sage.

Goldberg, D.P., Hobson, R.F., Maguire, G.P., Margison, F.R., O'Dowd, T., Osborn, M., & Moss, S. (1984). The clarification and assessment of a method of psychotherapy. *British Journal of Psychiatry, 144,* 567-580.

Goldberg, D., & Huxley, P. (1980). Mental illness in the community: A pathway to psychiatric care. London, New York: Tavistock.

Goldberg, D.P., Steele, J.J., & Smith, C. (1980). Teaching family doctors to recognise psychiatric illness with increased accuracy. *Lancet, II,* 521-523.

Good, M.J.D., & Good, B.J. (1982). Patient requests in primary care clinics. In N.J. Crisman & T.W. Maritzla (Eds.). *Clinically applied anthropology.* Boston: D. Reidel.

Goodwin, C. (1981). *Conversational organization: Interaction between speakers and hearers.* New York: Academic Press.

Gottman, J.M. (1979). *Marital interaction: Experimental investigations.* New York: Academic Press.

Gouldner, A.W. (1960). The norm of reciprocity: a preliminary statement. *American Sociological Review, 25,* 161-179.

Grams, G. (1987). *Personal communication.* Unpublished doctoral dissertation. University of Toronto.

Green, B.F., & Hall, J.A. (1984). Quantitative methods for literature reviews. *Annual Review of Psychology, 35, 37.*

Greenfield, S., Kaplan, S., & Ware, J.E. (1985). Expanding patient involvement in care. *Annals of Internal Medicine, 102*(4), 520-528.

Greenfield, S., Kaplan, S.H., & Ware, J.E., Jr. (1988). Patient participation in medical care: Effects on blood sugar and quality of life in diabetes. *Journal of General Internal Medicine, 3,* 448-457.

deGroot, A.D. (1962). *Methodologie. Grondslagen van onderzoek en denken in de gedragswetenschappen.* Mouton: 'sGravenhage.

Grose N. P., Goodrich, T. J., & Czyzewski, D. (1983). The development of professional identity in the family practice resident. *Journal of Medical Education, 58,* 489-491.

Guilford, J.P., & Fruchler, B. (1981). *Fundamental statistics in psychology and education.* London: McGraw-Hill.

Hall, J.A., & Roter, D.L., (forthcoming). *Good doctoring: The significance of talk between doctors and patients.* Manuscript under review.

Hall, J.A., Roter, D.L., & Katz, N.R. (1988). Correlates of provider behavior: A meta-analysis. *Medical Care, 26,* 657-675.

Hall, J.A., Roter, D.L., & Katz, N.R. (1987). Task versus socioemotional behaviors in physicians. *Medical Care, 25,* 399-412.

Hall, J.A., Roter, D.L., & Rand, C.S. (1981). Communication of affect between patient and physician. *Journal of Health and Social Behavior, 22,* 18-30.

Harrigan, J.A., Oxman, T.E., & Rosenthal, R. (1981, August). *Physicians' nonverbal behavior.* Paper presented at the American Psychological Association Convention, Los Angeles, CA.

Harrigan, J.A., & Rosenthal, R. (1983). Physicians' head and body positions as determinants of perceived rapport. *Journal of Applied Social Psychology, 13,* 496-509.

Haug, M., & Lavin, B. (1979). Public challenge of physician authority. *Medical Care, 17,* 344.

Haug, M., & Lavin, B. (1983). *Consumerism in medicine: Challenging physician authority.* Beverly Hills, CA:Sage.

Hayes-Bautista, D.E. (1976). Modifying the treatment: Patient compliance, patient control and medical care. *Social Science & Medicine, 10*, 233-238.

Haynes, R.B., Taylor, D.W., & Sackett, D.L. (1979). *Compliance in health care.* Baltimore: Johns Hopkins University Press.

Headache Study Group of the University of Western Ontario. (1986). Predictors of outcome in headache patients presenting to family physicians—A one year prospective study. *Headache Journal, 26*(6), 285-294.

Heaton, C.J., & Kurtz, S.M. (1988). Coordinated clinical skills assessment in the preclinical years: Helical progression makes sense. In I.R. Hart, and R.M. Harden (Eds.), Further development in assessing clinical competence. Montreal: Heal.

Helfer, R.E. (1970). An objective comparison of pediatric interviewing skills on freshman and senior medical students. *Pediatrics, 45*, 623.

Helman, C. (1984). *Culture, health and illness: An introduction for health professionals.* London: Wright.

Henbest, R. J. (1985). *A study of the patient-centred approach in family practice.* Unpublished dissertation, London, Ontario, University of Western Ontario.

Hess, J.W. (1969). A comparison of methods for evaluating medical student skill in relating to patients. *Journal of Medical Education, 44*, 934-938.

Heszen-Klemens, I., & Lapinska, E. (1984). Doctor-patient interaction, patients' health behavior and effects of treatment. *Social Science & Medicine, 19*, 9-18.

Holsti, O.R. (1969). *Content analysis for the social sciences and humanities.* Reading, MA: Addison-Wesley.

Hopkinson, K., Cox, A., & Rutter, M. (1981). Psychiatric interviewing techniques: III. Naturalistic study: Eliciting feelings. *British Journal of Psychiatry, 138*, 406-415.

Hulka, B.S., Kupper, L.L., & Cassel, J.C. (1975). Doctor-patient communication and outcomes among diabetic patients. *Journal of Community Health, 1*, 15-27.

Hulka, B.S., Cassel, J.C., & Kupper, L.L. (1976). Communication, compliance and concordance between physicians and patients with prescribed medication. *American Journal of Public Health, 66*(9), 847-853.

Inui, T.S., & Carter, W.R. (1985). Problems and prospects for health services research on provider-patient communication. *Medical Care, 23*, 521-538.

Inui, T.S., Carter, W.B., Kukull, W., & Haigh, V. (1982). Outcome-based doctor-patient interaction analysis: I. Comparison of techniques. *Medical Care, 20*, 535-549.

Inui, T.S., Yourtree, E.L., & Williamson, J.W. (1976). Improved outcomes in hypertension after physician tutorials: A controlled trial. *Annals of Internal Medicine, 84*, 646-651.

Irwin, W.G., & Bamber, J.H. (1984). An evaluation of medical student behaviors in communication. *Medical Education, 18*, 90-95.

James, W. (1958). *The Varieties of Religious Experience.* New York: The New American Library.

Jerrett, W. A. (1981). Lethargy in general practice. *The Practitioner, 225*, 731-737.

Kagan, N. (1975). Influencing human interaction—Eleven years with IPR. *Canadian Counselor, 9*, 74-97.

Kahn, G.S., Cohen, B., & Jason, H. (1979). The teaching of interpersonal skills in U.S. medical schools. *Journal of Medical Education, 54*, 29.

Kallen, D.J., & Stephenson, J.J. (1981). Perceived physician humaneness, patient attitude and satisfaction with the pill as a contraceptive. *Journal of Health and Social Behavior, 22*, 256-267.

Kaplan, S.H., Greenfield, S., & Ware, J.E. Jr. (April 1985). *Expanded patient involvement in medical care: Effects on blood pressure*. Paper presented at the National Conference on High Blood Pressure Control.

Kasteler, J., Kane, R., Olsen, D., & Thetford, C. (1976). Issues underlying the prevalence of "doctor-shopping" behavior. *Journal of Health & Social Behavior, 17*, 328.

Katon, W., & Kleinman, A. (1980). Doctor-patient negotiation and other social science strategies in patient care. In L. Eisenberg & A. Kleinman (Eds.), *The relevance of social science for medicine*, Boston: D. Reidel. Publishing, 253-279.

Katz, R. (1982). *Boiling energy: Community healing among the Kalahari Kung*. Cambridge, MA: Harvard University Press.

Kauss, D.R., Robbins, A.S., Abrss, I., et al. (1980). Long-term effectiveness of interpersonal skills training in medical schools. *Journal of Medical Education, 55*, 595-601.

Keen, S. (1970). *To a dancing god*. New York: Harper & Row.

Kestenbaum, V. (1982). The experience of illness. In V. Kestenbaum (Ed.), *The humanity of the phenomenological perspectives*. Knoxville: Knoxville University of Tennessee Press.

Kleinman, A. (1982). Patients treated by physicians and folk healers. *Culture, Medicine and Psychiatry, 6*, 405-423.

Kleinman, A., Eisenberg, L., & Good, B. (1978). Culture, illness and care: Clinical lessons from anthropologic and cross-cultural research. *Annals of Internal Medicine, 88*, 251-258.

Knopke, H.J. & Anderson. R.J. (1981). Developmental approaches to faculty careers in primary health care education. In H.J. Knopke & N.L. Diekelmann (Eds.), *Approaches to teaching primary health care*. St. Louis: C. V. Mosby.

Koestler, A. (1979). *Janus: A summing up*. London: Pan Books.

Konner, M. (1987). *Becoming a doctor—A journey of initiation in medical school*. New York: Viking Penguin.

Korsch, B.M., Gozzi, E., & Francis, V. (1968). Gaps in doctor-patient communication: I. Doctor-patient interaction and patient satisfaction. *Pediatrics, 42*, 855-871.

Kraan, H.F., & Crijnen, A.A.M. (1987). *The Maastricht history-taking and advice checklist: Studies of instrumental utility*, Amsterdam: Lundbeck.

Kurtz, S.M. (1983, April). A format for teaching information giving skills to health professionals. Education Resources Information Centre (ERIC), 222928.

Labov, W., & Fanshel, D. (1977). *Therapeutic discourse*. New York: Academic Press.

Laing, R.D. (1978). *"Knots" in knots*. New York: Penguin.   ·

Langer, E., & Rodin, J. (1976). The effects of choice and enhanced personal responsibilities for the aged: A filed experiment in an institutional setting. *Journal of Personality and Social Psychology, 34*, 191-198.

Larsen, K.M., & Smith, C.K. (1981). Assessment of nonverbal communication in the patient-physician interview. *Journal of Family Practice, 12*, 481-488.

Layton, I. (1963) There were no signs. In *Balls for a one armed juggler*. Toronto: McClelland and Stewart.

Lazare, A., Eisenthal, E., & Wasserman, L. (1975a). The customer approach to patienthood. *Archives of General Psychiatry, 32*, 553-558.

Lazare, A., Eisenthal, S., & Wasserman, L., & Harford, T. C. (1975b). Patient requests in a walk-in clinic. *Comprehensive Psychiatry, 16*, 467-477.

Le Baron, C. (1981). *Gentle vengeance—an account of the first year at Harvard medical school*. New York: Richard Marek.

Leff, J., Kuipers, L., Berkowitz, R. & Sturgeon, D. (1985). A controlled trial of social intervention in the families of schizophrenic patients: Two year follow-up. *The British Journal of Psychiatry, 146,* 594-600.

Levenstein, J.H.(1984). The patient-centred general practice consultation. *South Africa Family Practice, 5,* 276-282.

Levenstein, J.H., McCracken, E.C., McWhinney, I.R., Stewart, M.A., & Brown, J.B. (1986). The patient-centred clinical method. I. A model for the doctor-patient interaction in family medicine. *Family Practice, 3*(1), 24-30.

Levinson, D.J. (1978). *The seasons of a man's life.* New York: Ballantyne.

Ley, P. (1980). *Communication variables in health education.* London: Health Education Council Monographs.

Ley, P. (1982). Satisfaction, compliance and communication. *British Journal of Clinical Psychology, 21,* 241-254.

Ley, P. (1983). Patients' Understanding and recall in clinical communication failure. In D. Pendleton, & J. Haslow, (Eds.), *Doctor-patient communication* (pp. 89-107). London: Academic Press.

Like, R., & Zyzanski, S. J. (1986). Patient requests in family practice: A focal point for clinical negotiations. *Family Practice, 3,* 216-228.

Lipkin, M., Jr., Quill, T.E., & Napodano, R.J. (1984). The medical interview: A core curriculum for residencies in internal medicine. *Annals of Internal Medicine, 100,* 277-284.

Lipowski, Z.J. (1970). Physical illness, the individual and the coping process. *Psychiatry in Medicine, 1,* 91-102.

Loevinger, J. (1982). *Ego development: Conceptions and theories.* San Francisco: Jossey-Bass.

Maguire, P., Fairbairn, S., & Fletcher, C. (1986). Consultation skills of young doctors: Benefits of feedback training in interviewing as students persist. *British Medical Journal, 292,* 1573.

Maguire, G.P., Roe, P., & Goldberg, D. (1978). The value of feedback in teaching interviewing skills to medical students. *Psychological Medicine, 8,* 695-704.

Maguire, G.P., & Rutter, D.R. (1976a). History-taking for medical students. I. Deficiencies in performance. *Lancet, II,* 365-368.

Maguire, G.P., & Rutter, D.R. (1976b). Training medical students to communicate. In A.E. Bennet (Ed.), *The development and evaluation of a training procedure in communications between doctors and patients* (pp. 45-74). London: Oxford University Press.

Maguire, P., Tait, A., & Brooke, M. (1981). Effect of counselling on the psychiatric morbidity associated with mastectomy. *British Medical Journal, 281,* 1454-1456.

Marburg, E., Blakelock, E., & Roeper, P.J. (1979). Resentful and reflective coping with arbitrary authority and blood pressure. *Psychosomatic Medicine, 41,* 189-201.

Marinker, M. (1981). Clinical method. In J. Cormack, M. Marinker, and D. Morrell (Eds.), *Teaching General Practice.* Brentford, Eng: Kluwer.

Marks, J.N., Goldberg, G.P., & Hillier, V.F. (1979). Determinants of the ability of general practitioners to detect psychiatric illness. *Psychological Medicine, 7,* 337-353.

McCue, J. D. (1985). The distress of internship: Causes and prevention. *New England Journal of Medicine, 312,* 449-452.

McGaughey, K.J., & Stiles, W.B. (1983). Courtroom interrogation of rape victims: Verbal response mode use by attorneys and witnesses during direct examination vs. cross-examination. *Journal of Applied Social Psychology, 13*, 78-87.

McWhinney, I.R. (1985). Patient-centred and doctor-centred models of clinical decision making. In M. Sheldon, J. Brooke, & A. Rector (Eds.). *Decision making in general practice* (pp. 31-46). NY: Stockton Press.

McWhinney, I.R. (1972). Beyond diagnosis: An approach to the integration of behavioral science and clinical medicine. *New England Journal of Medicine, 287*, 384-387.

Meehl, P.E. (1954). *Clinical versus statistical prediction: A theoretical analysis and a review of the evidence.* Minneapolis: University of Minnesota Press.

Meeuwesen, L. (1986). *Verbal analysis of the medical interview of patients with psychosocial complaints.* Unpublished manuscript, Department of Clinical Psychology, Catholic University of Nijmegen, The Netherlands.

Mehrabian, A. (1969). Significance of posture and position in the communication of attitude and status relationships. *Psychological Bulletin, 71*, 359-372.

Mehrabian, A. (1972). *Nonverbal communication.* Chicago: Aldine-Atherton.

Miller, N.L., & Stiles, W.B. (1986). Verbal familiarity in American presidential nomination acceptance speeches and inaugural addresses, 1920-1981. *Social Psychology Quarterly, 49*, 72-81.

Mishler E. G. (1984). *The discourse of medicine: Dialectics of medical interviews.* Norwood, NJ: Ablex.

Mitchell, S.K. (1979). Inter-observor agreement, reliability and generalizability of data collected in observational studies. *Psychological Bulletin, 86*, 376-390.

Morgan, W.L., & Engel, G.L. (1969). *The clinical approach to the patient.* Philadelphia: W.B. Saunders.

Morrell, D. C. (1972). Symptom interpretation in general practice. *Journal of the Royal College of General Practitioners, 22*, 297.

Mount, B. M. (1986). Nurturing your personhood: A message for 1986 graduates. *Canadian Medical Association Journal, 135*, 291-293.

Mumford, E., Schlesinger, H., & Glass, G. (1982). The effects of psychological intervention on recovery from surgery and heart attacks: An analysis of the literature. *American Journal of Public Health, 72*, 141-151.

Nabarro, J. (1984). Unrecognised psychiatric illness in medical patients. *British Medical Journal, 289*, 635-636.

Naji, S.A., Maguire, G.P., & Fairbairn, S.A. (1986). Training clinical teachers in psychiatry to teach interviewing skills to medical students. *Medical Education, 20*(2), 140-147.

Nardone, D.A., Reuler, J.B., & Girard, D.E. (1980). Teaching history-taking: Where are we? *Yale Journal of Biology and Medicine, 53*, 233-250.

Needleman, J. (1985). *The way of the physician.* San Francisco: Harper & Row.

Norton, R. (1978). *Communicator style.* Beverly Hills, CA: Sage.

Nouwen, H.J.M. (1979). *The wounded healer.* New York: Image Books.

Odegaard, C. E. (1986) *Dear Doctor - A Personal Letter to a Physician.* Menlo Park, CA: The Henry J. Kaiser Family Foundation.

Orth, J.E., Stiles, W.B., Scherwitz, L., Hennrikus, D., & Vallbona, C. (1987). Patient exposition and provider explanation in routine interviews and hypertensive patients' blood pressure control. *Health Psychology, 6*, 29-42.

Parsons, T. (1951). *The social system.* Glencoe, IL: The Free Press.

Patrick, D.L., Scrivens, E., & Charlton, J.R.H. (1983). Disability and patient satisfaction with medical care. *Medical Care, 21*(11), 1062-1075.

Peabody, F. W. (1927). The care of the patient. *Journal of the American Medical Association, 88*, 877-882.

Pellegrino, E. (1983). The healing relationship: The architecetonics of clinical medicine. In E. Shep. (Ed.), *The clinical encounter*. New York: Reidel Press.

Pellegrino, E. (1979). *Humanism and the physician*. Knoxville: University of Tennessee Press.

Pendleton, D. (1981). Learning communications skills. *Update, 22*, 1708-1710, 1713-1714.

Pendleton, D. (1983). Doctor-patient communication: A review. In D. Pendleton & J. Hasler (Eds.), *Doctor-patient communication*. London: Academic Press.

Pendleton, D., & Arnston, P. (1985, August). *Training general practitioners to teach consultation skills: An evaluation study of a residential course*. Paper presented to the Summer Conference on Health Communication, Northwestern University, Chicago.

Pendleton, D., Schofield, T., Tate, P., & Havelock, P. (1984). *The consultation: An approach to learning and teaching*. Oxford: Oxford University Press.

Perry, W.G., Jr. (1970). *Forms of intellectual and ethical development in the college years—A scheme*. New York: Holt, Rinehart & Winston.

Perry, W.G., Jr. (1981). Cognitive and ethical growth: The making of meaning. In A.W. Chickering & Associates. *The modern american college*. San Francisco: Jossey-Bass.

Pfeiffer, R.J. (1983). Early-adult development in the medical student. *Mayo Clinic Proceedings, 58*, 127-134.

Platt, F.W., & McMath, J.C. (1979). Clinical hypocompetence: The interview. *Annals of Internal Medicine, 91*, 898-902.

Poole, A.D., & Sanson-Fisher, R.W. (1979). Understanding the patient: A neglected aspect of medical education. *Social Science and Medicine, 13A*, 37.

President's Commission for the Study of Ethical Problems in Medicine and Behavioral Research. (1982). Volume 1. Washington, DC: Government Printing Office.

Premo, B.E., & Stiles, W.B. (1983). Familiarity in verbal interactions of married couples versus strangers. *Journal of Social and Clinical Psychology, 1*, 209-230.

Preven, D.W., Kachur, E.K., Kupfer, R.B., & Waters, J.A. (1986). Interviewing skills of first-year medical students. *Journal of Medical Education, 61*, 842-844.

Psychiatric illness in medical Patients. (Editorial) (1979). *Lancet, II*, 478-479.

Putnam, S.M., Stiles, W.B., Jacob, M.C. & James, S.A. (1988). Teaching the medical interview: An intervention study. *Journal of General Internal Medicine, 3*, 38-47.

Putnam, S.M., Stiles, W.B., Jacob, M.C., & James, S.A. (1985). Patient exposition and physician explanation in initial medical interviews and outcomes of clinic visits. *Medical Care, 23*, 74-83.

Quill, T.E. (1983). Partnerships in patient care: A contractual approach. *Annals of Internal Medicine, 98*, 228-234.

Quinton, D., & Rutter, M. (1985). Family cathology and child psychiatric disorder: A four-year prospective study. In A.R. Nicol (Ed.), *Longitudinal studies. Child psychology and psychiatry*. Chichester: Wiley.

Rabin, D., Rabin, P.L., & Rabin, R. (1982). Compounding the ordeals of ALS: Isolation from my fellow physicians. *New England Journal of Medicine, 307*, 506-509.

Reiser, D.E., & Schroder, A.K. (1980). *Patient interviewing: The human dimension*. Baltimore, MD: Williams and Wilkins.

Report Card on HMO's: 1980-1984. (1985). San Francisco: Louis Hamis and Associates.

Research Committee of the College of General Practitioners. (1958). The continuing observation and recording of morbidity. *Journal of the College of General Practitioners, 1,* 107.

Riccardi, V.M., & Kurtz, S.M. (1983). *Communication and counseling in Health Care.* Springfield, IL: Charles C. Thomas.

Rodin, J. (1983). Behavioral medicine: Beneficial effects of self-control training in aging. *International Review of Applied Psychology, 32,* 153-181.

Rogers, E.M. (1983). *Diffusion of innovations* (3rd Ed.). New York: Free Press.

Rogers, C. (1951). *Client-centered therapy—Its current practice implications and theory.* Cambridge, MA: Riverside Press.

Rosenthal, R. (1984). *Meta-analytic procedures for social research.* Beverly Hills, CA: Sage.

Rosenthal, R., Hall, J.A., DiMatteo, M.R., Rogers, P.L., & Archer, D. (1979). *Sensitivity to nonverbal communication: The PONS test.* Baltimore, MD: Johns Hopkins University Press.

Rosser, J., & Maguire, P. (1982). Dilemmas in general practice: The care of the cancer patient. *Social Science and Medicine, 16,* 315-322.

Roter, D.L. (1985). *The Roter method of interaction process analysis.* Unpublished manuscript, Department of Behavioral Sciences and Health Education, Johns Hopkins University, Baltimore, MD.

Roter, D.L. (1977). Patient participation in patient-provider interaction: The effects of patient question-asking on the quality of interaction, satisfaction, and compliance. *Health Education Monographs, 5,* 281-315.

Roter, D.L., Hall, J.A., & Katz, N.R. (1987). Relations between physicians' behaviors and analogue patients' satisfaction, recall, and impressions. *Medical Care, 25,* 135-154.

Roter, D.L., Hall, J.A., & Katz, N.R. (1988). Patient-physician communication: A descriptive summary of the literature. *Patient Education and Counseling, 12,* 99-119.

Russell, R.L., & Stiles, W.B. (1979). Categories for classifying language in psychotherapy. *Psychological Bulletin, 86,* 404-419.

Rutter, M., Cox, A., Egert, S., Holbrook, D., & Everitt, B. (1981). Psychiatric interviewing techniques: VI. Experimental study: Four contrasting styles. *British Journal of Psychiatry, 138,* 456-465.

Rutter, M., & Maguire, G.P. (1976). History-taking for medical students: II. Evaluation of a training programme. *Lancet, 2*(Sept. 11), 558-560.

Rutter, M., & Cox, A. (1981). Psychiatric interviewing techniques: I. Methods and measures. *British Journal of Psychiatry, 138,* 273-282.

Sackett, D.L., Haynes, R.B., & Tugwell P. (1985). *Clinical epidemiology: A basic science for clinical medicine.* Boston: Little, Brown.

Sacks, O. (1984). *A leg to stand on.* London: Duckworth.

Sacks, O. (1973). *Awakenings.* Garden City, NY: Doubleday.

Sacks, H., Schegloff, E.A., & Jefferson, G. (1974). A simplest systematics for the organization of turn-taking for conversation. *Language, 50,* 696-735.

Samph, T., & Templeton, B. (1978, July). *Progress report: Interpersonal skills project.* Paper presented at the American Board of Family Practice.

Sandelin, Singa. (1981). *Self and Education.* Commentationes Physico-Mathematicae/Societas Scientiarum Fennica Helsinki.

Sapir, M. (1982). *Le groupe Balint, passe et avenir den l'experience Balint: Histoire et actualite.* Paris: Bordas.

Schouten, J.A.M., et al. (1982). *Anamnese en advies. Nieuwe richtlijnen voor informatie-uitwisseling tussen arts en patient.* Brussel: Stafleu, Alphen a.d Rijn.

Shrout, P.E., & Fleiss, J.L. (1979). Intraclass correlation: uses in assessing rater reliability. *Psychological Bulletin, 86,* 420-428.

Schulz, R. (1976). Effects of control and predictability on the physical and psychological well-being of the institutionalized aged. *Journal of Personality and Social Psychology, 33,* 563-573.

Searle, J.R. (1969). *Speech acts: An essay in the philosophy of language.* Cambridge, MA: Cambridge University Press.

Shaw, P.M., & Garth, D.H. (1975). Teaching the doctor-patient relationship to medical students. *British Journal of Medical Education, 9,* 176-181.

Siegler, M. (1982). The patient-physician accommodation: A central event in clinical medicine. *Annals of Internal Medicine, 142,* 1899-1902.

Smith, R. M. (1982). *Learning how to learn—Applied theory for adults.* Chicago: Follett.

Smith, C.K., Polis, E., & Hadac, R.R. (1981). Characteristics of the initial medical interview associated with patient satisfaction and understanding. *Journal of Family Practice, 12,* 283-288.

Snow, L.F. (1974). Folk medical beliefs and the implications for care of patients. *Annals of Internal Medicine, 81,* 82-96.

Snow, L.F. (1983). Traditional health beliefs and practices among lower class black Americans. *Western Journal of Medicine. 139,* 820-828.

Sprunger, L.W. (1983). An analysis of physician-parent communication in pediatric prenatal interviews. *Clinical Pediatrics, 22,* 553-558.

Starfield, B., Steinwachs, D., Morris, I., Bauer, G., & Siebert, S. (1979). Patient-doctor agreement about problems needing follow-up visit. *Journal of the American Medical Association, 242,* 344-346.

Starfield, B., Wray, C., Hess, K., Gross, R., Birk, P.S., & D'Lugoff, B.C. (1981). The influence of patient-practitioner agreement on outcome of care. *American Journal of Public Health, 71*(2), 127-132.

Stein, H. (1985). What is therapeutic in clinical relationships? *Family Medicine, 17*(5), 31.

Stephens, G.G. (1982). *The intellectual basis of family practice.* Tucson: Winter.

Stetten, D. (1981). Coping with blindness. *New England Journal of Medicine, 305, 458.*

Stevens, J. (1974). Brief Encounter. *Journal of the Royal College of General Practice, 24,* 5-22.

Stewart, A.L., Hays, R.D. & Ware, J.E., Jr. (1988). The MOS short-form general health survey. *Medical Care, 26*(7), 724-735.

Stewart, M.A. (1984). What is a successful doctor-patient interview? A study of interactions and outcomes. *Social Science & Medicine, 19,* 167-175.

Stewart, M. (1983). Patient characteristics which are related to the doctor-patient interaction. *Family Practice, 1,* 30-36.

Stewart, M.A., Brown, J.B., Levenstein, J.H., McCracken, E., & McWhinney, I.R. (1986). The patient-centred clinical method. 3. Changes in residents' performance over two months of training. *Family Practice—An International Journal, 3,* 164-167.

Stewart, M.A., McWhinney, I.R., & Buck, C.W. (1979). The doctor-patient relationship and its effect upon outcome. *Journal of the Royal College of General Practice, 29,* 77-82.

Stiles, W.B. (1978). Verbal response modes and dimensions of interpersonal roles: A method of discourse analysis. *Journal of Personality and Social Psychology, 36,* 693-703.

Stiles, W.B. (1978-1979). Discourse analysis and the doctor-patient relationship. *International Journal of Psychiatry in Medicine, 9*(3&4), 263-274.

Stiles, W.B. (1981). Classification of intersubjective illocutionary acts. *Language in Society, 10,* 227-249.

Stiles, W.B. (1986). Development of a taxonomy of verbal response modes. In L. Greenberg & W. Pinsof (Eds.), *The psychotherapeutic process: A research handbook.* New York: Guilford.

Stiles, W.B. (1989). Evaluating medical interview process components: Null correlations with outcomes may be misleading. *Medical Care, 27,* 212-220.

Stiles, W.B., Au, M.L., Martello, M.A., & Perlmutter, J.A. (1983). American campaign oratory: Verbal response mode use by candidates in the 1980 American Presidential primaries. *Social Behavior and Personality, 11,* 39-43.

Stiles, W.B., Orth, J.E., Scherwitz, L., Hennrikus, D., & Vallbona, C. (1984). Role behaviors in routine medical interviews with hypertensive patients: A repertoire of verbal exchanges. *Social Psychology Quarterly, 47,* 244-254.

Stiles, W.B., Putnam, S.M., & Jacob, M.C. (1982). Verbal exchange structure of initial medical interviews. *Health Psychology, 1,* 315-336.

Stiles, W.B., Putnam, S.M., & Jacob, M.C. (1984, May). *Question-asking by patients in initial medical interviews: Sequential analysis of verbal antecedents and consequences.* Paper presented at the Midwestern Psychological Association Convention, Chicago, Illinois.

Stiles, W.B., Putnam, S.M., James, S.A., & Wolf, M.H. (1979a). Dimensions of patient and physician roles in medical screening interviews. *Social Science & Medicine, 13A,* 335-341.

Stiles, W.B., Putnam, S.M., Wolf, M.H., & James, S.A. (1979b). Interaction exchange structure and patient satisfaction with medical interviews. *Medical Care, 17,* 667-681.

Stiles, W.B., Putnam, S.M., Wolf, M.H., & James, S.A. (1979c). Verbal response mode profiles of patients and physicians in medical screening interviews. *Journal of Medical Education, 54,* 81-89.

Stiles, W.B., & Sultan, F.E. (1979). Verbal response mode use by clients in psychotherapy. *Journal of Consulting and Clinical Psychology, 47,* 611-613.

Stiles, W.B., Waszak, C.B., & Barton, L.R. (1979). Professorial presumptuousness in verbal interactions with university students. *Journal of Experimental Social Psychology, 15,* 158-169.

Stiles, W.B., & White, M.L. (1981). Parent-child interaction in the laboratory: Effects of role, task, and child behavior pathology on verbal response mode use. *Journal of Abnormal Child Psychology, 9,* 229-241.

Stimson, G.V., & Webb, B. (1975). *Going to see the doctor: The consultation process in general practice.* London: Routledge and Kegan Paul.

Stoeckle, J. D. (1987). *Encounters between Patients and Doctors - An anthology.* Cambridge, MA: MIT Press.

Suchman, A., & Matthews, D. (1988). What makes the doctor-patient relationship therapeutic? Exploring the connexional dimension of medical care. *Annals Internal Medicine, 108,* 125-130.

Svarstad, B.L. (1976). Physician-patient communication and patient conformity with medical advice. In D. Mechanic (Ed.), *The growth of bureaucratic medicine: An inquiry into the dynamics of patient behavior and the organization of medical care* (pp. 220-238). New York: John Wiley.

Szasz, T.S., & Hollender, M.H. (1955). A contribution to the philosophy of medicine. *Archives of Internal Medicine, 113,* 585-592.

Tahka, V. (1984). *The patient doctor relationship.* Sydney: Adis Health Science Press.

Tait, I. (1979). *The history and function of clinical records.* Unpublished M.D. dissertation thesis, University of Cambridge.

Terasaki, M.R.T., Morgan, C.O., & Elias, L. (1984). Medical student interactions with cancer patients: Evaluation with videotaped interviews. *Medical and Pediatric Oncology, 12,* 38-42.

Thomasma, D. (1982) A cognitive approach to the humanities in primary care. *Family Medicine, 14,* 18.

Thompson, J.A., & Anderson, J.L. (1982). Patient preferences and the bedside manner. *Medical Education. 16,* 17-21.

Thorndike, R.L. (1982). *Applied psychometrics.* Boston: Houghton, Mifflin.

Tinsley, H.E.A., & Weiss, D.J. (1975). Interrater reliability and agreement of subjective judgments. *Journal of Counseling Psychology, 22,* 358-376.

Traux, C.B., & Carkhuff, R.R. (1967). *Toward effective counseling and psychotherapy.* Chicago: Aldine.

Tuckett, D., Boulton, M., Olson, C., & Williams A. (1985). *Meetings between experts: An approach to sharing ideas in medical consultations.* London: Tavistock Publications.

Tumulty, P.A. (1978) The art of healing. *Johns Hopkins Medical Journal 143,* 140-143.

Vaccarino, J.M. (1977). Malpractice: The problem in perspective. *Journal of the American Medical Association, 23,* 861-863.

Von Bertallanfy, L. (1968). *General systems theory.* New York: Braziller.

Waitzkin, H. (1985). Information giving in medical care. *Journal of Health and Social Behavior, 26,* 81-101.

Wakeford, R. (1983). Skills training in United Kingdom Medical Schools. In D. Pendleton & J. Hasler (Eds.). *Doctor-patient communication* (pp. 233-248). London: Academic Press.

Ware, J.E., Jr., Davies, A.R., Kane, R.L., et al. (1978). *Effects of differences in quality of care on patient satisfaction and behavioral intentions: an experimental simulation.* Paper presented at Research in Medical Education Annual Meeting, New Orleans.

Wasserman, R.C., & Inui, T.S. (1983). Systematic analysis of clinician-patient interactions: A critique of recent approaches with suggestions for future research. *Medical Care, 21,* 279-293.

Wasserman, R.C., Inui, T.S., Barriatua, R.D., Carter, W.B., & Lippincott, P. (1983). Responsiveness to maternal concern in preventive child health visits: An analysis of clinician-patient interactions. *Developmental and Behavioral Pediatrics, 4*(3), 171-176.

Wasserman, R.C., Inui, T.S., Barriatua, R.D., Carter, W.B., & Lippencott, P. (1984). Pediatric clinicians' support for parents makes a difference: An outcome based analysis of clinician-parent interaction. *Pediatrics*, *74*, 1047-1053.

Wasson, J.H., Sox, H.C. Jr., & Sox, C.H. (1981). The diagnosis of abdominal pain in ambulatory male patients. *Medical Decision Making*, *1*, 215-224.

Weinberger, M., Greene, J.Y., & Mamlin, J.J. (1981). The impact of clinical encounter events on patient and physician satisfaction. *Social Science and Medicine*, *15*, 239.

Werner, A., & Schnedier, J.M. (1974). Teaching medical students interactional skills: A research-based course in the doctor-patient relationship. *New England Journal of Medicine*, *290*(22), 1232-1237.

West, C. (1983). "Ask me no questions...": An analysis of queries and replies in physician-patient dialogues. In S. Fisher, & A.D. Todd (Eds.). *The social organization of doctor-patient communication*. Washington, DC: Center for Applied Linguistics.

West, C. (1984). *Routine complications: Troubles with talk between doctors and patients*. Bloomington: Indiana University Press.

White, K. L. (1988). *The Task of Medicine*. Menlo Park, CA: The Henry J. Kaiser Family Foundation.

White, K. L., Williams, F., & Greenberg, B. (1961). Ecology of medical care. *New England Journal of Medicine*, *265*, 885.

Whitehead, A.N. (1926). *Science and the modern world*. Cambridge: Cambridge University Press.

Wilber, K. (1983). Eye to eye. The quest for the new paradigm. New York: Anchor/Doubleday.

Wilbush, J. (1981). Climacteric symptom formation: Donovan's contribution. *Maturitas*, *3*, 99-105.

Williams, R.B., Kimball, C.P., & Williard, H.N. (1972). The influence of interpersonal interaction on diastolic blood pressure. *Psychosomatic Medicine*, *34*, 194-198.

Williams, G.H., & Wood, P.H.N. (1986). Common-sense beliefs about illness: A mediating role for the doctor. *Lancet*, *2 (8521)*, 1435-1437.

Willson, P., & McNamara, J.R. (1982). How perceptions of a simulated physician-patient interaction influence intended satisfaction and compliance. *Social Science & Medicine*. *16*, 1699-1704.

Wolraich, M., Albanese, M., Stone, G., Nesbitt, D., Thomson, E., Shymansky, J., Bartley, J., & Hansen, J. (1986). Medical communication behavior system: An interactional analysis system for medical interactions. *Medical Care*, *24*, 891.

Woolley, F.R., Kane, R.L., & Hughes, C.C. (1978). The effects of doctor-patient communication on satisfaction and outcome of care. *Social Science & Medicine*. *12*, 123-128.

Wright, H.J., & MacAdam, D.B. (1979). *Clinical thinking and practice: Diagnosis and decision in patient care*. Edinburgh: Churchill Livingstone.

Wu, W.C., & Pearlman, R.A. (1988). Consent in medical decision making: The role of communication. *Journal of General Internal Medicine*, *3*(1), 9-20.

Index

Active and passive interviewing, 74, 100-106

Affective ratings of interviews, 180, 192-193, 211, 216-217, 233-234

Agreement between the patient and doctor, 83, 200, 230

Anthropological approach, 33, 65, 77

Attitude change of the physician or student, 58-63, 111

Audiotape, 121-122, 124, 184, 187, 232

Balint Groups, 31-32, 41, 58-63, 78, 147

Behavior Science, 30-33

Biopsychosocial model, 18, 32, 87, 98, 246

Checklist, 123, 128, 162-165, 167-177

Clinical method, 18, 25, 107

Coding interactions, 180, 211-222, 233

Collaborative research, 209, 223, 227, 256

Communication, doctor-patient, 19, 58, 155, 163-165, 179, 248

Communication skills, 18, 123, 124-125, 128-137, 153-166, 169

Communication skills training, 54-55, 58-63, 253; attitude change, 58-63, 138-139, 146; courses, 121-122, 126, 139, 141-145, 153-166; evaluation, 122-123, 125-137, 144-152, 154, 162-166, 167-177; feedback, 121-122, 125-126, 134, 137, 139-144, 147, 155, 162-166; simulated patients, 124-127, 141-143, 145, 158-161; task for consultation, 114, 139, 141-145, 156

Compliance, 86, 94, 97, 136, 139, 143, 172-173, 180, 187, 191-192, 200, 225-226, 228-229

Conduct, 73, 96-97

Consultations: style of, 74-75, 143-144

Content, 73, 92, 160-162, 172, 180, 211-212

Content categories, 180, 211-212

Context, 22, 73, 94

Courses, 58-63, 121-122, 126, 139, 141-145, 153-166

Curriculum, 52, 86, 122, 138, 145, 163-166

Developmental/descriptive studies, 180, 197-202

Developmental issues, 253; personal, 44-46; cognitive, 47-48; tasks, 48-51

Diabetes, 181, 232

Diagnosis, 59, 79, 82, 107, 119, 133-134, 160, 167

Disease vs. illness, 14, 18, 73, 79, 87, 107-111, 119-120

Education: communication skills, 54-56, 58-63, 122, 124-137, 138-152, 153-166, 253; postgraduate/resident, 41, 50-51, 53, 122, 138-152, 168; undergraduate medical, 14, 41, 51-53, 122, 124-137, 138, 153-166, 167-177

About the Editors

MOIRA STEWART is an Associate Professor in the Department of Family Medicine and the Centre for Studies in Family Medicine at The University of Western Ontario, London, Canada. She is an Epidemiologist who for the past 13 years has applied her research skills to two general topics: stress in relation to health and communication between patients and doctors. She has published numerous articles in *Social Science and Medicine, Medical Care, Family Practice: An International Journal, Canadian Medical Association Journal*, and *Journal of the Royal College of General Practitioners*. She has been particularly active in fostering an international network of teachers and scientists of communication in medicine through the International Conference on Doctor-Patient Communication, the Society for General Internal Medicine, Task Force on the Medical Interview, and the North American Primary Care Research Group's Interest Group on Doctor-Patient Communication.

DEBRA ROTER is an Associate Professor in the Department of Health Policy and Management Division of Behavioral Science and Health Education of the Johns Hopkins School of Hygiene and Public Health. She has been actively involved in interaction analysis research in the medical encounter for the past ten years. A product of that work has been the development of an original method of process and content analysis of audiotapes of medical encounters. The Roter Interaction Analysis System (RIAS) has become increasingly popular with investigators due to its practical considerations and predictive validity. For the past five years she has been a member of the Society for General

Internal Medicine, Task Force on the Medical Interview. In that capacity she has coordinated a large multisite collaborative research project to analyze communication dynamics through tape recordings of routine, primary care encounters in a variety of practice settings and geographic locations across the United States and in Canada. This work has produced a set of 550 audiotapes of medical encounters with extensive patient and physician exit interviews. Few studies have undertaken such a diverse, empirically based investigation of communication dynamics, and this rich data set is likely to provide many new insights. She has recently published articles in *Medical Care, Journal of General Internal Medicine, Patient Education and Counseling,* and *Evaluation and the Health Professions.*

About the Contributors

PAUL ARNTSON is Chair and Associate Professor in the Department of Communication Studies at Northwestern University. He spent a year at Oxford University Medical School working with Course Organizers and Trainers in Postgraduate Education for General Practice. He has been published widely in communication journals. His work includes articles on the psychosocial aspects of epilepsy, self-help groups, and perceptions of control in doctor-patient encounters, particularly among elderly patients.

HOWARD BECKMAN is Associate Professor in the Division of General Internal Medicine at the Wayne State University School of Medicine. As a member of the Coordinating Committee of the Society of General Internal Medicine Task Force on the Medical Interview, his interests have focused on developing practical techniques to help physicians become more effective partners in their patients' care. He has conducted workshops for the American College of Physicians, the Society of General Internal Medicine, and the International Communication Association. His work has been published in books as well as such journals as the *Annals of Internal Medicine*.

FERNAND BLONDEAU is Associate Professor of Family Medicine at Laval University, Quebec. Doctor Blondeau is involved in the University's behavioral sciences program at the undergraduate and graduate level. He also organizes continuing medical education activities using the Balint method. He is a certificant of the College of Family Physicians of Canada.

JUDITH BELLE BROWN is a Clinical Assistant Professor in the Department of Family Medicine at the University of Western Ontario. With teaching and research interests in Doctor-Patient Communication she has presented local and national workshops to residents and faculty, and has been published in such journals as *Family Practice: An International Journal, Canadian Medical Association Journal* and the *Canadian Family Physician*. Brown received her M.S.W. from Smith College and is currently a Ph.D. candidate in social work at Smith.

WILLIAM B. CARTER is an Associate Professor of Health Services at the University of Washington. With interests in health promotion and disease prevention, health status measurement, and the health behavior of patients and providers, he has been published in books and such journals as *Clinical Research, Medical Care, Health Services Research, American Journal of Public Health, Organizational Behavior and Human Decision Making*. Carter received his Ph.D. from the University of Washington.

ERIC J. CASSELL, an internist and Clinical Professor of Public Health at Cornell University Medical College, is widely recognized in the medical field for his contributions to the study of communications in medicine and medical ethics. His first book, *The Healer's Art*, has achieved the status of an underground classic. His two-volume book *Talking with Patients* was the result of more than ten years of research. He is now completing a book on *The Nature of Suffering and the Goals of Medicine*.

ANTONY COX is Professor of Child and Adolescent Psychiatry at the University of Liverpool and was formerly in the Department of Child and Adolescent Psychiatry at the Institute of Psychiatry, London, U.K. His research interests include epidemiology, infantile autism, interviewing techniques, links between adult and child mental disorder, and the evaluation of intervention.

ALFONS CRIJNEN is Senior Resident in Psychiatry and Child Psychiatry at the Municipal University of Amsterdam and a former general practitioner and Assistant Professor at the State University of Limburg (Department of Social Psychiatry). He conducts research in psychiatric education and has a Ph.D. in Medicine on reliability and validity studies in measurement of medical interviewing skills.

SUSAN FAIRBAIRN was educated at the universities of Edinburgh, Strathclyde, and Stirling. She is currently Research Associate in the Cancer Research Campaign Psychological Medicine Group, Manchester University, where she is undertaking research on nurses' and doctors' communication skills with cancer patients. She has been published in medical and nursing education and in environmental psychology. She is a Tutor in Social Psychology for the Open University. With Gavin Fairbairn she is joint editor of *Psychology, Ethics and Change* (RKP, 1987) and *Ethical Issues in Caring* (Gower, 1988).

PROFESSOR CHARLES FLETCHER was educated at Eton, Cambridge, and St. Bartholomews Hospital, London. As the Nuffield Research Fellow in Oxford, he did the first clinical trial of penicillin. He was Professor of Clinical Epidemiology at the Postgraduate Medical School in 1968 and has written widely on aspects of epidemiology, particularly chronic bronchitis and emphysema. He has had two books published, *Communication in Medicine* (Oxford University Press, 1973) and the *Natural History of Chronic Bronchitis and Emphysema* (Oxford University Press, 1976). He is currently Chairman of the Education Section of the British Diabetic Association and is a past president of the Action of Smoking in Health (ASH).

RICHARD FRANKEL is Assistant Professor of Medicine at Wayne State University where he coordinates behavioral science training. He has been published and lectured widely in the area of doctor-patient communication and has been active in the Society of General Internal Medicine Task Force on the Medical Interview. His major area of interest is in qualitative research utilizing participant expertise and the application of findings to health care outcomes. Recently awarded a Fulbright Senior Research Fellowship for study in Sweden, Frankel received his Ph.D. in Sociology from the Graduate Center of the City University of New York.

JACQUES FRENETTE is Associate Professor of Family Medicine and Director of the Family Medicine Residency Program at Laval University, Quebec, Fellow of the College of Family Physicians of

Canada, and former president of the College's Section of Teachers. Dr. Frenette has shown much interest in the study of the doctor-patient relationship. He is a member of the International Balint Society.

SHELDON GREENFIELD, M.D., is a Professor of Medicine and Chief of the Division of Health Services Research at the Tufts University Medical School and is a Senior Scientist at the Institute for the Advancement of Health and Medical Care. His research has been primarily focused on the assessment of the quality of both the technical and interpersonal aspects of medical care. He has recently completed the development and testing of generalizability measures of disease severity and co-morbidity in two national health policy studies. He continues his interest in the assessment of organizational influences on the outcomes of health care as Medical Director of the National Study of Medical Outcomes. Dr. Greenfield is published primarily in the areas of clinical policy and health services research.

TJAARD IMBOS is a statistician and psychometrician and Assistant Professor at the Department of Educational Research, State University of Limburg. He is coauthor of the Maastricht "progress test of medical knowledge," a measurement method with predictive validity for future medical competence.

THOMAS S. INUI is a Professor of Medicine and of Health Services at the University of Washington, Division Head in General Internal Medicine, and Director of the University's Robert Wood Johnson Clinical Scholars Program. He received his M.D. and Sc.M. (Health Services) from Johns Hopkins University. His research and publications emphasize health-related behavior, ambulatory care management, clinical epidemiology, and clinically applied health services research.

SHERRIE H. KAPLAN, Ph.D., MPH, is the Director of Research Grant Development at the Institute for the Advancement of Health and Medical Care at the New England Medical Center, and is an Adjunct Assistant Professor at the Harvard School of Public Health. Her research has been primarily focused on the development and testing of interventions aimed at changing the doctor-patient relationship and on the development and testing of quality of life outcome measures and measures of preferences for control in the context of the doctor-patient relationship. She is currently the Principal Investigator on two grants to study the effects of interventions designed to improve doctors' and patients' negotiation skills on patients' health outcomes and physicians' satisfaction with practice among community-based private practice physicians and their patients. She is also a coinvestigator on the National Study of Medical Care Outcomes, in the context of which she is studying the effects of doctors' and patients' interpersonal style on patients' health outcomes in different systems of care. Dr. Kaplan aims her publications primarily at clinical and health services audiences and is published in clinical and public health journals.

BARBARA M. KORSCH is a pediatrician who is currently serving as Head of the Division of General Pediatrics at Childrens Hospital of Los Angeles, California, and is a Professor of Pediatrics at the University of Southern California, Los Angeles, California. Her current activities, besides being responsible for a general pediatric service, include continued research and teaching in the field of doctor-patient communication. Dr. Korsch initiated her studies of doctor-patient communication in the 1950s and has continued these studies in many other clinical settings with various associates through the last several decades. She has numerous publications, has spoken at many universities in the United States and abroad, and has received a number of distinctions and awards in recognition of her contributions to this emerging field of investigation. Dr. Korsch is a graduate of Smith College and Johns Hopkins Medical School and has received training in pediatrics and child psychiatry at a number of academic institutions.

HERRO KRAAN is Associate Professor of Psychiatry at the State University of Limburg, Netherlands (Department of Social Psychiatry). He designed an experimental clinical program in psychiatry for undergraduates in the Maastricht medical curriculum. He conducts research on affective disorders in primary care. He received a Ph.D. in medicine for his studies on the reliability and validity of a measure of medical interviewing skills.

SUZANNE M. KURTZ is Associate Professor of Communication in the Faculties of Education and Medicine, University of Calgary, Canada. Focusing on clinical skills evaluation, and the development of communication curriculum, she has worked for more than a decade with medical students and residents, practicing physicians, nurses, allied health professionals (including health workers in developing countries), and patient self-help groups to improve communication in health care. Her book, *Communication and Counselling in Health Care* (with Vincent M. Riccardi, 1983), reflects these interests. She received her Ph.D. in speech communication from the University of Denver.

JOSEPH H. LEVENSTEIN is the Head of the Unit of General Practice, University of Capetown, and Chairman of the Research Committee of Academy of Family Medicine of South Africa. He has 60 publications. He is the winner of several awards, including the Louis Leipoldt Award for the best article in the *South African Medical Journal* in 1976, the Noristan Gold Medal for contributions to science in 1983, and the Fehler Fellowship for outstanding contributions to Family Medicine in 1987. He has lectured and taught at several universities throughout the world.

MACK LIPKIN, JR. is Director of the Division of Primary Care in the Department of Medicine at New York University School of Medicine and Associate Professor of Clinical Medicine. He directs the Task Force on the Medical Interview of the Society of General Internal Medicine. The author-editor of ten books and numerous articles, he publishes *Medical Encounter* and does research on the medical interview, the family in health and illness, health services, and patient and medical education. He trained at Harvard College and Medical School, did an Internal Medicine residency at the University of North Carolina in Chapel Hill, a residency and fellowship in Medicine and Psychiatry at the University of Rochester, and was visiting research fellow at the Rockefeller Foundation.

MARK F. LONGHURST is Associate Professor of Family Medicine at the University of British Columbia. As Director of Residency Training until 1987, he worked extensively with the educational development of family doctors. His interest and publications have focused on the doctor-patient relationship in journals such as *Canadian Medical Association Journal, Canadian Family Physician,* and *Humane Medicine.* He is currently working on a book *Images of Illness.* Longhurst received his MDCM at McGill University and his M.Cl.Sc. in Family Medicine at the University of Western Ontario.

PETER MAGUIRE is Senior Lecturer in Psychiatry at Manchester University and Director of the Cancer Research Campaign Psychological Medicine Group. He has been published widely in books and professional journals, such as the *British Medical Journal* and *Medical Education*, on psychological problems in cancer patients and training in interviewing skills. He is currently researching affective disorders in cancer patients, the effectiveness of counseling, and training in counseling skills.

ERIC C. MCCRACKEN is an Associate Professor of the Department of Family Medicine at the University of Western Ontario. He graduated from the University of Glasgow in 1953. He practiced family medicine in a rural area of Scotland until 1956 when he commenced practice in metropolitan Toronto. In 1978 he joined the Department of Family Medicine, the University of Western Ontario, and is presently the Director of the Southwest Middlesex Health Centre, a rural unit of the Department of Family Medicine. Dr. McCracken's areas of special interest are native health problems, the problems of addicted health professionals, and the doctor-patient interaction in family medicine. His work has been published in the *Canadian Family Physician*, *Family Practice: An International Journal*, and the *Canadian Journal of Public Health*.

IAN MCWHINNEY is Professor of Family Medicine at the University of Western Ontario. He received his medical degree from Cambridge University in 1949 and spent fourteen years in general practice in England before coming to Western in 1968. His interests include the philosophy and history of medicine, the diagnostic process, and the natural history of disease. He has been published on these subjects in the *Lancet*, the *New England Journal of Medicine*, the *Canadian Medical Association Journal*, the *Proceedings of the Royal Society of Medicine*, the *Journal of Medicine and Philosophy,* the *Journal of Medical Education*, and the *Journal of Family Practice*.

SAMUEL M. PUTNAM is an Associate Professor of Medicine at Boston University, affiliated with Bedford VA Hospital, and codirector of the Task Force on the Medical Interview of the Society of General Internal Medicine. His primary interests are in investigating the interaction between patients and clinicians and in teaching interviewing to medical students and residents. In collaboration with William Stiles of Miami University and Jane Young of the University of Southern Maine, his studies have appeared in *Medical Care* and *The Journal of General Internal Medicine*.

THEO SCHOFIELD is a general practitioner in Shipston-on-Stour, Warwickshire, England, and is Lecturer in General Practice in the Department of Community Medicine and General Practice at the University of Oxford. He was formerly Associate Regional Advisor to the Oxford Region Vocational Training Scheme where he worked with others to write *The Consultation—An Approach to Learning and Teaching*, which has been published by Oxford University Press. His research interests also include health promotion in primary care, the continued care of chronic diseases, and performance review in practice. Dr. Schofield has a B.M. from Oxford and is a Fellow of Royal College of General Practitioners.

WILLIAM B. STILES is Professor of Psychology and Director of the Psychology Clinic at Miami University in Oxford, Ohio. His research interests include verbal processes in psychotherapy and medical interviews. He has been published in such journals as *Medical Care*, *Psychotherapy*, *Health Psychology*, *Journal of Consulting and Clinical Psychology*, *British Journal of Clinical Psychology*, and *American Psychologist*. He received his Ph.D. in psychology from the University of California, Los Angeles.

CEES VAN DER VLEUTEN is a psychometrician and Assistant Professor at the Department of Educational Research, State University of Limburg. He is a prolific author in national and international educational journals. He is preparing a Ph.D. thesis on the measurement of the physicians' skills.

JOHN E. WARE, JR., Ph.D., is a senior scientist at the Institute for the Advancement of Health and Medical Care at the New England Medical Center. His research has focused on the development and validation of outcome measures of health status and patient satisfaction and on the application of these measures in health policy research and clinical studies. In RAND's Health Insurance Experiment, Dr. Ware examined the effects of different health care financing and organization arrangements on health status and patient satisfaction. He is currently the Principal Investigator for the National Study of Medical Care Outcomes, examining variations in practice styles and outcomes for patients with chronic disease treated in different systems of care and by different provider specialty groups. He is published primarily in clinical and health policy journals.

W. WAYNE WESTON is Professor of Family Medicine at the University of Western Ontario, Director of Education for the Department of Family Medicine and Director of the university's Office of Health Sciences Educational Development. With a special interest in medical education and doctor-patient communication, he has been published in several journals and led numerous local and national workshops for faculty in these areas. He received his MD degree in 1964 from the University of Toronto.

JAAP ZUIDWEG is a general practitioner and a Research Fellow at the Department of Social Psychiatry, State University of Limburg. He conducts studies in measurement of medical interviewing skills. He is preparing a Ph.D. thesis on general practitioners' competence in the management of diabetes mellitus.